Creating Chaos

Creating Chaos

Covert Political Warfare,
from Truman to Putin

Larry Hancock

O/R

OR Books

London · New York

All rights information: rights@orbooks.com
Visit our website at www.orbooks.com

Published by OR Books for the book trade in partnership with Counterpoint Press.
Distributed to the trade by Publishers Group West.

First printing 2018

Cataloging-in-Publication data is available from the Library of Congress.
A catalog record for this book is available from the British Library.

ISBN 978-1-944869-87-8 paperback
ISBN 978-1-944869-88-5 e-book

Typeset by Lapiz Digital Services, Chennai, India.

Contents

Introduction

Diplomacy, foreign relations, and the conduct of both political and actual warfare between states are addressed within the academic discipline of political science as well as being part of the education and training of Foreign Service and diplomatic personnel. Beyond academia, the practices of the darker and covert side of statesmanship and foreign relations are of practical concern in the day-to-day work of national intelligence communities around the world.

Creating Chaos focuses on and explores the dark side of statecraft, the covert use of power in international relations. It specifically deals with activities and practices by which one nation targets another—considered as an adversary or as a threat—with practices of secret, deniable political warfare. Elements of this darker side of foreign relations can be found in one of the earliest treatises on statecraft, *The Prince*, a sixteenth-century work by diplomat Niccolò Machiavelli. Much of Machiavelli's analysis offers direct, highly pragmatic and notably immoral recommendations for successful rulers. As an example, he maintains that the first priority of any ruler should be a continual study of the art of war; its practice represents the sole "art" mandatory for a ruler.[1]

While Machiavelli discusses certain aspects of deniable action, such as the suborning of nobles (whom he then describes as obviously unreliable, to be dealt with cautiously or eliminated once their aid is no longer needed) much of his rather infamous reputation derives from his avocation that a successful ruler must know both right and wrong—and choose to do wrong whenever circumstances dictate: "Hence it is necessary for a prince wishing to hold his own to know how to do wrong and to make use of it or not according to necessity....It will be found that something that looks like virtue, if followed would be his ruin, whilst something else which looks like vice, yet followed, brings him security and prosperity."[2]

We will find that particular attitude appearing continually in this exploration of both historical and contemporary political warfare—as relevant to the decisions of presidents as to princes, kings, and queens. However, other of his admonitions appear to have been more often ignored than not. Machiavelli cautions that no ruler can ever securely govern a hostile populace, simply because those in opposition will out-number those content with his leadership. Also, a ruler who obtains sovereignty through the assistance of foreign nobles will always be dealing with those who consider themselves his equals; such a ruler will govern with far more difficulty than if he had acquired sovereignty by popular favor. The most successful ruler can maintain himself easily, simply by ensuring the people are not oppressed.[3]

As we will see in our exploration of political warfare during the Cold War era, those particular points often seem to have been ignored—even if they were highlighted by the individuals directly involved in successful operations. One of America's first covert foreign regime change efforts during the Cold War was overseen by Kermit Roosevelt Jr., the senior Central Intelligence Agency officer in its Middle East division. Roosevelt was deemed to have directed what was at the time considered to be an extremely successful project—the Iranian coup of 1954.[4] When debriefed on the operation, Roosevelt was adamant that the CIA must never attempt another such covert project unless both the army and the majority of the people in the targeted nation wanted what the United States itself desired as the outcome. Roosevelt pragmatically concluded that if that were not certain, then covert political warfare should not even be considered as an option—the president should just send in the Marines. Pragmatic advice, given by someone in a position to know, which seemingly fell on deaf ears.

Creating Chaos is not a book about Cold War espionage, deniable military operations, or military warfare. Instead it is first a detailed examination of covert political warfare as it was conducted both by both the United States and Russia during the twentieth century, the era of the ideological Cold War between the Eastern and Western Blocs. It then moves into the twenty-first century, exploring the transition period which followed the collapse of the Soviet Union and contemporary political warfare practices in what has become a role reversal in the activities of the two nations.

Some readers may be surprised to find that it was the United States, rather than Russia, which most frequently turned to major covert political action projects during the Cold War, focusing on reversing Soviet geopolitical influence first in Eastern Europe and then globally. Beginning in the late 1940s and continuing through the 1980s, American political warfare was highly focused, conducted by special task groups with relatively short term, disruptive missions.

Initially such projects involved specific activities intended to create internal chaos and destabilize Eastern European nations which had come under Russian control following World War II. Specialized CIA psychological warfare and paramilitary groups were formed to conduct deniable operations, with the intent of encouraging and supporting internal resistance movements, and creating schisms which would undermine Russian influence. Following that early period of "containment" efforts, operations became much more far ranging, responding to what were perceived as potential Soviet "beachheads" in nations around the globe. Much more aggressive practices, including regime destabilization, surrogate warfare, and actual regime change came into play to remove any such beachheads that did come into place.

The full story of American deniable political warfare has become visible through the massive release of both State Department and Central Intelligence Agency documents, the most covert elements being forced into public scrutiny by a series of congressional inquiries and supplemented by aggressive citizen use of the Freedom of Information Act of 1966, by which agencies are forced to respond to public records requests.

It is now possible to examine and describe the decision process which led America to commit to practices in which it had little experience, practices totally outside the rule of law and international legal agreements. Beyond that, the practices themselves can be dissected, illustrated by specific intervention projects and traced though the evolutionary process which in many cases led from simple economic and political action intended to destabilize targeted regimes to formal projects intended to bring about actual regime change. In several instances this involved covert paramilitary action using deniable American military assets and surrogate agents and fighters.

In contrast to the American turn to the "dark side" and covert regime change projects, during the Cold War the Soviet Union enjoyed the foreign policy advantage of simply following along behind a global wave of anti-colonialism and an explosion in nationalist politics within Dutch, French, and British global empires. Russia was able to move openly in supporting newly independent nations, many of them avowedly neutral or openly opposed to the prior dominion of European powers. In the context of a strongly expressed anti-colonialist foreign policy, Russian support for newly independent nations was generally quite overt; mutual trade pacts were signed, diplomatic agreements completed, weapons shipments initiated and, as necessary, Russian military advisors appeared in-country. The Soviet Union was also able to take advantage of growing Western fears over what was depicted as an almost unstoppable wave of global communist expansion, the red menace. In a number of instances, American fears led to a rejection of appeals for neutral relationships, forcing nations firmly into the Soviet bloc, dependent on both economic and military support from Russia.

Yet, as we now know, the Soviet Union did continue its own active and highly focused program of political warfare, targeting Western Bloc nations they considered their primary military adversaries—the United States, Britain, and to a lesser extent France. Immediately following World War II the Soviets also conducted a number of economic and psychological warfare actions intended to block neutral Scandinavian nations from moving fully into the Western Bloc.

But overall, Russian Cold War-era political warfare activities against its primary adversaries were much more subtle and generally far less visible. They are revealed in FBI documents, by information (and documents) from former KGB officers, and by the investigations of counterintelligence units in Western nations including Canada, Mexico, and Britain. *Creating Chaos* examines and illustrates the ongoing Russian "active measures" practices—including the manipulation of individuals through financial coercion and blackmail and a variety of psychological/information warfare activities.

Soviet active measures were intended to covertly and subtly shape American public opinion and political policy. They were supported by the use of forged and planted documents as well as the insertion of false news and misinformation into the Western media. Historically, examples of Russian success in document fabrication can be found long before the Soviet era. One striking example comes from the first years of the 20th century, in the form of the infamous *Protocols of the Elders of Zion*. That document, first published in Russia in 1903, was created with the intent of enabling a domestic Russian government campaign of anti-Semitism. It purported to be a historical record of a meeting in which Jewish leaders laid out their plans for global economic control and cultural hegemony, to be achieved through the subversion of Gentile morals. While created for internal political purposes, the document was convincing enough to find its way into campaigns against

Jews around the world. In the United States, Henry Ford paid for the printing and distribution of half a million copies in the United States; it also became a political tool for the Nazis during their rise to power in Germany.

Active measures also involved the ongoing recruitment of both knowing and unknowing "agents of influence," and individuals which Russian intelligence personnel described as "useful idiots"—those who could facilitate the distribution of information through particular connections and associations and potentially make introductions to more significant "targets."[5]

As a fundamental part of its exploration of political warfare, *Creating Chaos* offers a tutorial on the tools and tradecraft of covert practices, showing the evolution of both, and in particular their rapid evolution when the internet emerged in the initial decades of the twenty-first century. While many of the basic practices have not changed since their development and formalization during the imperial competitions of the first global empires, recent events suggest that they have actually become both more deniable and more successful. One of the goals of this work is to provide the history and context required to recognize political warfare practices in contemporary affairs.

With that in mind our exploration will pay particular attention to the tactics of "deniability," in particular the uses of economic, trade, and finance networks as both "covers" and enablers for covert political and paramilitary activities. That story begins during the Cold War, with the CIA's involvement with America's post-World War II global economic reach and the business leaders associated with its trade networks. The voluntary and undocumented, covert use of trade and financial networks is actually nothing new. It has always been—and remains—a key to deniable political warfare. That continues to be as true now as it was during the centuries of jousting among the first global empires.

Accommodation and cooperation by those in charge of major commercial business networks appear to be a key enabler in much of the deniable warfare activity of first the United States under Roosevelt though Reagan and more recently the Russian Federation's destabilization and hybrid warfare actions under Putin. The activities of a particularly close personal associate of Vladimir Putin, Yevegeny Prigozhi, illustrate the power of deeply layered financial networks. Initially Prigozhi, known as "Putin's chef," was best known as a member of a Putin clique described in the Russian media as a frequent recipient of major government contracts, a path to considerable wealth in the new Russia. In turn, he became one of the individuals whose business enterprises served as major conduits for funds going into deniable Russian political warfare, ranging from the insertion of paramilitary personnel into the Ukrainian conflicts, the funding of information warfare against the United States, and most recently the support of private Russian military firms operating within Syria.[6] The use of Prigozhi and his business connections as covers for deniable action is within the best traditions of the commercial cover practices developed by the Central Intelligence Agency in the earliest years of the Cold War with the Soviet Union.

The American Cold War experience with the use of covert economic and financial networks offers an important insight into both the risks and negative consequences associated with such commercial "entanglements," including the criminal activities which continually develop during ostensibly deniable activities. When leaders decide that their best options include, as Machiavelli put it, "making use of the wrong," their immediate purposes may indeed be achieved, though the ultimate consequences might be extremely negative and long-lasting.

It would be comforting to find that America and Russia have learned something from the decades of the Cold War, from the negative consequences of destabilizing targeted governments to the covert intervention to replace them with preferred regimes. Reality has shown that hope to be woefully optimistic. Perhaps that should have been no surprise given the personal warnings of some of those most directly involved in the earliest "engagements" of the Cold War. One was George F. Kennan, whose insights as a Foreign Service officer date back as early as 1960.

In 1946 Kennan had served as the chargé d'affaires in Moscow. Based on his own firsthand experience and certain recent and alarming speeches by Soviet leader Joseph Stalin, Kennan cabled an extended warning to his superiors in Washington. The 8,000-word message pointedly described the Soviet view of world affairs as being "neurotic."[7] His assessment as the professional on the scene in Moscow fueled the fears that led to the first major postwar American covert political action programs. He portrayed the Russians as obsessed by centuries of foreign incursion and driven to use every possible means of undermining any potential external threat. It was a deeply pervasive fear of the outside world, a fear exponentially magnified by the extensive destruction inside Russia and millions of casualties in the recent war.[8]

Kennan pictured that fear as driving the Soviets to undermine and destabilize Western powers. He anticipated that future Soviet international policy would be one of unremitted political warfare—involving extensive psychological warfare, massive propaganda efforts, and covert destabilization actions designed to increase Western political uncertainties and tear apart wartime alliances. He also anticipated that the Soviets would constantly probe and push to exacerbate fears and political chaos in adjacent nations. He painted a picture of a unique and terrifying confrontation, equivalent to war. His conclusion was that there could be "no peaceful coexistence" between the West and Soviet Russia. His cable produced an uproar in Washington and was circulated by Secretary of Defense James Forrestal to a variety of senior officers in all the armed services.[9]

Time and further experience led Kennan to modify his initial dramatic assessment of the political warfare between East and West. With twenty-five years of foreign relations service, built largely on his Cold War experience, his final observations are especially meaningful in setting the context for our exploration of covert political warfare. Kennan pointed out that "...international life normally has its strong competitive elements. It did not take the challenge of communism to produce the current situation...I think there is no international relationship between sovereign states which is without its elements of antagonism, its competitive aspects. Every government is in some respects a problem for every other government and it will always be this way as long as the sovereign state, with its supremely self-centered rationale, remains the basis for international life."[10]

Such insights extend from Machiavelli to Kennan, over the centuries. The histories of kingdoms, empires and nations demonstrate that political warfare is a constant; it appears to be a temptation that simply cannot be resisted regardless of its long-term consequences. From that perspective, we would all be well served by being continually alert to its practices.

Chapter One:
The Games of Queens, Kings, and Presidents

Covert political warfare, a practice of empires and nations, of kings, queens, and presidents—warfare without armies, combat without body counts, victory at little to no expense with virtually no risk. Whether used for offensive economic and territorial gains or for the defense of national sovereignty and interests, it's a temptation few leaders have successfully resisted.

We will examine its twentieth and twenty-first century appearances in great detail, in specific projects and operations by both the United States and Russia, as well as in the routine "active measures" conducted primarily by individuals from both nations, at times working under diplomatic cover, and operating out of embassies, consulates, and legations. The tools and tradecraft used in deniable activities are also important topics given that they evolved specifically to obfuscate and conceal political warfare of all stripes. Yet while the tools have evolved dramatically over time, many of the basic practices remain much the same.

Operatives recruit "agents of influence" within the targeted nation, to be used in both knowing and unknowing actions which are intended to favorably shape foreign policies from within—as well as to disrupt established political and military alliances. Various types of propaganda, disinformation, and misinformation are used in psychological warfare to undermine public confidence in the targeted nation's governance, in its military—or in both. Surrogates are recruited for those same activities, and in the most extreme instances are used in conjunction with covert paramilitary operations and even overt military pressure to bring about actual regime change.

These basic practices have a very long history, but their scope expanded dramatically during the eras of global exploration and empire building. Numerous examples are found in the eighteenth and nineteenth century competitions among imperial powers; they are especially well-illustrated in the confrontation between imperial Russia and Great Britain in their struggles for economic domination and political control across the Balkans, Arabia, and into Asia and the Indian sub-continent.

As early as 1791, nearing the end of her reign, Catherine the Great of Russia secretly considered plans to take control of India from the British, as part of Russian military action against the Persians intended to regain control of territories in the Caucasus for the Russian Empire. In what might be considered a classic act of psychological warfare, Catherine added the Crimean Khanate to her empire with no overt use of force at all, simply by declaring it as a fact.[1] She ordered posters placed at key public locations throughout the region, declaring to the Crimeans' that she was happy to receive them as Russian subjects. Having long been dissatisfied with the less than benevolent attentions of the Turkish Empire, the locals accepted this announcement by the empress as fact and raised no objections.

A sampling of other activities from the era of "The Great Game" provides an introduction to certain elements of the basic tradecraft and tools which reoccur in contemporary times. For example, a common strategy for both the Russians and the British was to begin the political shaping process though the use of economic influence, offering technologies and luxury goods which were only available from the more developed European nations. Trade pacts became the entrée for establishing personal contacts, extending political influence, and building alliances with local rulers. They also served as tools to recruit willing local agents in the pursuit of subtle economic and political influence.

Russian political agents were repeatedly sent into virtually unexplored tribal regions on highly dangerous missions. For the purposes of travel, they disguised themselves as local tribesmen or traders from adjacent territories. Ultimately their goal was to contact local rulers to offer gifts, messages of friendship, and promises of military and economic alliance. The bait was commerce, and the agents were carefully instructed to observe and prepare not only notes on the strengths of the local defenses but also as much economic intelligence as possible. Another constant, a standby in all such covert activities, was the admonition that if they failed in their mission and were imprisoned or even executed, the Russian government would completely disavow and disown any relationship with them.[2]

In later years Russia would turn to the use of "scientific expeditions" as covers for covert political missions. The British preferred to detach military or political officers from active duty, allowing them to go on "shooting leave"—which also provided a measure of deniability. A number of dynamic and enterprising young officers were lost on such hunting expeditions. Others proved quite successful, on occasion establishing alliances and pacts exceeding both expectations and their instructions.

While the British initially focused on expanding their territorial and economic control on the Indian subcontinent, Russian political action proved quite successful in expanding the czar's broader reach. In 1836 British diplomat John McNeill forcefully brought that Russian imperial success to the attention of the British public in a booklet titled *The Progress and Present Position of Russia in the East*. It contained maps that dramatically illustrated that the Russian Empire had increased the number of its subjects from fifteen to fifty-eight million, advancing its borders some five hundred miles towards Constantinople and one thousand miles towards Tehran.[3]

Efforts by the British Empire to push back against Russian territorial expansion peaked when it began to seem likely that Russian political manipulation might spur a major Afghan incursion into India, triggering a general uprising by Muslim co-religionists. Historically India had suffered through several similar incursions coming out of Afghanistan through the Khyber and Bolān Passes in the Pamir mountain ranges. British diplomatic messages of the time reflect the actions which would be required, introducing a term which will become quite familiar, even in contemporary times: "We have long declined to meddle with the Afghans, but if the Russians try to make them Russian, we must take care that they become British."[4]

British political, and later direct military, involvement in Afghanistan was often opposed by the governor-generals of India, especially since they were forced to bear the economic and military burdens of such actions. Any turn towards "forward policies" became a matter of great internal debate among the British leadership.[5] Interestingly, we will find similar debates over a hundred years later during the Cold War, with little change in terminology—advocates of preemptive covert political action during the Truman and Eisenhower administrations would declare themselves for "forward leaning" policies to block the spread of political influence by the Soviet Union.

Another Great Game gambit from the days of the czars provides further insight into practices which will become familiar over time. British India was not the only target of economic and political opportunity for Imperial Russia. Indeed, Czar Nicholas II focused on the concept of Russia developing itself as an economic power as well as a military force to be reckoned with in world affairs. In support of that idea, his finance minister Count Sergei Witte offered a plan that would enable Russia to achieve economic hegemony from the "shores of the Pacific to the heights of the Himalayas." The plan would allow Russia to dominate the affairs of both Asia and Europe. Overtly it would involve the construction and economic leveraging of the world's longest railroad, some 4,500 miles from Moscow to Vladivostok and Port Arthur on the Pacific. Such an accomplishment would offer overland shipping competition to Britain's control of the sea lanes.

While construction of this Trans-Siberian Railway proceeded, an additional but covert element was added, initiating basic political warfare against China and Tibet under the cover of a new commercial trading company. The trading company and its secret political objectives had been proposed to Czar Alexander III shortly before Nicholas's ascension to the throne, and Witte felt it would be an ideal complement to the railway effort.[6] The trading company would conduct its operations along the route of the rail line but with the secret objective of creating wide-scale revolt against Manchu dynasty domination of the outlying areas of the Chinese Empire. The political destabilization effort would place pressure on the Chinese throne, generating Russian leverage for concessions from the region's Manchu governors. In addition, the trading company was to extend its efforts not only to areas of Mongolia but towards establishing Russian political influence in Tibet.

To what extent this particular covert political action program was successful will likely remain a matter of speculation. It is known that the trading company was established and capitalized with two million rubles. British sources in India also began to report a number of suspected Russian agents, all apparently associated in some fashion with the operators of the trading company, traveling between Saint Petersburg and Lhasa, the capital of Tibet. During the same period Russia did indeed obtain Chinese concessions to establish its first warm water naval facility at Port Arthur; it also obtained territorial control of the area around Port Arthur. Even more important, the Chinese acceded to the Russian connection of the Trans-Siberian Railway to Port Arthur, a major strategic gain for the czar's empire.

It is important for our understanding—and identification—of covert political action practices to appreciate that the practices themselves change relatively little over time. The tradecraft is modified, the tools evolve with technology, but the practices remain basically the same. That continuity is illustrated in the political warfare directed against British India after the fall of Imperial Russia and the establishment of the new Union of Soviet Socialist Republics.

Driven by ideology and with the full support of Russia's communist leaders, the new Asian initiative was a very public Soviet undertaking. In 1917 the Council of People's Commissars declared a major goal of creating revolutions "in all countries, regardless of whether they are at war with Russia, in alliance with Russia, or neutral."[7] In support of that effort, even while faced with immense internal challenges to support its citizens, the Council allocated two million gold rubles to that revolutionary agenda.

One of the most obvious targets for the revolutionary communist initiative was the British Empire, in particular India, the jewel in the British crown. India continued to provide vast economic support to the empire but had revolted against foreign rule before and might well do so again. In pursuit of that goal, the Soviet leadership turned to what is commonly the first practice in any course of covert political action—psychological warfare. It began with a series of planted rumors that hundreds of trained Indian agitators had already been dispatched into the country to inflame long held objections to foreign rule, and spread the message of communist empowerment of the local peoples. Other warnings were quoted to a Comintern (Communist International) official, reportedly disclosing that a special training school in Samarkand was preparing hundreds of native revolutionaries to be sent into India.[8]

To be effective, false stories like these need to make it into the popular news, and indeed they did, appearing in major Indian and British newspapers and provoking widespread concern. In fact, such schools would later be developed and native agitators would eventually be dispatched into India, but that would take time. The rumors and gossip, the stories planted in the press, all worked much more quickly and offered a far broader public impact.

Beyond illustrating the ease of media manipulation for psychological warfare, the effort illustrates what is one of the most important foundations of covert action in general, that of deniability. One of the most basic types of deniability—and one especially preferred by national leaders during both the Cold War and in more contemporary times—is that of "separation," distancing the acts of individual citizens and groups from official government policy and sanctioned actions.

It was impossible for the Soviet Union to deny the goals and actions of the Comintern, those were quite open and publicly proclaimed. But when other nations challenged that it represented an aggressive action, the Soviet response was that the Comintern was an international organization, its actions reflected an ideological movement.[9] Even though its leaders and officials were Soviet government officers, in regard to their actions as members of the Comintern, they were simply acting freely within their rights as private citizens.

Such blatant deniability deceived few people and no foreign nations. The immediate British response was forthright and uncharacteristically direct in diplomatic terms. The British Foreign Minister, Lord Curzon, was quoted as stating that "when the Russian government desire to take some action more than usually repugnant to normal international law and comity they ordinarily erect some ostensibly independent authority to take the action on their behalf...the process is familiar and ceases to beguile."[10]

A very accurate assessment in 1921. Yet in terms of official foreign policy the Russian denial tactic proved viable, if disingenuous. In retrospect it might even seem somewhat laughable, but in terms of deniability that sort of bipolar government stance would continue to surface repeatedly in both American and Soviet covert actions during the Cold War. And while not totally beguiling, it continues as a quite obvious element of contemporary political warfare in the early twenty-first century.

Although initial planted rumors regarding trained, native infiltrators and agitators were largely untrue, in time the Soviets did prepare and insert a number of surrogate agitators into India. Given the nature of covert action and in order to establish both separation and deniability, the use of indigenous surrogates (either actual locals or political exiles) is a standard practice when political warfare takes the final step, moving beyond manipulation and shaping of the adversary's foreign policies to actively attempting to bring about a change in governance and political rule—what today is referred to as regime change.

Beginning in the summer of 1921 trainees from the Moscow-based "Toilers of the East" communist training program began to move into India, using Persian passports. More were sent the following year, with an estimated two dozen attempting entry through 1923. In addition, large quantities of revolutionary literature were mailed into India and considerable funds were channeled through the Soviet diplomatic legation and trade missions in Kabul, Afghanistan. The British actually recovered a large number of hundred pound notes issued through Lloyd's bank in London, which they were able to trace back to a Russian trade official.[11]

With advance warning of the Comintern's intentions, the British and Indian authorities began a program of aggressive interrogations and mail interceptions, successfully exposing the Russian effort and producing headlines in the *Times* of London, calling out the "Bolshevik Plan for India" and "A Revolutionary Programme."[12] The combination of openly announcing a regime change agenda while attempting to carry it out with secret agents proved not to be a particularly effective approach—a historical lesson which the American government totally failed to appreciate in launching certain of its own regime change activities during the Cold War.

The covert activities of the Russian diplomatic and trade personnel illustrate another tactic routinely used in covert political action. It was certainly not something unique to the Russians; the British would use the same practice extensively. It is simply one of the first steps in any political action program. As one British intelligence memorandum describes, the ideal covert political operative should be a trader, a salesman, traveling extensively in the pursuit of his business. Of course the identities of such agents would be extremely closely held, and such agents would be totally disavowed.[13] Commercial actors could never be connected to official diplomatic missions or be treated differently than any other business person, but they proved to be far more effective and certainly more deniable than personnel associated with government affairs or with a diplomatic mission, who would of course normally be suspected and very likely held to some level of observation.

Trade and commercial activities clearly offer initial points of personal contact, establishing channels for recruiting agents of influence and developing potential leverage for manipulating relationships. When policies proceed to more aggressive, and necessarily even more deniable activities, commercial and financial entities may also be used as covers for personnel, to secretly move funds for operations and to establish critical and covert logistics mechanisms. To illustrate how complex such commercial enabling activities can be, and how subtly they come into play, we can move forward in time, to before the Cold War and just prior to World War II.

By 1940, President Franklin D. Roosevelt was faced with a quandary that would become familiar to many of his successors—dealing with national adversaries he perceived to be an imminent threat but which the American public had no desire to militarily engage. He had been able to turn to long-established relationships with the British to move against the threat from Germany, but aggressive Japanese moves in the Pacific (including the occupation of Manchuria and its ongoing war with China) posed a quite different challenge. One possibility for acting against Japanese territorial ambition evolved out of a very private Chinese approach to Roosevelt. The approach came in the form of personal contacts by Dr. T. V. Soong, acting on behalf of his brother-in-law Chiang Kai-shek, head of the Nationalist Government of the Republic of China and leader of its armed forces. Soong was financially involved with the Bank of China and a variety of Chinese trade activities with the U.S. (primarily conducted through the Universal Trading Corporation). Soong's position as one of China's wealthiest men had brought him into close personal relationships with both Treasury Secretary Henry Morgenthau Jr. and Navy Secretary Frank Knox. It would be Morgenthau and Knox who provided the personal introductions that ultimately produced a covert project agreed to by both Chiang and Roosevelt, independently acting as the leaders of their respective governments.

The secret agreement was to lead to the deployment of American fighters and bombers in China, purchased by the Chinese and flown by privately contracted American volunteers. It was ostensibly to be a totally private, commercial arrangement. The fighters would go into action against Japanese bombers, as well as support Chinese ground forces. However, Roosevelt privately expressed the hope that bombing missions flown against Japan from Chinese bases would raise concerns of the Japanese public as to the consequences of the foreign aggressions being carried out by the war party which had taken control of the Japanese government.[14] If done quickly enough it might even pause or delay what appeared to be an imminent Japanese threat to the British in Singapore.

Of course such bombing missions would have had little major military impact, and they would have served primarily as a tool of psychological warfare. Still, even a small number of B-17 bomber raids, targeting Japanese cities and likely using firebombing, would have been a tremendous surprise and created serious public shock. From that perspective the plan was tactically sound. The impact of such missions out of China would have shattered the domestic Japanese propaganda that the island nation was immune to foreign attack irrespective of its own military actions. After the American war with Japan had actually begun, the Tokyo Raid of April 1942, led by Lt. Colonel James Doolittle, was launched with much the same objective.

The psychological shock of bombing missions flown against Japan from China would also have been magnified by the threat of actual American strategic bombing of Japan, and Roosevelt determined that threat needed to be added to the overall strategy. It was certainly within his power as commander in chief to order the deployment of a strategic bombing force with the capability of attacking Japan, and Roosevelt moved to do exactly that. To that end heavy American bombers, Army B-17s, were to be deployed to the Philippines. In fact, a number of aircraft intended originally to operate out of Hawaii and provide long-range sea surveillance were instead sent to the Philippines. The intent was to demonstrate a strategic bombing threat which would deter the Japanese, already involved in expanding Japanese imperial holdings beyond Manchuria and China.

Army Chief of Staff George C. Marshall advised the American commanders in the Philippines that establishing a B-17 force there was of great strategic importance, establishing a strong deterrent and threatening the flank of any further Japanese movement southward from their new bases in Indochina towards Malaya and into the rich Dutch territorial possessions. Roosevelt also made sure that this overt military leverage was publicly visible to the Japanese. Media outlets were used to promote the image of growing American air power in the western Pacific, with the intent of ensuring such stories were repeated by Japanese newspapers.

A *New York Times* article in October 1941 described—and illustrated—the possibility of bombing the Japanese islands from a number of points, including Chungking, China and Hong Kong. Beyond that, in a highly unusual move, General Marshall conducted a closed-door briefing for a number of major American newspapers and magazines. The subject was America's plan for an air war against Japan, to be conducted from bases in both the Philippines and China.[15]

The potential of these bombing missions projected a message of deterrence and it was simple enough for Roosevelt to direct the buildup of a bombing force in the Philippines. From a "psyops" perspective, it was enough to get that message into the American media and on to Japan. But actual American air operations in China would have been something far different, especially with an official American position of neutrality in China and a public not at all willing to go to war. At this point in time the isolationists still wielded a great deal of national political clout and formal measures such as the Neutrality Act circumscribed any kind of overt effort to aid China.

Roosevelt's solution was to secretly turn to commercial and business connections in order to enable the Chinese portion of a deterrent stance against Japan. Exactly how he managed that provides us with an excellent illustration of the ways private businesses, trade relationships, and "layered" financial transactions can be used to enable deniable activities. In this particular instance, the project proved especially feasible because the Chinese government was willing and ready to agree to virtually any arrangement which would bring American aircraft and personnel into its fight against the ongoing Japanese invasion.

Personal relationships based in pre-existing business and social connections also contributed to the acceptance of what was in truth a highly risky project—politically at least—for President Roosevelt. Fortunately for the Chinese, Soong had already developed those types of connections to two of Roosevelt's key cabinet advisors. That put him in a very special position, able to present proposals to and receive endorsements from Morgenthau and Knox, who were at the most senior level of American policy making. By the fall of 1940, Soong had convinced both men that America must come to China's aid, even if it had to do so covertly. Morgenthau's private papers reveal a great number of details about his plans to establish a "Special Air Unit" which would operate bombers from Eastern China to attack Tokyo and other Japanese cities.[16]

Given that this was essentially a deniable military project, it differs in some respects from purely political warfare operations, but it exposes certain aspects of operational activities that are common to both. One, being that the materials and personnel involved cannot be found to be officially purchased or employed by the government that is actually initiating the action. In regard to the Special Air Unit the solution was to have all the American-made aircraft and materials purchased by Chinese companies, and paid for with Chinese funds. The aircrews and support personnel, having "resigned" from the U.S. Army Air Force, would have to be employed by Chinese companies; they could be referred to as either volunteers coming to the aid of the Chinese people, or as soldiers of fortune.

This approach is a constant in deniable actions through the Cold War period and beyond. Not limited to the United States, it includes Russian "volunteers" flying MIG aircraft over Korea in the 1950s and extends to the "little green men" in Crimea and Eastern Ukraine in the present. It is of course necessary to obfuscate connections to the materials and personnel in a deniable project, and the same caution applies to hiding the money that pays for it all. Money for the initial Special Air Unit purchases came directly from bank credits guaranteed by the American government.[17] Later, circumstances would allow the Roosevelt administration to actually extend a $100 million loan to China from the United States.[18]

Soong's company, Universal Trading Corporation, bought the aircraft and engines and served as a representative for another company, China Defense Supplies Inc. Intentionally named to sound like a Chinese company, China Defense Supplies was simply a legal shell organized by Thomas Corcoran, who served as its legal counsel. Corcoran was well-connected in Washington DC, working as a lawyer, a lobbyist, and a speechwriter for FDR. David McKean, the author of a biography of Corcoran (*Peddling Influence: Thomas "Tommy the Cork" Corcoran and the Birth of Modern Lobbying*), described him as Roosevelt's most trusted advisor and companion, often acting as his emissary in Washington circles. Corcoran's brother David served as president of China Defense Supplies, while Roosevelt's elderly uncle Frederic A. Delano acted as the company's "honorary counselor."

As part of its cover, the company established its offices within the Chinese Embassy in Washington, DC. However, for practical purposes, such a project could not have been enabled without the use of American business connections in China itself. That critical link was fulfilled by William D. Pawley, long active in overseas aviation companies in both Cuba and China, and the head of the Intercontinent Corporation of New York. Pawley was well established in China, having managed the China National Aviation Corporation and then, using Intercontinent as a holding company, partnering with the Chinese government in the creation of Central Aircraft Manufacturing Company (CAMCO), which functioned as a purchasing company for the government. CAMCO also operated a number of aircraft assembly, maintenance, and repair facilities in China itself.

Hearing of the China Defense Supply purchase of some hundred American-manufactured P-40 fighters, Pawley inserted himself into the Special Air Unit project, obtaining an agreement to assemble, service, and test-fly the planes being shipped into China. This provided effective cover for American personnel going into the unit, as they simply became employees of Pawley's CAMCO. Roosevelt directly facilitated that process by authorizing Special Air Unit representatives to directly contact U.S. Army and Navy pilots, offering them assurances that they could resign their commissions, take the private jobs overseas, and later return to their military careers with equivalent or possibly even higher ranks.

Given the political risks of the project those contacts and promises were made verbally and the funds involved, which came from U.S. presidential discretionary accounts, were transferred with no paper records. The private papers of Secretaries Morgenthau and Knox refer to "hush-hush" meetings on the subject and the need to leave no official paper trails of any sort.[19] Roosevelt also issued a secret, oral executive order directing covert military assistance in the formation of the new air unit without consultation with or notification of Congress.[20] This is especially revealing in that it would prove to be a precedent followed by successive U.S. presidents. Decades later, FDR's actions would even be cited as precedent and justification for certain actions of President Ronald Reagan in respect to covert operations against the legal government of Nicaragua.

Roosevelt's efforts did indeed produce a "Special Air Unit" in China, and its fighter element became publicly known as the American Volunteer Group (AVG-1). The unit's members became famous as the Flying Tigers, led by Claire Lee Chennault. When America officially declared war against Japan, Chennault rejoined the American military as a major general, commanding the 14th U.S. Army Air Force. What was much less widely known was that plans were also underway for AVG-2, the bomber element of the special air group, the unit which would have delivered on the threat of bombing Japan.

The formation of that unit had been delayed due to bomber aircraft allocations, with both the regular Army Air Force and Britain irate over losing bomber production to any Chinese sales. In September 1941, Chennault was in the process of sending Lockheed Hudson bombers to China for AVG-2, as well as recruiting and beginning overseas transport of aircraft crews.[21] By mid-November, at the same time George Marshall was conducting his secret media briefing on plans for a potential air war against Japan, the first set of crews destined for AVG-2 was in San Francisco, waiting to depart for China. In retrospect it seems that Roosevelt's strategy for developing strategic bombing as a deterrent would most likely not have affected Japanese war plans, but within a month the Japanese attacks on Hawaii and in the Philippines spelled the end to the formation of AVG-2. The disaster in the Philippines destroyed the entire B-17 bombing force that was being established there.

At the time Roosevelt's secret Chinese Special Air Unit project was something very new to America. Covert operations had little place in the nation's history. That would change dramatically within a single decade. In fact, some of the individuals from that project became active in certain of the nation's first Cold War-era covert political and military operations. Both Corcoran and Pawley became influential within Washington power circles beyond the Roosevelt presidencies.

Pawley was appointed by President Harry S. Truman as a U.S. ambassador, first to Peru and then to Brazil. He became quite close to President Dwight D. Eisenhower, as well as to very senior CIA officers such as Allen Dulles. In 1954 Eisenhower appointed Pawley to a top-secret five-member advisory panel chartered to review and evaluate all aspects of American intelligence, including the operations of the CIA and all other intelligence groups. That panel presented its findings directly by way of personal reports to the president.[22]

"Tommy the Cork" Corcoran was close not only to Roosevelt but also to Eisenhower. He represented a number of corporations, among them United Fruit Company, one of the largest American companies doing business across Latin America.[23] With his access to both the senior levels of the CIA and presidential administrations, he became a primary source of political intelligence—and commercial influence. We now know that his opinions were critical to triggering the decision for one of America's very first postwar political warfare operations, a deniable intervention in Guatemala which began as a psychological warfare effort, moved to destabilizing that nation's governance, and ultimately turned into a full-scale regime change effort.[24] [25]

American political warfare against Guatemala, which will be explored in considerable detail, illustrates what would become all too familiar—projects initiated as limited political warfare which grew into full-scale hybrid warfare and involved surrogate paramilitary action and even overt American military involvement. However, the intervention in Guatemala did not come about until well into the 1950s, after America had committed itself to deniable actions totally outside its own laws and its long-established moral positions in international affairs.

During World War II the United States had proved it could militarily engage and defeat any combination of foreign powers, but within no more than two years after the victories against Germany and Japan, its leaders came to fear that the nation was threatened by something beyond conventional warfare. It was a threat which could not be fought openly and cleanly. The Truman and Eisenhower administrations reached the conclusion that America faced an existential threat—from not just the Soviet Union but from an ideology.

Chapter Two:
Going Dark

America's entry into deniable political warfare was a move driven both by fear and a certain amount of sheer panic. During the war in the European theater the Allied powers had simply acceded to Russia's move to take military and political control over the Baltic nations of Latvia, Estonia, and Lithuania. At the time this was viewed as purely a tactical military move, part of the common allied effort against Nazi Germany. But as early as 1945, President Roosevelt was beginning to lose confidence in any meaningful long-term alliance with the Soviets. It began with a personal note from Soviet leader Joseph Stalin accusing the Western Allies of being willing to sell out Russia in a separate peace agreement with Germany.

American relations with the Soviets only grew worse. Stalin followed with more accusations that Russia was being provided with misleading intelligence intended to undermine the Red Army's advance. Roosevelt privately remarked that it appeared to be impossible to work with the Soviet leader: "We can't do business with Stalin," he said, describing him as "not a man of his word."[1] In response, during May 1945, the "Casey Jones" aerial photomapping project was initiated over Western and South Central Europe. Its mission was to produce the comprehensive maps that would be needed for a bombing effort to blunt any western advance the Red Army might be ordered to make after the defeat of Germany.[2]

After finally repelling German invasion forces, Russia indeed surged westward, in massive and overwhelming strength. They occupied Hungary, Albania, Bulgaria, Romania, and East Germany. Although they did stop short, holding to an agreed upon dividing line in Germany, it became clear they considered those territories to be permanently under their control. As the war ended, backed by the power of the massive Red Army, Stalin quickly moved to establish both Russian political and economic hegemony over a broad sweep of the Eastern European and Baltic nations. Stalin made it quite clear to the other allied nations that Soviet control was going to be permanent, openly declaring that "whoever occupies a territory imposes its own social system."[3]

Given its new atomic weapons and the successes of its wartime bombing efforts, the American military had an answer to further overt Russian military advances. General Lauris Norstad's Army Air Forces Air Staff for Plans moved to expand on preliminary work that had been done in the summer of 1945. The result was a document entitled "A Strategic Chart of Certain Russian and Manchurian Areas." In reality it was an early strategic targeting study, anticipating the need for long-range bombing of the Soviet Union. Such a campaign would surely require the power of atomic weapons, and in line with that thinking it was proposed that the 509th Composite Group, used in the atomic bombing of Japan, be maintained intact during the postwar period. That proposal was accepted and the 509th—the only unit operating the special B-29 bombers configured for atomic attacks—was retained and stationed well within the interior of the United States, in New Mexico.

By October 1945, the Air Staff for Plans called for a bombing campaign against Russia that would have included between twenty and thirty atomic bombs. That was considered to be a realistic estimate of the number of weapons that could be immediately constructed using available uranium ore and atomic isotope production facilities at Oak Ridge, Tennessee and Hanford, Washington. The attack targeting charts designated fifteen key Russian cities, aircraft staging areas, and flight paths. An appendix listed the number of bombs required to completely destroy each city—six each for Moscow and Leningrad.[4][5]

The implicit threat of a further Red Army advance was taken quite seriously. Both the Soviets and the United States had performed major military demobilizations but the size of the Red Army as a whole still doubled that of the American forces in uniform and in Europe the Soviet manpower advantage was simply overwhelming.[6] Still, given atomic weapons and an effective strategic bombing campaign, America could at least hope to oppose any open military moves by Stalin and the Soviet Union, at least in regards to the seizure of new territories and the open warfare that would ensue.

In stark contrast there appeared to be no solution whatsoever to the problem of the new Russian political/military dominance of Eastern Europe. Political change began occurring so rapidly that the West was continually shocked by ongoing events, especially given that some of the countries initially appeared to be functioning in an independent, democratic fashion following the end of the war. Still, as a result of the Yalta Conference of February 1945, those same nations had indeed been designated to be within the sphere of interest of the Soviet Union.

Soviet tactics within its new sphere were direct, sophisticated, and brutal, based in lessons learned during the communist consolidation of power inside Russia. One of the first steps was to take control of internal affairs under the cover of security; state police were converted into Soviet surrogates under control of Russian sympathizers and directed by Russian Internal Security Officers (MVD/Ministry of Internal Affairs). Romania provided a terrifying example of how quickly Soviet dominance could be imposed. When the Red Army moved into Romania the public and official Soviet government position was that the Soviet Union "had no intention of changing the social system existing in

Romania." Yet at the end of the war it proceeded to do just that, assuming total domination of Romania's economy and governance, with the country being declared a People's Republic and totally reorganized as a communist state in the form of the Soviet Union.[7]

The heavy-handed and unapologetic imposition of Russian political dominance shocked and surprised the United States, fueling fears that Russia would turn to exporting its own ideological revolution and a communist social system even more broadly. Of course, the United States had experienced its own domestic Red Scare immediately following World War I. At that time President Woodrow Wilson responded with a heavy hand of his own, moving aggressively to confront what he characterized as "the poison of Bolshevism." Wilson's secretary of state was even more animated in his characterization, describing Communism as "the most hideous and monstrous thing the human mind has ever conceived," supported only by the "criminal, depraved, and the mentally unfit."[8]

President Herbert Hoover's campaign against American communism included use of the commonly called Sedition Act (actually a series of amendments to the Espionage Act) of 1918, which made illegal normally free speech and any expressions which questioned or cast doubts on the war effort or interfered with the sale of government bonds. The new legal code specifically targeted the use of "disloyal, profane, scurrilous, or abusive language" about the United States, its flag, or its military. Expressions of contempt for the government were also forbidden. The same standards were applied to any material sent through the U.S. mails. Conviction resulted in sentences from five to twenty years. The amendments were removed in 1920 but in the interim estimates describe some 1,500 prosecutions and up to 1,000 convictions.[9]

Beyond Hoover's moves to suppress the communist movement through controls on speech and propaganda sent though the mails, he directed Attorney General A. Mitchell Palmer to seize and deport suspected radicals, anarchists, and revolutionaries. Palmer, driven by the same fears as the president and much of his administration, warned the nation that radicals were planning to literally seize the government in an orchestrated revolution. Under Hoover's direction Palmer ordered a series of law enforcement operations, known as the Palmer Raids, which arrested thousands of immigrants and resulted in the actual deportation of hundreds of individuals. Hoover also ordered the army to move against incidents of labor and racial unrest as well as intervene in work strikes—some twenty-five times during 1919 and 1920.[10]

That first American Red Scare involved a certain element of panic, but it was a domestic matter and law enforcement and the military could be directly deployed to deal with it. Suspected radicals, communists, or sympathizers could be tried, convicted, locked up, or in some cases simply deported. But beginning in 1946 a new type of Red Scare emerged, and this time the threat appeared to be global in nature.

That type of international challenge was something entirely new for the United States. Historically, America's foreign policies had been relatively traditional, largely formal, and in the tradition an imperial approach, albeit in terms of economic rather than political empire. In a number of instances major American law and banking firms had worked in conjunction to support favored governments, ensuring loans to sustain pro-American leaders. That had been especially true in America's own hemisphere, with major loans to the governments of Bolivia and Columbia in the 1920s.

During the 1930s this approach had become more structured, with the newly formed Council on Foreign Relations (composed of the elite of the American international legal and banking firms) identifying nations which were particularly receptive to the expansion of global American economic interests. During the 1930s and 1940s its members, including future Secretary of State John Foster Dulles, confidentially authored and provided six hundreds memos on policy recommendations to the U.S. State Department.[11]

Investment, finance, legal structures, and commercial economic expansion had been the foundation of what was felt to be American international policy. Of course, as with other "empires," on a number of occasions American corporate interest had been combined with so called gunboat diplomacy. Localized military interventions had been particularly common in Latin America, most often directly stimulated by access to American policy makers by the financiers and law firms who held concerns over their clients' investments.

One particular example illustrates the general practice of gunboat diplomacy.[12] In 1917 a series of violent labor protests threatened the interests of American companies with holdings in sugar, mines, and railways in Cuba. Those companies were all clients of America's largest international law firm, Sullivan & Cromwell. As it happened, a firm associate (John Foster Dulles) had an uncle (Robert Lansing) who was serving as a legal advisor to the State Department—a position of considerable influence. Following a breakfast with his uncle, in which Dulles focused on business problems in Cuba, the State Department moved to address the issue. State requested Navy Department support and two destroyers with complements of Marines were dispatched. The Marines were landed on both the northern and southern coasts of Cuba, in areas controlled by revolutionaries. The American forces moved into the countryside and suppressed the labor protests as well as all other anti-government activities, effectively occupying those regions of Cuba for some five years. That intervention resolved the labor problems and also suppressed what had been an incipient revolution against a pro-American government in Cuba.

In the immediate postwar years of 1946 and 1947, it quickly became clear that traditional American diplomacy was going to have no effect at all on Joseph Stalin and the Soviet Union. American diplomats found that they could not even hold dialogues with Soviet representatives since every point had to be relayed to Moscow and no responses would be given until the Kremlin, or Stalin himself, weighed in on the exact wording. When the responses did arrive they were generally expressed in ideological polemic, leaving little if any room for negotiation. The emerging communist states in Eastern Europe were regarded in Moscow as being under Soviet sovereignty, and that sovereignty was being guaranteed by the force of the Red Army. The only real question was just how far that sovereignty might be extended.

Immediately following World War II, Greece remained immersed in a civil war with communist guerilla forces, forces increasingly supported and supplied by pro-Moscow regimes in Albania and Yugoslavia. An increasing number of American transport aircraft were being intercepted, threatened, and even shot down during transit flights near the Yugoslavian border. Turkey, neutral throughout the recent war, faced Russian territorial claims and the Soviet Navy was deployed to pressure the Turks to allow Russian ships unrestricted access to the Mediterranean through the Turkish Straits. Russia appeared intent on extending pressure across its borders in the entire Middle East. The Allies had agreed to remove all forces from Iran at the conclusion of the war. However, Stalin was maintaining a military presence in Iran and openly providing support to pro-Soviet separatists in revolt against the central Iranian government.

It seemed that in addition to the ongoing fear of a further Red Army advance westward within Europe, America was facing the prospect that Stalin had more far-ranging intentions, extending to all of Russia's border states. In February 1947, Secretary of State George C. Marshall warned congressional leaders—as part of a $400 million aid request for Turkey and Greece—that "it is not alarmist to say that we are faced with the first of a series [of Soviet political warfare actions] which might extend Soviet domination to Europe, the Middle East, and Asia.[13] The postwar United States had suddenly become a global power, dealing with geopolitical crises around the world. It was immediately clear that the United States had an immediate need to collect both global military and political intelligence on an entirely new scale.

During most of its history America had collected foreign intelligence in a relatively limited fashion, using military attachés detailed to foreign diplomatic missions and contacts established by Foreign Service officers within those missions. As described earlier, that sort of activity was simply an accepted corollary of long-established diplomatic relations. All nations engaged in it, to a greater or lesser extent, with global empires such as Britain, Russia, and France being particularly adept in such intelligence work.

However, in the late 1930s, as events in Europe increasingly indicated that widespread warfare was on the horizon, President Roosevelt had become quite open to alternative sources of information. We reviewed one instance of access to the president in regard to the covert Special Air Unit project in China. But there were others with special access. A group of senior American international corporate, legal, and banking leaders, with obvious self-interest in the global political order, established their own working council to share sensitive information gained from their high-level contacts in the world's capitals.[14]

Many of the participants had very special international connections and a number had intelligence and military experience. In what became an important precedent for later, deniable Cold War operations, a number of such individuals—including William "Wild Bill" Donovan (later head of the Office of Strategic Services during World War II) and Allen Dulles (future director of the CIA)—became personally involved in foreign intelligence collection. Some individuals undertook missions with specific direction from Roosevelt himself. All willingly provided and used corporate business covers for intelligence collection activities.

As World War II ended, key members of that same elite international business community began to openly warn of the Soviet threat to the established global order, both in a political and an economic sense. In doing so they established and advocated their own ideological position—based in humanity, fair play, and most especially freedom—as the antithesis of the totalitarianism inherit in Soviet style "people's republics." John Foster Dulles continued to be one of the most adamant and prolific voices speaking out against the threat of world communism. Over time he moved from preparing confidential position papers for the Council on Foreign Relations to much broader public forums, facilitated by his personal association with magazine magnate Henry Luce.

Luce's media outlets were widely viewed as giving him a preeminent voice in shaping American public opinion. They included *Time* (one million subscribers), *Life* (four million), and the business audience subscribing to *Fortune*. Beyond print media the Luce reach included *The March of Time* radio program (eighteen million listeners) and millions more who watched its newsreel version. Beginning in 1945 and 1946 Luce gave John Foster Dulles access to that audience, representing as much of a third of the nation's literate adult population. And Dulles made active use of it, touting views he shared with Luce in a series of urgent and frightening articles warning not only of the threat posed by the red menace but its basic, essentially immoral and evil nature.[15]

Out of the headlines, and known to only the highest levels of government and the military, fears of aggressive Soviet espionage and covert political action against the West had been magnified by revelations of the extent of Russian wartime spying, in particular the almost unbelievable penetration of the most secret American military development of the war. Unbelievably, the details of both the isotopic materials required for atomic weapons production and the actual Manhattan Project atomic bomb designs had been acquired by Soviet intelligence. First exposed in leads from a Russian cipher code clerk in Canada, investigations revealed that sympathetic scientists had worked with Russian military intelligence agents (GRU) to provide exact Manhattan Project information.

That information ranged from the actual locations of the American atomic plants and the production rates of the radioactive materials used in the bombs to the technical details of the critical masses of atomic materials required, the weapons fabrication procedures, the design of the bomb cores, and even the specifics of the explosive initiators. It had all been documented and passed to the Soviets. By the end of the war the Soviets did not have an actual atomic bomb, but the penetration had been so extreme that they knew a great deal about how to build one.[16]

In the public view, as 1947 passed, the political and media voices urging action against Soviet expansionism and political warfare were increasingly joined by internal calls within the American government for more drastic action, in particular on the part of the American intelligence community. By the fall of that year President Truman had agreed to that need and signed into law the National Security Act, which not only created what was hoped to be a more unified body of military command through the work of a new Joint Chiefs of Staff organization but a Central Intelligence Agency, tasked with consolidating and reporting intelligence directly to the president.[17]

While Truman himself intended the tasks of the CIA to be limited, certain language in its charter provided great leeway for its work and would serve as the legal justification for covert operations. At the time of this writing in 2018, the National Security Act of 1947 and the legal code that supports it continue to provide the basis for American covert and deniable activities, extending to both political warfare and classified military operations. In his later years Truman spoke about being increasingly frustrated by how the CIA had evolved into a "Cloak and Dagger Outfit!" rather than remaining simply a tool for keeping the president informed on international security matters.[18]

The National Security Act of 1947 also created the National Security Council (NSC), acting under the chairmanship of the president. And while Truman would later deny any personal responsibility for cloak-and-dagger operations, it was during his presidency that deniable political warfare most definitely began. The new National Security Council immediately determined that the possibility of a communist government taking control in Italy was not only a real possibility but a potential disaster for the West.

The political situation in Italy was seen as the most imminent threat facing the United States in terms of the advance of Soviet influence. That Italy was seen by the NSC as the most troubled spot in the developing political warfare with Russia is indicated by the fact that its very first report was devoted to the country. The top-secret NSC 1/1 report entitled "The Position of the United States with Respect to Italy" was issued on November 17, 1947. Its assessment was dire. The situation was such that, in the event of a communist electoral victory, America had begun planning to deploy troops to support anti-communist forces in what was anticipated to be an Italian civil war.[19]

NSC 1/1 noted that "The Italian Government, ideologically inclined toward Western democracy, is weak and is being subjected to continuous attack by a strong Communist Party." It also stated that the United States should "actively combat communist propaganda in Italy by an effective information program and by all other practical means; overt humanitarian aid, military assistance to the Italian government, and an intense program of deniable political action and covert psychological warfare were all part of the plans developed for a rapid American intervention in Italian politics."

The NSC followed up with another directive in December 1947. NSC 4/A authorized the initiation of covert political warfare programs, stating that the CIA would conduct "psychological operations" while the State Department would oversee "informational activities."[20] This document was so sensitive that only two copies were made; one remained with the CIA director, another went to George Kennan at the State Department. Secrecy was essential, the United States was about to move into activities clearly beyond its own traditions of fair play and respect for the democratic process. It was going over to the dark side, to deniable warfare, engaging in the same conduct its adversaries were; the old standards no longer applied.[21]

During 1948, the new Central Intelligence Agency, responding to events in Italy and France, moved into America's first major covert political warfare missions. In doing so it initiated a series of activities which had long been standard practices for the ages-old imperial intelligence services, political action practices adapted by the Comintern following the communist overthrow of the czarist government, practices still actively being carried out by the Soviets in Eastern Europe and elsewhere. In Italy and France, CIA operatives would recruit surrogates, suborn government officials, use local media for propaganda purposes, and conduct a program of psychological warfare. They would also unabashedly attempt to manipulate free elections. All measures relatively new to America but simply baby steps compared to what was to come later.

In the first months of 1948 the political situation in Italy was perceived as being so desperate that one internal memorandum from the secretary of state provided a truly radical option, advising the Italian government to declare the Italian Communist Party illegal and to exclude it from the pending elections—even though such a move would no doubt provoke violence and possibly even an attempted revolution.[22] Contingency plans were also being made for U.S. Navy evacuations of United States citizens from various points in Italy. The assumption was that either a communist electoral victory or government moves to forestall such an event would bring riot and chaos to Italy.[23]

The CIA's Italian emergency action program aimed at forestalling such a disaster consisted primarily of money covertly provided to Italian centrist parties, to the tune of one million American dollars. The money bought posters, flyers, and covered both campaign and personal expenses.[24] Letter campaigns were financed and radio broadcasts warning of the dangers of a Communist Party election victory were carried out. The Luce media empire even entered the fray, with an April 19, 1948 *Time* cover story on the elections, warning Americans (including Italian-Americans) of the dangers of a Communist victory and supporting the Christian Democracy party leader in the elections.

But the CIA was not alone in offering deniable monetary support to groups in the Italian election. In practices similar to those we traced through the Great Game, money was funneled from the Soviet compound in Rome directly to the Communist Party of Italy.[25] The amounts grew as the elections neared and an ongoing stream of financial support went into party recruiting, campaigning, and to individual party leaders and candidates. Stalin himself was reportedly personally involved and in communication with the Italian party leaders.[26]

The initial CIA money and media operation in Italy proved to be surprisingly successful. A more modest effort in France, along with extensive aid measures, blocked the communist labor efforts there. American political action in Italy then moved into a sustaining effort, with the CIA spending approximately $5 million in covert funds annually to maintain American influence and "shape" Italian elections. That effort, strongly supported by Clare Booth Luce (the American envoy to Italy from 1953–55) continued on into the early 1960s.[27] Ironically, shortly after her nomination to the post, Luce was asked by a reporter if she would make a prediction on an upcoming Italian election or offer advice to the Italian voters. Luce replied quite simply: "We don't like people or other nations to interfere in our elections. Why should they?"[28] Later she remarked to a friend that it would be best if she maintained a low profile, and, if asked, she simply indicate that the United States does not interfere in other people's affairs.

While events in Italy had been seen as an imminent danger, within months the reality of the early 1948 communist "constitutional coup" in Czechoslovakia had taken hold as a major concern not only for America but all of the Western Bloc nations. A series of challenges over

Czechoslovakia's general election initially led to widespread protests. Then, to everyone's shock, a communist interior minister had moved to orchestrate a restructuring of the government and the end result was total Communist Party control.

The experience was another dramatic example of how quickly a centralized, organized Communist Party movement could literally overwhelm a variety of independent or opposing factions, parties, and groups. Communist militants had quickly occupied non-communist ministries and civil servants were prevented from entering and carrying out routine governance. The Czech Army took a position of inaction in respect to civilian control, but in their place trade union militias armed themselves and quickly blocked any public protest. A general strike was threatened, and the Red Army, deployed at the nation's borders, was offered in support of the "popular" revolution.

Further elections were banned and from that point on the new government simply implemented a model of governance based on the Soviet system. Opposing political parties were dissolved, restrictions were placed on any foreign travel, businesses were nationalized, and currency control impoverished much of the nation's business and professional classes. The overwhelming American reaction to the Czechoslovakian experience was that once communists took positions in any government they had the ability to take control, therefore any government with an active Communist Party was at risk.[29]

It seems worth noting that the Russian practice of staging units of the Red Army as a large and intimidating military force, available but ostensibly not actively taking part during regime change activities, would later be copied by the United States during several Eisenhower regime change projects. It proved exceptionally effective in Guatemala in 1954 and totally ineffective in Cuba in 1961. In contrast, following postwar events in Eastern Europe, it would generally disappear from Russian tactics of the Cold War, only to appear again in the Crimea and Ukraine in the second decade of the twenty-first century. In the first instance it would prove quite effective, in the second it appears to have largely failed.

The level of American concern over what appeared to be Soviet-supported political chaos in the long-established international order rapidly escalated. During the early spring of 1948 President Truman had come to view the global changes as a basic war of ideologies. National security historians describe Truman's view as being that it mattered little whether Soviet military forces or even Soviet officials were present at all.[30] That view was formally stated in a National Security Directive (NSC 7) in March 1948 that led with the blunt assumption: "The ultimate objective of Soviet directed World Communism is the domination of the world."[31]

Both the State Department and the Central Intelligence Agency felt that it would be their responsibility to play the primary role in the new American political action initiatives opposing that domination. State because of its responsibility in regard to international relations and the CIA due to the fact that deniable psychological warfare, within its charter, would obviously be a major component of such projects. The State Department weighed in first, with a position paper (May 4, 1948) from its Policy Planning Committee (PPC); the paper largely reflected the personal views of PPC committee head George Kennan.[32]

Those views are particularly instructive in that Kennan found covert political action to be both historically justified and a practical necessity in regard to the realities of international relations. In particular Kennan noted that political warfare had long been an accepted practice of the British and the Russians, in fact the Soviet Union consistently used its practices and at the time its conduct of such operations was "the most refined and effective of any in history."[33] Clandestine support of friendly surrogates, "black" psychological warfare, and the active encouragement of resistance—even inciting, aiding, and abetting revolutionary movements were mandatory if the United States was going to attempt to forestall "the full might of the Kremlin's political warfare."[34]

Without an explicit reference to the example of the Soviet Union and the pre-war Comintern, Kennan went on to propose the creation of highly visible and independent "liberation committees." These committees would be publicly separate from the American government, would conduct broad appeals for membership and volunteer funding, and would provide a credible source for a wide variety of propaganda messages. In reality, they would simply be covers for a far more aggressive set of covert actions ranging from psychological warfare to direct paramilitary action should it be required as a last resort.[35]

While Kennan would have liked the State Department to have assumed control of the new political warfare initiative, clearly the legal justification—under the National Security Act of 1947—and the most obvious resources for such projects were within the Central Intelligence Agency. In a compromise, State was given the role of policy guidance in regard to major new projects and the CIA was assigned to the actual, dark and deniable operational aspects of carrying out such missions. That agreement was formalized with NSC 10/2, which spelled out responsibilities and created a new Office of Special Projects. OPC functioned with policy and planning direction from State and operational support from the CIA.[36] Its projects and functions were authorized to include propaganda, economic warfare, and—as required—"direct action" including infiltration, sabotage, demolition, evacuation (exfiltration), and support and assistance for resistance organizations and guerilla groups within the targeted countries.

This American move into the dark side of political action was largely directed against the rapid expansion of Soviet control in Eastern Europe, with the intent of destabilizing governance in the targeted nations, of weakening Soviet political influence and, at its most optimistic, stimulating and supporting counter-revolutions. Much thought (and money) was focused on propaganda and psychological warfare, there were efforts to insert exiles and refugees to collect intelligence and hopefully to organize guerilla-type opposition to communist rule.

Yet, in a striking error, little attention was given to the policy (and military) commitments that would come into play should revolution against Communist regimes actually occur—something almost certain to bring about Soviet military intervention.

Chapter Three:
Containment

With the full concurrence of President Harry Truman and the issuance of National Security Council Directive 10/2, the United States was going to war, covertly and with deniable operations in direct contrast to its officially stated public policies—using practices authorized within the legal codes derived from the National Security Act of 1947. In later years Truman expressed regret that the CIA had gone into cloak-and-dagger work, but anyone reading Directive 10/2 should have had no illusions about what was to happen, and no doubt that it would be done using both operational and financial covers.

The financial aspects of those covers were enabled by wording in the National Security Act of 1947 which had essentially freed the CIA from the standard legal constraints of reporting and accounting for government spending. Specifically: "…the sums made available to the Agency may be expended without regard to the provisions of law and regulations relating to the expenditure of government funds…"[1] That gave the Agency the ability to determine its own financial practices. In many instances it did follow normal government accounting practices internally for routine operations and for its own personnel. However, in other instances major covert expenditures were signed off only with authorizations from key senior officers and largely undocumented. In terms of the newly authorized containment activities, it was particularly helpful that the newly created Office of Policy Coordination also had access to unvouchered administrative "counterpart funds," funds available to the very public Marshall Plan European assistance program, which received some $200 million annually.[2]

Housing the new containment initiative under the benignly named Office of Policy Coordination (a change from its original designation as the Office of Special Projects) was just the first step in coving up the joint State Department/CIA's new clandestine operations. In later years similar innocuous designations such as Directorate of Operations or Directorate of Plans would be given to the CIA division responsible for psychological and paramilitary operations, including those aimed at actually overthrowing democratically elected governments. For the purposes of our exploration of covert political warfare, the OPC's "containment" initiative provides us with an introduction to tools and tradecraft but equally importantly to the types of layered cover structures used to shield the financing and operational activities involved. Initially those covers seem baffling—reasonably so, given they are constructed for just that purpose—but after a time they become not only obvious but repetitive. For example, many of the financial covers used in the containment operations in Eastern Europe are little different in principal than those which were used decades later to cover Reagan era covert action against the government of Nicaragua.

The first point to make is that certain aspects of propaganda and psychological warfare have to be conducted in public. Radio broadcasts, leaflet distribution, newspaper and magazine articles—any mass media tools—are all quite public and in respect to official deniability need to have a credible source other than an agency of the government that is expected to deny official involvement. The Soviet Union had dissolved the original Comintern during World War II but restored it as the Cominform (Communist Information Bureau) in 1947, utilizing it once more as a similar cover for supporting and routing funds to communist parties and national fronts around the world.

The Cominform's reach was extremely broad and its scope global. Its affiliates included the World Peace Council, World Federation of Democratic Youth, World Federation of Scientific Workers, International Union of Students, International Order of Journalists, and the International Association of Democratic Lawyers. New and revitalized practices allowed the Soviet government to leverage supposedly independent political parties, labor unions, academic unions, and similar surrogates to accomplish its propaganda programs. In ostensibly neutral countries its outreach to students, academics, and journalists proved especially effective given that it consistently conducted propaganda advocating world peace, anti-colonialism, and anti-imperialism. Such messaging was often well received in the postwar developing nations; it also worked effectively in the face of the explosive and increasingly obvious postwar growth of American economic hegemony.

Beginning in 1949, the Office of Policy Coordination turned to a public cover somewhat more limited than the Cominform, but one which provided deniability for its campaign against the new Soviet satellite nations in Eastern Europe. Given that the containment program's fundamental goal was to "liberate" nations that had fallen under Communist Party domination, the first public move in the campaign was to organize a series of liberation committees. These would be composed of exiles, refugees, and American citizens desiring to support liberation efforts. They ostensibly served to establish political leadership and a common forum for organizing a public voice for national groups speaking out against the new totalitarianism in their native countries. However, with or without the knowledge of members and donors, the groups would actually become fronts, conducting very public activities but also providing covers for a series of covert, deniable activities.[3]

To a large extent the State Department under George Kennan was the driving force in the public organization of the fronts. It also assisted in directing their overt activities while the OPC largely operated in their shadow. In April 1949, Kennan inaugurated that effort with a memorandum to Secretary of State Dean Acheson, in which he asked for permission to found the National Committee for a Free Europe (NCFE).[4] The committee, led by future CIA Director Allen Dulles and other philanthropic, industrial, and legal elites, was to be a "principal instrumentality" in the brand new containment project. Only a handful of people knew that NCFE was actually the public face of an innovative psychological warfare project being undertaken by the CIA. That operation, which soon gave rise to Radio Free Europe, would become the public face of the new containment efforts in Eastern Europe.

The NCFE was publicly supported by a host of well-known Americans including General Dwight D. Eisenhower, Arthur Schlesinger Jr., and Cecil B. DeMille. One of its major missions was fundraising, conducted by the Crusade for Freedom. Donated monies ostensibly supported a number of very public activities and the Crusade for Freedom was very active, producing donations of two to three million dollars annually through the early 1950s.

In reality both the NCFE and the public donation program provided operational and financial covers for a series of covert Office of Policy Coordination activities, including an extensive effort to organize, sustain, and direct the activities of various expatriate "national councils" targeting the new Soviet satellite nations. Given that the United States was officially maintaining relations with those nations, the hosting of governments in exile, as had been done during World War II, was not feasible. However, it was hoped that the national councils might bring respected figures into the effort to destabilize governance in the satellites and possibly even within Russia itself.

That hope began to fade as the national councils quickly ran into considerable difficulty. The NCFE found itself totally unable to sufficiently reconcile pre-existing political and personal differences to even form councils for the Yugoslav and Polish exiles. As of 1952 the same held true for the Romanians, and the councils that had been formed for the Czechoslovaks and Hungarians were in disarray and highly factionalized. A 1953 review of the psychological warfare effort concluded that efforts to organize effective national councils had been frustrated by continual "bickering" and "jealousies" among the member politicians.[5]

This early experience with national committees composed of émigrés and exiles might have been taken as a warning of just how difficult such groups would be to organize or effectively use in either political warfare or actual regime change operations. Given the political differences, the ideological differences, and the willingness to revive both old grudges and conflicts, it was certainly a poor leading indicator for future efforts. The experience also revealed that such individuals were quick to sense the covert intelligence connections to their groups, to boast about official support, and to take disagreements either to the media or to sympathetic members of Congress.[6]

Other OPC activities at first appeared to hold far more promise. In particular it was the NCFE's sponsorship of radio broadcasts, first via Radio Free Europe beginning in 1950, and later via Radio Liberty, which specifically targeted the Soviet Union. Great care was taken to provide for financial cut-outs to obscure the actual CIA funding of Radio Free Europe. This was a closely held secret, unknown to members of the boards of the Crusade for Freedom and Radio Free Europe who had no idea that considerable monies were coming from the CIA. It would not be until 1971, when the CIA's relationship was exposed, that Agency funding ceased.[7] Documents would eventually reveal that the NCFE offices (in a well-appointed third-floor space in Manhattan's Empire State Building) routinely received a weekly Agency support payment in the form of a check, carried to them from the offices of Henry Sears's Wall Street investment firm.[8]

Radio as a psychological tool was certainly not something new. As early as 1917 the Bolsheviks had attempted limited propaganda broadcasts, and the Soviets had applied much more aggressive radio efforts towards Finland in support of their effort to annex that country, following up with an actual invasion. During World War II, Germany, Japan, Great Britain, and the United States had routinely aired propaganda. English-language broadcasts from Germany and Japan had specifically targeted American servicemen, often in a very selective fashion, including unit- and operation-specific messaging.

While the U.S. Army had been involved in a variety of psychological warfare activities during the war, applying those practices during peacetime (and doing so covertly) was something very new. OPC personnel were faced with learning messaging techniques and practices on the job.[9] Radio Free Europe evolved quickly, from almost brute-force anti-communist messaging in the earliest days to a much less strident tone as each national, language-specific broadcast attempted to sound exactly like local media while offering a truly alternative view of both national and world events.

The scope of broadcasting dramatically escalated over time, from one transmitter in 1950 to twenty-six in 1953. Almost every Soviet satellite nation was being targeted by Radio Free Europe, with source information from eight news bureaus and a staff of 256 Americans and over 1,500 foreign employees devoted to the individual national language broadcasts.[10] The Soviets were not at all pleased with such airwave saturation and set up massive radio jamming operations. In more than one instance they were also suspected of intimidating or assassinating broadcast personnel. Mass production of shortwave radios was also restricted inside Russia.

As with any psychological warfare effort, the effect of the radio broadcasts could be magnified with access to detailed intelligence about the target. One of the participants was a Polish former intelligence officer who had prior access to dossiers on leading communists now in senior positions in the Polish communist government. The files included specific details of personal and financial corruption. A series of targeted broadcasts exposed them, resulting in a purge that established a more "moderate" regime.[11] It was an excellent example of classic political warfare at its most successful—chaos had been created within a regime which destabilized its ability to govern.

Still, with Soviet control over the availability of radios and with extreme jamming efforts, OPC's radio reach was limited. No matter how good its émigré and exile-sourced information from inside the United States and in Europe, it was limited by the tools available for getting its message beyond Eastern Europe's new Iron Curtain. While the open media in the West provided virtually unlimited opportunities for Soviet propaganda and disinformation, the OPC remained limited to long-distance shortwave transmissions using Radio Europe, Radio Liberty, and pirate radio.

For want of other alternatives, the OPC turned to a communications method that could not be jammed. Balloons carried leaflets, broadsheets specifically targeted individual communist leaders, and newspapers and even forged currency were launched in huge numbers over the borders of the closest satellite nations. Over 300 million leaflets and newspapers were dropped over denied areas through the early 1950s. Obviously this sort of highly public psychological warfare was strongly protested by the nations being overflown, as well as by the Soviet Union.

The official American response, one previously used by the Comintern and later the Cominform, was simply the standard gambit used in deniable warfare of all types, and one which continues today. The balloons and their contents had been launched by private citizens volunteering in pursuit of freedom, paid for with donations. None of it had anything to do with the United States or its official diplomatic relations with the nations making the protests. In the meantime, the weekly checks continued to be delivered to the third floor of the Empire State Building.

Within OPC itself other officers newly recruited from the wartime Office of Strategic Services (OSS) carried out highly compartmentalized projects involving missions of a much more paramilitary nature.

Led by Frank Wisner (former chief of OSS operations in Eastern Europe), the effort started from scratch, including such extremes as purchasing intelligence from former Nazis and extensively recruiting operational personnel, including infiltration personnel, from refugee populations.

The officers involved viewed themselves as already being at war with the Soviets, their mission described by former CIA Director William Colby as that of saving Western freedom from communist darkness. In its first years, OPC officers were generally second-in-command at overseas American embassies and were given a high degree of autonomy with access to almost totally non-accountable funding, including unvouchered "counterpart funds" hidden within the Marshall Plan's European relief program administrative budget. It was viewed as a desperate effort for a desperate time. That desperation was perhaps most obvious in the ongoing efforts to insert agents and entire teams across the satellite nation borders.

Ground insertions and airdrops were conducted on an ongoing basis, with the hope that the effort would support guerilla and resistance groups already working against communist regimes in the targeted nations, possibly triggering major insurgencies or even anti-communist revolution. Yet dozens of teams and hundreds of personnel simply disappeared into the East. Some were heard from briefly as team radio messages lured in new groups—which were immediately captured. It was years before it was learned that most missions were compromised by Soviet agents with access to operational plans. In the end, the denied area insertion operations proved to be a horrific fiasco.

One retired U.S. Army officer who had been involved with the "black" insertion efforts into Eastern Europe summarized that experience: "I went down to the airfield each time an agent team was to be inserted into a target country...to do a final equipment check and wish them luck...at the time none of them I was responsible for made contact after being inserted."[12] The officer would later function in the same capacity, supporting years of similar covert insertions into North Vietnam, yet another effort which proved to be a total fiasco for all involved.[13]

Perhaps the most shocking aspect of the overall OPC effort is found in what we now know about the abortive Hungarian Revolution of 1956, a general uprising against communist governance and Soviet political control. At the time there was a widespread belief that Western propaganda and the new, clandestine political action campaign might indeed have the potential of triggering revolutions within satellite nations. Certainly, the CIA was suspected of playing a serious role in the Hungarian uprising. While the American public might have liked to think (at least initially) that this had been the case, there is no doubt that the Soviets themselves assumed it to be true. In a Presidium of the Supreme Soviet session of October 28, statements were made that American intelligence was obviously more active in Hungary than were the Soviets.

Yet with decades of study and new document releases, we know that the Hungarian uprising was a total shock to the CIA.[14] The uprising itself provides a dramatic illustration of the utter lack of planning—or political commitment—to American action in the event of any actual revolution against Soviet hegemony in Eastern Europe. The CIA had no intelligence operation in Hungary, the OPC had no response to actively follow up on the revolutions it was attempting to incite, and both the Truman and Eisenhower administrations had developed no policy or contingency plans should the OPC efforts succeed. Other than a fevered, emotional expression of outrage, there simply was no American response as Soviet tanks rolled into Hungary and over its popular insurgency.

Finger-pointing followed and the CIA went to great lengths preparing internal studies relating the true state of affairs, exposing the almost total lack of operational intelligence not only in regard to Hungary but as to the Soviet Union as well. A CIA Clandestine Service history of 1958 was explicit: "This breath-taking and undreamed-of state of affairs not only caught many Hungarians off-guard, it also caught us off-guard, for which we can hardly be blamed since we had no inside information, little outside information, and could not read the Russians' minds."[15]

American lack of planning and participation in the uprising is detailed by Charles Gati in his book *Failed Illusions: Moscow, Washington, Budapest and the 1956 Hungarian Revolt.*[16] Gati obtained portions of two previously secret CIA histories dealing with CIA operations in Hungary. Excerpts from those studies are now available online at the National Security Archives, hosted by George Washington University. The documents confirm that the CIA had only a single Hungarian-speaking officer in-country, working within the American diplomatic staff in Budapest. His duties were almost entirely related to support tasks for that role, including conducting interviews with visitors to the nation. Specifically, the CIA affirmed that during October and November 1956 no activities were being conducted inside Hungary that constituted a true "intelligence operation."

A National Security Archives review of the available CIA documents, edited by Thomas Blanton and Michael Byrne, also addresses the view of the time that there must have been some type of American assistance to the insurgency, either by the CIA or the OPC.[17] Given the OPC's mission, it would certainly have seemed that its teams must have been deployed into Hungary, inciting or participating in the uprising. At the least, weapons, ammunition, and some level of covert military support would have been expected. Yet the internal CIA inquiries confirm that staff were instructed from headquarters that the only operational role in the uprising, and with what turned out to be an interim, independent Hungarian regime, was to be intelligence collection. As to arms and military supplies, the documents indicate that it was not a subject of discussion even as a contingency—during the uprising no inquiries were made regarding the availability of weapons.

While there had been an earlier effort to recruit and train Hungarian expatriates, and even attempts to form volunteer groups, many had been lost in the earlier failed insertions and reconnaissance missions. Such insertions had become increasingly difficult and by 1953 cross-border operations were virtually untenable. The most that was done was to move available volunteers to the border of Hungary in an effort to collect information about what was going on during the revolt. Some may have penetrated inside, but their mission was limited to field intelligence collection.[18] In retrospect and with the internal documents now available, it appears that a major disconnect had evolved within the dual missions of the OPC by the time of the Eisenhower administration. A disconnect very possibly encouraged by the difference between Eisenhower's assertive campaign rhetoric regarding "rolling back" communism and his much more realistic private views acknowledging the absolute need not to provoke open warfare with the Soviets.

The nature and depth of that disconnect is explored at length in Ronald D. Landa's "Almost Successful Recipe: The United States and East European Unrest prior to the 1956 Hungarian Revolution."[19] Landa makes a strong case that by 1952-53 American policy was oriented towards political warfare that would simply reduce Soviet influence on its satellites in Eastern Europe, minimizing centralized Soviet bloc control and evolving more nationalist governments, on the model of Tito's Yugoslavia. While the governments themselves might remain socialist/communist in orientation, the goal would be to move them towards more autonomy, increasingly breaking lockstep control from Moscow and including the potential of destabilizing if not actually fragmenting the Warsaw Pact.

Eisenhower is privately on record speaking out against the provocation of futile and bloody uprisings that would only provoke stronger military control—and repression—from Moscow. Documents from Psychological Strategy Board meetings of the period express the selection of tactics and messages which simply encourage "disunity." Even CIA Director Allen Dulles is on record in 1953 stating, "you don't have uprisings in a totalitarian state…you don't revolt in the face of tanks, artillery, and tear gas…revolutions are now at the top, with the Army going to one side or the other."[20]

The Hungarian experience exposes the reality that a major American political warfare project intended to destabilize Russian satellite governments—containing and hopefully minimizing further Soviet political influence—had expanded to include a deniable paramilitary effort intended to actually instigate and support resistance, insurgencies, and even revolution. But it had done so without any specific commitment at the presidential level under Truman and Eisenhower, much less any detailed plans for action should those efforts actually succeed.

Certainly, both presidents talked about containing and even pushing back Soviet political advances in Europe. This had become a standard political talking point, primarily of Republicans, during the early 1950s.

Given the private, pragmatic views of President Eisenhower, available dialogues within the Psychological Strategy Board (composed of senior staff from the State Department, CIA, and Joint Chiefs of Staff),[21] and remarks by the CIA director, the lack of any overt American response to the Hungarian uprising is quite understandable. However, at the time it was certainly a shock to the American public, and apparently to certain paramilitary elements of the OPC as well.

While the OPC had indeed created some elements of disunity and destabilization in certain of the targeted satellite nations, primarily through its radio broadcasting efforts, its goal of creating unified national councils of expatriates and émigrés had fallen far short of expectations. Its early paramilitary efforts were almost totally ineffectual, verging on sacrificial. And national policy had passed it by, acknowledging the fact that, at best, political warfare against the satellites was evolutionary rather than revolutionary. There would be no roll-back there; the Hungarian uprising had demonstrated that the Red Army was available to intervene against any uprising at the time of Moscow's choosing. In the longer term, the failure of the OPC effort also had a deeply personal element. Its chief, Frank Wisner, entered into a deep depression soon after the Soviet crackdown, and after his retirement from the CIA, he committed suicide in 1965.

Yet America most definitely still considered itself faced with an international crisis, and engaged in a very real and dangerous ideological war, even if it was largely a cold one. The Soviet threat was seen as existential, and President Eisenhower, with ongoing and forceful urging from Secretary of State John Foster Dulles, was not about to back off from the challenge. The United States might not be able to dislodge the Soviets from Eastern Europe, but it could certainly act to stop them elsewhere. And as to tactics, things were going to get much nastier. If the efforts of the OPC had been shadowy and deniable, the CIA was going to go much further into the dark side of political warfare.

Chapter Four:
Political Action

The more aggressive practices of political warfare—active measures programs, destabilization activities, hybrid warfare, and even regime change operations—are the exception in international relations. What is normal, even among historically friendly nations, is a relatively benign form of ongoing political action we can refer to as "shaping," a concept derived from the military usage of the same term. In combat, it is used in regard to "battlespace shaping" and involves creating an image (as perceived by the adversary) of the relationship between two forces—an image that may not be real but which will prove favorable in combat to the side performing the shaping.

The comparable practice of shaping the perceptions of relationships between governments is a task for diplomatic and foreign service professionals, a basic element of foreign relations. Shaping practices can be either positive or negative. Regimes which are favorable or seen to be at risk of adversary influence need to be approached positively, with the building of economic relationships, circulating information highlighting mutual bonds and making connections to persons of influence. Both America and the Soviet Union actively engaged in a positive imaging and shaping campaign across Europe in the years immediately following World War II, competing for influence over the voting populace and in the new postwar governments.

With both Greece and Turkey under political pressure by the Soviets as the war ended, the United States had immediately begun food and economic assistance programs to both nations during 1946. It also moved to address the larger hunger and reconstruction needs of a devastated Europe with the massive Marshall Plan/Economic Recovery Program in the summer of 1947. Certainly, humanitarian motives were fundamental to that effort—a huge $13 billion expenditure sending food, fuel, staple goods, and machinery to nations that had been laid to waste by the end of the war. The populations of Germany and France in particular were under immense stress in regard to lack of food, fuel, and the basic necessities of life. But there is also no doubt that the Marshall Plan was intended to address the immediate issues of hunger and public distress that would have placed the established governments of several nations at risk to the resurgent communist parties gaining momentum in popular elections.

Under Stalin, Russia was taking every advantage of the positive image created by its military victories over Germany to proclaim the superiority of the Soviet system. The Soviet Union also began massive propaganda campaigns in Europe, spending more in messaging to France alone than America was spending on information campaigns over all of Europe.[1] Along with the Soviet propaganda, the disdain for French business collusion with the Germans during the war combined with the lack of food, supplies, and overall economic stress to provide a major advantage for the Communist Party, which moved into a majority position in the postwar elections of 1946 and 1947. The established anti-communist and centrist political majority was also in great risk in Italy, with combined Communist and Socialist parties receiving some 40 percent of the vote in national elections.[2] The situation appeared to be breeding the same dangers that had first emerged immediately after World War I, summarized succinctly by Secretary of State Robert Lansing in 1918, "Empty stomachs mean Bolsheviks; full stomachs mean no Bolsheviks."[3]

The Soviets certainly recognized the competing political action aspects of the Marshall Plan programs and moved aggressively to prevent Eastern Bloc nations from participating. Stalin's view of the situation was imminently pragmatic, he felt that economic distress in Europe offered a real opportunity for Communist Party gains, and Soviet influence.[4] American aid had been offered to several of the new Soviet satellite regimes and certainly they were in dire need. However, Stalin strongly opposed any agreements which would allow Soviet satellites to actively participate in the Marshall Plan. Directions to stay away from the program were issued to the regimes in Czechoslovakia, Poland, and East Germany. Even Finland was pressured not to join. More directly, Stalin instructed the Communist regimes in its new Eastern European Bloc nations to actively sabotage the aid and recovery program.[5]

As an alternative, Russia fielded its own less well-funded effort, designating its relief and recovery efforts as the Molotov Plan. The Soviet plan was something far less than the Marshall Plan in actual aid; it focused on a new set of trade agreements with the obvious intent of strengthening economic ties and binding the nations now within its realm of political and military influence. The Molotov economic programs were also more obviously moves of political action since any of its new satellites who had fought on the German side were also required to pay reparations to Russia. Soviet demands for immediate and extensive reparations had a particularly dire effect on recovery in East Germany.

ITALIAN ELECTIONS 1948

The United States had embarked on a serious effort to establish positive foreign relations with Italy, even though the nation had been a major ally of Germany in the recent war. Its approach to the postwar government was quite supportive, particularly so in the face of what the

U.S. State Department viewed as a very real communist threat to the nation's established power structure. The threat of a communist victory in the 1948 Italian elections resulted not only in aggressive State Department "positive shaping" activities but also one of the first major covert political actions by the new Central Intelligence Agency. These activities are a particularly good illustration of the first level of covert practices, carried out by CIA political officers operating directly out of American diplomatic facilities.

During the winter of 1947 and spring of 1948, a great effort was made by the State Department to expedite aid to Italy under the new Marshall Plan, and also to stabilize the Italian currency by assisting the central government in fighting inflation. Aid was to be provided in Italian lira to maintain the value of the currency, the amount totaling over 600 billion lira. In essence, "control over the lira fund would mean control of the Italian economy."[6] The overriding goal was to stabilize the economy while at the same time ensuring that food and fuel were available in sufficient quantity so that shortages did not become an overriding political problem. Special attention was paid to allowing recovery funds to be used against items already included in the Italian government's budget, especially for short-term projects which would begin to immediately circulate currency and demonstrate growth.

In terms of image and psychological shaping, a combination of American and locally produced materials was brought into play. However, great care was taken to ensure that only local actors—political parties, media companies, spokespersons—actually circulated the materials to the Italian public. Propaganda and psychological warfare were viewed as the province of the Italian government and the political parties being supported.[7] Materials used in the information media campaign included the standard tools of the period (leaflets and posters to be distributed by the favored anti-communist political parties) as well a mass media outreach of radio broadcasts and newsreels.

As an example, the Italian government was active in widely distributing a newsreel titled *Thanks, America* developed by the Italian firm of Pallavicini.[8] One of the programs with the largest reach was broadcast over Radio Audizioni Italiane (RAI), Italy's national public broadcasting company. RAI was owned by and operated under the supervision of the Italian Ministry of Economy and Finance. The program intentionally avoided controversial issues and was essentially a "friendship program" featuring well-known American performers such as Bing Crosby, Walter Pidgeon, and Dinah Shore, with each making at least limited remarks in Italian. Responses from the Italian listeners showed this both surprised and pleased them. The program included references to American aid and a fundraising effort for the families of Italian flyers injured or killed in World War II. The Italian president of the National Association of Families of Fallen and Mutilated Aviators expressed great appreciation and many families of the flyers were quite moved.[9]

Food shortages, especially of cereal grains, were a particular concern for the Italians. This was a special problem for America, since it was essentially trying to balance its own grain exports across all the Marshall Plan nations' needs. While Italian diplomatic personnel emphasized the urgency of grain aid, the only U.S. recourse was to refer them to alternative, and more expensive, Argentinian sources. However, in an effort to avoid any negative political consequences, the State Department went so far as to participate in a joint press release affirming that projections for May 1948 showed that imports both from America and alternative sources would be sufficient to maintain cereal rations until domestic Italian production was able to return to required levels.[10]

The release affirmed that, if developments threatened the projected supply levels, the United States would make every effort to allocate and ship any emergency quantities required. The State Department memorandum that discusses that joint release notes that it would actually be very unlikely for the United States to up its shipments, and encouraged the Italian government to make every effort to continue pursuing alternative grain sources. The State Department also moved to assist the Italians in diversion of wheat going to Britain from Australia in order to improve their grain stocks during the summer months.[11] From a foreign relations standpoint such a move would also help to demonstrate the potential of cooperation among those nations in the Marshall Plan while reinforcing the image of the United States as being actively involved in pursuing Italian interests.

In addition to these economic and information activities, CIA political officers also covertly provided at least a million dollars in direct funding for favored, centrist political parties. The payments enabled a burst of meetings, leafleting, and advertising activities immediately prior to the national elections, and ensured that in the longer term the candidates in those parties would become positive agents of influence in future relations between the two nations. Of course, such donations had to be carried out deniably since they were in direct violation of the stated American foreign policy of non-interference in foreign elections and the democratic process in general. As noted earlier, a series of American ambassadors to Italy were careful and consistent in publicly declaring that the United States did not interfere in other people's elections.

The State Department did its own analysis of trends occurring immediately before the Italian election of 1948, reporting back to Washington that the American political action programs appeared to be surprisingly effective, and that a major swing against the Communist and Socialist parties appeared to be in play.[12] American economic aid programs and the diplomatic warning that a Communist government would not be extended aid were singled out as major factors contributing to the apparent swing away from Communist candidates. The report also noted that the flood of posters and leaflets had been very noticeable, reflecting what appeared to be a measurable difference in the final campaign push by the parties involved.

In addition, American military aid and support for a renovated and reinvigorated Italian Army appeared to have considerable impact, especially with ongoing radio broadcasts and even parades featuring newly constituted military formations. At the same time the events of early 1948 in Czechoslovakia, with a Communist Party takeover following a "failed" election, had raised fears as to what could happen when a communist political party took substantial control over government ministries and potentially the military. That message had been very effectively communicated through a variety of American and Italian media outlets.

American political action in the Italian election of 1948, and in the years to follow, gives us a picture of what became basic political action practices during the Cold War. It might well be considered a classic operation in terms of political warfare and certainly sets a baseline from which to compare American interventions throughout the rest of the era.

REGIME CHANGE IN IRAN

American involvement in Iran was heavily influenced by a worldview which settled into place early in the Eisenhower administration and was soon firmly established. The aggressive covert action political program there would stem from the demand for pushback against Soviet influence expressed in the Jackson and Doolittle Committee Reports, and it was strongly enabled by the personal worldview of Secretary of State John Foster Dulles and his ability to influence the strategic foreign policy decisions of President Eisenhower.

The CIA's participation in the Iranian political events of 1953 has been written about extensively over several decades. It was positioned as one of the first aggressive, and successful, CIA covert regime change operations. Although American involvement was officially denied at the time, it was not covert enough to escape broad public attention, both domestically inside Iran as well as in the United States. It also appears that the CIA may have taken the opportunity to promote the operation both within the Eisenhower administration and internationally to enhance its reputation.

That speculation stems from the appearance of a widely read *Saturday Evening Post* article of November 6, 1954, "The Mysterious Doings of the CIA."[13] The article begins by referring to the recent events in Iran in 1953 as a "CIA triumph," the "successful overthrow…of old, dictatorial Premier Mohammad Mossadegh…and a return to power of this country's friend Shah Mohammad Riza Pahlevi." It goes on to justify the American political action as a response to a "blackmail" effort by Mossadegh, rejected by President Eisenhower—with consequences. The article touts mysterious meetings in Switzerland between Allen Dulles, Ambassador to Iran Loy W. Henderson, and two men ostensibly accompanying the twin sister of the Shah. These occurred while Mossadegh was "consorting" with the Russian diplomatic delegation in Tehran. At the same time, Brigadier General Norman Schwarzkopf Sr. was making a circuit of Middle Eastern nations, ending up in meetings with Major General Fazlollah Zehedi and the Shah. Schwarzkopf had been posted to Iran during World War II to organize security for the Shah and stayed there though 1948, working with "elements of the Army" loyal to the Shah and countering plots to overthrow his rule.

The article relates considerable detail on events inside Iran, giving the timing of an attempt by the Shah to dismiss Mossadegh as prime minister and the appointment of General Zehedi as his successor. It relates a seizure of power by Mossadegh and the subsequent flight of the Shah from the country. It also elaborately describes a large street procession, which suddenly turned into a pro-Shah demonstration, and the Army's move to join in seizing Mossadegh and returning the Shah to power. Certainly, some of the information could be assumed to be accurate although no sources are given. Later years would reveal that much was certainly not. Perhaps the most historically questionable statements are at the end of the article, with its conclusion and effusive praise for the CIA in its success: "The strategic little nation of Iran was saved from the closing clutch of Moscow" due to the action of the CIA in developing and nurturing "indigenous Iranian legions" within Iran.

The *Post* article reportedly had considerable impact within Iran, helping to reinforce the perception that the United States had not only intervened in its internal affairs but that both the Shah and Zahedi were either virtual puppets of the United States or at best agents of American interest.[14] Beyond that, the depth of detail in the article seems to suggest either a concerning leak of operational security information (especially given the naming of Schwarzkopf and Zehedi as key CIA assets) or a CIA leak intentionally planted with the domestic media for the purposes of propaganda. It certainly made the CIA appear virtually omnipotent, able to carry out regime change with at most a handful of meetings and a few weeks of political action. What it did not mention was that the U.S. State Department was also deeply involved in the coup activities, and it most certainly does not point out, as confirmed only in 2017, that the operation as initially planned and agreed to by the State Department and CIA had actually failed.

The article's simplistic story of CIA covert political action conducted over the period of only a few weeks—removing a dictatorial prime minister who had unsuccessfully attempted to blackmail the president of the United States and who was busily working with Russian diplomats to make Iran into a Soviet satellite—did fit well within the public's worldview of the era. In retrospect and with the history now available, combined with the 2017 release of actual State Department and CIA documents on the events, we have a far more accurate picture of over two years of both British and American political action which ended with the regime change of August 1953. This story is vital to our full understanding of political warfare practices, including what worked, and what definitely did not. The tale that can now be told is far more convoluted and a good deal less impressive than the one in the *Saturday Evening Post*.

In political terms the Iranian regime change of 1953 was the outgrowth of a series of ongoing domestic political conflicts among several factions, including the sometimes pro-Soviet and sometimes anti-Soviet Tudeh Party. Iranian political history in the period is far too complex to relate here, but it is well detailed in released documents and political studies.[15] Although overly simplistic, the basic context of the political crisis of 1953 can be described in terms of a surge in nationalist politics, considerable anti-colonial emotion first towards the British and ultimately towards the West in general (due to its solidarity with Britain in their aggressive oil concession negotiations with Iran), and a fundamental split inside the country between those involved with long-established political order and those promoting change. However, in terms of political action, the crisis of the summer of 1953 actually began in 1952, with a series of British actions that seriously destabilized the Iranian economy.

Although conceding certain points in oil negotiations to the Iranians, some four basic disagreements remained, the most emotional element being the British demand that the oil fields be operated by British companies and managers rather than by Iranians, even if the Iranians were given nominal authority over their nation's oil production. Such a demand was viewed as being insulting at best, and at worst an indication that Britain had no intention of truly accepting Iranian sovereignty in regard to its most valuable natural resource. The United States certainly appreciated the Iranian concerns in the British oil negotiations and initially had remained relatively neutral. However, it moved to an implicit support of the British position as a more nationalistic Iranian position developed.

With much of the previously secret State Department and CIA communications on the subject now available for review—including more than one National Security Council deliberation—the evolution of the American position can be seen. The following is based on those documents; readers can review them online at the National Security Archives and at the State Department.[16]

As early as March 1951, the State Department and CIA assessment of the Iranian political situation had reached a point where the Iranian "ultranationalists," who were pursuing a hard line in the oil negotiations, were deemed a serious threat to the established order. While the pro-Soviet Tudeh Party was listed as a concern, its actions were seen as supportive of a broader nationalist, anti-British coalition. The Shah was perceived as ineffectual, with the only real hope of stability being in traditionalist elements of the Iranian Army. Communications from the CIA station in Tehran can generally be found to be the most alarmist and argued that nationalization of the oil industry could well lead to an outreach to the Soviets for technical support and increased Soviet influence among not only the Tudeh but the nationalists in the Iranian parliament.

A CIA Directorate of Plans paper of that same month outlined the worst possible scenario for Iran, one which would bring it directly into the Soviet orbit as a satellite state. That paper is especially revealing, as it provides insight into the standard political warfare tool kit of the CIA and the OPC. It outlines a plan for intensified overt and covert propaganda supporting the Shah, coordination with the State Department to establish a political coalition, and additional assistance "in the form of money, personnel and technical aid to the police and security forces in Iran."[17] The failings of the leading nationalist, Mossadeghe, were recognized in the paper, but given his popularity, the proposed strategy was to focus propaganda on certain of his followers, associating them with Soviet influence: "The approach should be against his conspicuous followers, to emphasize the idea that they are deceiving and misleading the grand old patriot." Clandestine publications targeted several individuals, while others were portrayed as creating "disorder and anarchy."

The approach involved "black propaganda," using forged and planted documents. "Instructions could be 'discovered' directing Tudeh Party members, following the recent success of the 'Tudeh plot,' to carry out open revolt. (This might bring a measure of unity to the country and provoke the security forces to take harsh measures against the Tudeh Party.) Leaflets, newspaper articles, forged copies of *Mardam* (the Tudeh paper) should assign full credit to the Communists for the success of the plot against Razmara. 'Instructions' could also be discovered listing the persons slated for liquidation after Tudeh assumption of power. These lists would include important religious and political leaders as well as important tribal chiefs."[18]

In contrast, lists had been prepared which included the "heads of departments of the Ministry of War and commanders of divisions… definitely pro-U.S."; individuals who would welcome any catalyst to prevent disintegration of internal security. The Directorate of Plans proposal noted that "the names of these officers are known to us. Such of these groups as proved amenable could be covertly supplied with money, arms, matériel, food, and possibly personnel."

Black propaganda, targeted disinformation, the forgery and planting of incriminating documents, misdirection, along with the covert provision of money, arms, and material, and possibly the infiltration of personnel to indigenous surrogate groups—these were all standard practices, to become increasingly familiar, and certainly not unique to American political action. The CIA paper covered these basics in March 1951. To what extent any of those proposed activities were actually initiated by the local CIA station prior to 1953 is uncertain, although clearly the station was identifying both targets and surrogates. More formal proposals and ultimately a sanctioned project would come later, as the British failure to negotiate drove Iran further into economic crisis during 1951 and 1952.

What the National Security Council did propose, in a draft of March 14, 1951 (approved by the president on March 24), was joint planning with the United Kingdom for a program to counter communist subversion in Iran by increasing support for pro-Western political factions. Plans were also to include paramilitary and military options in the event of a communist regime's rise to power in Tehran. The NSC recommended that the two nations should "correlate political action" and conduct "special political operations." Clearly the intent was for the U.S. to work with British personnel, leveraging their more in-depth experience in Iran, as well as their access to "agents of influence."[19] America did not first move to political action in Iran in the summer of 1953, as the *Saturday Evening Post* had described, it had joined with Britain in coordinated actions beginning in the spring of 1951.

A proposal from CIA Director Allen Dulles gives us further insight into exactly what practices were already in progress or going into play as of March 1951. To some extent they are similar to what was described earlier in regard to Italy. However, certain additions become necessary when the operations are being conducted without the support of the regime actually in power. Dulles pointed out that the CIA officers "are severely restricted in Iran owing primarily to the hampering effect of increased distrust of the West, including the US." Under those conditions, the CIA station in Iran was currently focused on

> increased subsidization for selected Iranian newspapers, extending guidance and money to Iranian elements opposed to ultra-nationalism and terrorism, establishing the feasibility of establishing new, pro-Western political parties and taking steps to discredit and if possible disrupt forces hostile to U.S. security interests, and exploring the possibility of establishing…a radio station for clandestine broadcasts which would reach at least certain parts of Iran.[20]

The wording in Dulles' memorandum for the Office of National Estimates seems to suggest that the CIA Tehran station clandestine staff were already engaged in and proceeding with the sorts of practices listed in the Directorate of Plans paper of that same month in 1951.

As the initial American assessment had presumed, nationalist fervor in Iran led to the nationalization of the Anglo-Iranian Oil Company and the Abadan refineries in March 1951. The British viewed the action literally as theft, declaring the oil production to be their property. State Department documents show that there was some consideration by the British of using military force to occupy the oil fields and refineries but that action was not taken. Instead Britain withdrew its oil company personnel and deployed the Royal Navy in a blockade of the port of Abadan. It also imposed a series of economic sanctions on British exports to Iran, the list including key building supplies such as steel as well as a series of basic commodities. In addition, Iranian assets in British banks were frozen. State Department documents show that the U.S. was quite aware of the impact of the British move, estimating that some eighty thousand Iranians would become unemployed and at least 40 percent of national revenues lost.

Initially the Iranian leadership looked to replace the British technicians with personnel from other Western nations. However, there was unanimous refusal to cooperate in operating a nationalized industry. The lack of support further inflamed public emotion against both Britain and the United States. The American response was especially striking because in previous instances the United States had frequently supported Iran in negotiations to control its oil resources, especially when the Soviets had made a strong move to take over the oil concessions immediately following World War II. As oil concession negotiations dragged on, CIA political action in Iran continued. An October 9, 1951 operations memorandum listed planting informants within the Tudeh, outreach to the Iranian clergy for anti-communist statements, the publication and distribution of a "black propaganda book" describing a Soviet attack against Islam, an expanded psychological warfare program (amount of funding still redacted) including printing presses and a printing establishment, and preliminary fieldwork to put field personnel into certain tribal areas for the purpose of organizing regional resistance to any communist insurgency.[21]

In March 1952 the continuing oil concession negotiations finally floundered completely, with the British totally refusing to give up on the issue of its technicians and engineers operating the Iranian oil fields and refineries. It became increasingly clear that there was no way that the Iranian government could pick up the shortfall in its budget, which included risk to government salaries and payments to contractors. By summer, the British took measures to further add to economic warfare against Iran, with the Royal Navy intercepting an Italian tanker and forcing it into the British protectorate of Aden on grounds that the oil was stolen property. The news was conveyed to other shippers and within a short period had virtually closed off Iranian oil exports.

By the spring of 1953, both the Iranian economy and political situation had moved to a point of imminent crisis. With access to actual documents, including the transcript of a vital National Security Council meeting involving President Eisenhower, we have a true understanding of a diplomatic outreach from Prime Minister Mossadegh, one quite different than described in the *Saturday Evening Post* article of 1954. Mossadegh, clearly running out of options, was proposing the possibility that the United States might either buy Iranian oil or at least supply technicians to help with operation of the oil fields. Interestingly, the NSC dialogue also registers the total British objection to any such proposal. There were no threats in the feelers to Eisenhower, although it was clear that in extremity Iran could dramatically reduce its oil prices or even turn Iran to the Soviets for technical assistance. There was some discussion of "friendly gestures" towards Iran, quickly squelched by Secretary of State Dulles, who referred to America becoming "senior partners" with the British in the Middle East—suggesting that the

United States could under no circumstances undermine oil negotiations and contracts.[22]

It appears that Mossadegh's requests for American assistance were indeed privately submitted and equally privately rejected by President Eisenhower. Almost immediately the American rejection appeared in Iranian newspapers, dramatically undermining Mossadegh.[23] While the U.S. ambassador personally denied to Mossadegh that his government would have leaked such privileged communication, the letter itself was broadcast over the Voice of America radio show, clearly as a part of the psychological warfare program against the premier. It was reportedly a very successful tactic, specifically weakening Mossadegh's support within Iran's parliament.[24]

It is also known from the documents that, as of March 31, the CIA station in Tehran was in contact with and reporting on a pending military coup which would place General Fazlollah Zahedi in the position of prime minister. It also reported that the military officers involved were all confident of the full support of the American Embassy in Tehran. While that coup did not occur, ongoing communications from the Embassy presented Zahedi as the most active contender, with the broadest support, to oust the nationalistic prime minister. The CIA station recommended supporting Zahedi and felt that he had a good chance of success. Zahedi himself is reported as being perfectly willing to accept American intervention in support of an insurgency. And by June, although we have no specific NSC document authorizing it, an officially sanctioned regime change operation began—designated as TPAJAX.

The first step in the operation, one we will learn to be common, was to find the appropriate cut-out to contact the key agent of influence, in this case General Zahedi. In terms of deniability, the cut-out had to conduct the approach as a private individual, not as a representative of the American government. And in the case of TPAJAX, as of the end of June 1953, the cut-out would be designated as Brigadier General Norman Schwarzkopf Sr., a private citizen, then administrative director, Department of Law and Public Safety for the State of New Jersey. His cover was a simple one, a vacation to old friends around the Middle East and in particular a stop in Tehran, where he would visit old military acquaintances from his service there during and immediately following the end of World War II. General Zahedi was simply one of those old friends.[25] Interestingly enough, although Zahedi was named in the *Saturday Evening Post* article of 1954, Schwarzkopf's actual Iranian contact remains redacted in all the TPAJAX documents released in 2017.

It was only during July 1954 that elements aligned for actual regime change under TPAJAX. First Prime Minister Mossadegh, under extreme financial and political pressure for the ongoing economic crisis, dismissed the Majlis (the Iranian Parliament), calling for new national elections. Constitutionally the parliament had the responsibility of nominating prime ministers, which were confirmed by the monarchy (the Shah). However, legally the Shah could decline a nomination or even select the prime minister of his choice. That provided the legal context to replace Mossadegh, and with American covert contacts and encouragement the Shah was persuaded to issue such a degree directly to Mossadegh. The problem was that Mossadegh had already made it quite clear that he rejected the Shah's authority to make such a change in the government.

It would be the military that would determine whether or not such an order would be obeyed, so despite the matter of legalities, any coup against Mossadegh was going to require its approval. And by mid-July, Zahedi assured his CIA contacts that the necessary military support was in place. The plan for TPAJAX had solidified; the Shah would dismiss Mossadegh and appoint no immediate successor. General Zahedi would assume the role of temporary military governor until a suitable Majlis could be convened, which would then appoint him prime minister. The military assets to be involved, the names of their commanders, and the individuals to be included in the new Zahedi government were reported in a CIA Director of Plans memorandum of July 16.[26] An arrest list was prepared for opposing members of the Majlis as well as for key Tudeh members, and facilities to be seized by Zahedi's forces were identified. The CIA station in Tehran was also organizing appropriate demonstrations of public support for the coup and the Shah.

However, from mid-July on, events proceeded at their own pace rather than as defined by the plan. Ongoing efforts including personal contacts by General Schwarzkopf were made to persuade the Shah to officially act. But when he did, on August 16, leaked information allowed Mossadegh to anticipate the order removing him from the premiership. He rejected it and jailed the officer delivering it. The planned military action was called off. Members of the coup had been informed that Mossadegh was aware of their plans and a flare was fired as a signal to delay widespread military action. Mossadegh announced his decision to retain his position, continuing his plans for a new popular election. General Zahedi went into hiding and TPAJAX appeared to have failed.

On August 17, the CIA station in Tehran communicated with Washington, stressing that the basic elements of the planned insurgency were still in place. The decree from the Shah had dismissed the old government under Mossadegh and military support for the Shah remained strong. Zahedi himself took steps to make sure that the Shah's decree was made visible to both the Iranian and the world press. The wording of the decree, as telegrammed back to Washington, quite clearly put his full support behind the general: "View of fact situation of nation necessitates appointment of an informed and experienced man who can grasp affairs of country readily, I therefore, with knowledge I have of your ability and merit, appoint you with this letter Prime Minister. We give into your hands duty to improve affairs of the nation and remove present crisis and raise living standard of people." A message from the Shah himself (who had fled Iran under fear of arrest) was widely broadcast: "Beloved people: In past 28 months Dr. Mossadeq has been given by me greatest support and encouragement in hope he would serve nation but in all this time he has created nothing but greatest poverty, disunity and chaos. Has also spent best part time libeling patriots and statesmen who tried help Iran."[27]

Clearly the anti-Mossadegh propaganda campaign had been thoroughly prepared and remained in action, regardless of the failure of the initial military coup. The CIA station message of August 17 also mentioned that popular fears of Tudeh influence were strong and could lead to mob violence in the streets. While the well-planned TPAJAX coup of August 16 had aborted, the CIA station assessment that its basic elements were still very much in play, even if not immediately visible, was correct. There were no popular demonstrations supporting Mossadegh, but the Tudeh Party did take to the streets, loudly demonstrating opposition to the Shah and raising considerable fear that the premier had indeed begun to accept their support. Premier Mossadegh responded by sending police forces to put down further Tudeh demonstrations, clearing the streets for a time.

As we will find in most instances of deniable regime change, once such operations begin—especially those using internal agents of influence and local military surrogates—they tend to take on lives of their own. One of the most dramatic instances of that can be seen in what was intended to be a purely political change in South Vietnam a decade later. What President John F. Kennedy had approved as a totally nonviolent action to remove and replace the Diem regime actually resulted in the murder of both the South Vietnamese leader and his brother. The history of deniable regime change shows that virtually all projects were described and approved as "bloodless"—something that in reality almost never happened.

Differences in opinion and commitment between the State Department and the CIA are also commonly found, with the State Department frequently much more cautious while CIA headquarters tried, often unsuccessfully, to manage real-time events. Furthermore, local CIA stations and field officers—strongly and personally committed to the projects—were acting at their own initiative. A CIA cable from Washington to Tehran on August 18 noted that the State Department had already reached the tentative stance that TPAJAX had failed and that there should be no further participation in operations against Mossadegh which could expose American opposition to his regime. However, the cable gave no specific directions and left the door open for opposing views from the ambassador and the CIA station chief in Tehran.

Other documents make it clear that the ambassador and others continued to talk with the Shah, and it seems clear that the CIA station itself remained involved with both Zahedi and other elements that had been put in place to support the action against Mossadegh. While the specific schedule for TPAJAX had failed, pro-Shah street demonstrations occurred the following day, clearly beginning with small groups already contracted and paid for their participation.[28] Instead of suppressing them, the military joined in and ultimately moved aggressively and directly against Mossadegh. The units involved were those earlier listed in Zahedi's plan, including both brigades and tank units.

At the end of the day on August 19, General Zahedi was in control and an invitation for the Shah to return to the country was extended. Ultimately TPAJAX had succeeded much as planned, delayed only by an early leak on the initial target day. In response, Ambassador Henderson immediately cabled Washington with a request to make $5 million available to Zahedi in order to secure his regime by meeting the Iranian government payroll commitments, thereby deflating the economic crisis Mossadegh had faced.

PRACTICES AND CONSEQUENCES

To this point we have explored certain basic practices of political action involved with foreign relations, observing that at some level political shaping is simply routine, involving a variety of activities intended to establish relationships of trust with individuals who either can or may in the future influence the foreign policies of a nation. Experienced intelligence agencies spend considerable time building dossiers on those who may rise into positions of influence, not necessarily contacting them directly but using cut-outs who can provide details or later make introductions. As we saw in early examples from the Great Game, individuals engaged in foreign trade were often selected to collect information or were targeted for future use. In more contemporary times, media and academic figures (who often become policy advisors) have been targeted for manipulation or outright recruitment as possible agents of influence.

In the beginning it's always a matter of building positive mindshare. Personal contacts can range from simple social relations to ones that become much more controlling. It's a subtle process, often well disguised over a long period of time. In the case of Iran, during World War II the British had suspected Zahedi (then commander of the Isfahan division) of German sympathies. He was arrested in 1942 and interned in Palestine until the war ended. In the years following the war he became head of the Iranian National Police, during the period in which Schwarzkopf was consulting on security for the Shah and working with the police force. For a time Zahedi, as a nationalist, actively supported Prime Minister Mossadegh, but after Zahedi violently suppressed a protest in mid-1951 (with two hundred killed and two thousand wounded) the prime minister removed him from his position. Change is indeed a constant, and dossiers can become quite lengthy until just the right set of circumstances emerge.

When events go beyond routine shaping—when political action and "active measures" are sanctioned—propaganda, psychological warfare, and in particular the selective use of large amounts of money provided to indigenous political parties or even surrogate agitators come into play. The national election of 1948 in Italy illustrated one of the most basic types of political warfare. As to consequences, it appears that once the meddling starts it becomes very hard to break away. As noted, in Italy the United States became committed to an expensive, ongoing series of covert payments and actions which entangled it in Italian politics for years.

Political action in Iran had moved to the next level, involving military surrogates, not simply helping to keep a government in place but conducting regime change. TPAJAX assumed a life of its own, resulting in the removal of a prime minister, the undermining of the nation's parliamentary and electoral process, and the creation of an unstable alliance between the reigning monarch and the nation's senior military figures. While it may have been deniable, American involvement was clearly visible to all parties involved, and intervention established a legacy of mistrust. KGB sources record the fact that ongoing suspicion of the CIA reached as high as the Shah himself.[29]

Soviet propaganda in the Middle East leveraged the story of the American and British intervention in Iran. Equally importantly, the KGB prepared and planted a number of false documents, carefully designed to inflame fears of further American political action, even of potential regime change operations. In 1955 a forged communication, purportedly from Allen Dulles to the U.S. ambassador in Tehran, belittled the Shah and suggested action against him. The Soviet residency (staffed with KGB political action officers much like the CIA stations within the American diplomatic missions) circulated the forgery among Iranian political and media figures with the anticipated result that a copy did get to the Shah.[30] The Shah in turn demanded an explanation from the American Embassy, which denied it and claimed it a forgery. However, in light of earlier experiences and with the Shah's ongoing impression that the CIA director was making demeaning remarks about him, he reportedly remained unconvinced.

Again, in 1960, the Russian active measures personnel prepared a forged Pentagon communication ordering regional intelligence collection from American missions, with the purpose of preparing for future regime change as necessary. This time the message was leaked by a "supposedly disaffected" Iranian working for the American Embassy. Word of the message made it to the Shah, who again called in the ambassador, with the same result as before. Actually, not quite the same result; this time the Shah personally ordered several of his own officers—suspected of being pro-American—dismissed.[31]

The consequences of even relatively bloodless political action, as in Italy and Iran, often proved quite expensive, at times embarrassing, often long-lasting, and almost always far more public than anticipated. But there are other levels of political warfare, some far more dark and much more bloody.

Chapter Five:
Regime Change

There are two major aspects of political warfare. One relies on covertly, deniably, and peacefully shaping the behavior of another state so that its economic and military policies and even its manner of governance are complimentary to your state's goals and interests. Machiavelli expressed the absolute pragmatism of such a viewpoint—a ruler's actions are not a matter of wrong or right, they are a matter of necessity. If any action brings security or prosperity, it is simply necessary.

From that perspective, the second aspect of political warfare is obvious. If the other state's practices cannot be positively shaped, then it becomes a potential adversary or potential tool of an enemy. In that case the regime is a threat and must be dealt with more assertively. If all else fails, it must be overthrown and its rulers replaced. Machiavelli discusses various methods of doing that, ranging from open warfare to covertly arranging for revolt and replacement of rulers. In contemporary times we have come to generally refer to such practices—whether done overtly or covertly—as regime change.

Beginning in the 1950s and through the early decades of the Cold War, America and Russia were in quite different positions in regard to regime change, not simply in Eastern Europe but globally. In the years following World War II the long-established global power structure, largely based on the imperial reach of America's wartime allies, had begun to collapse. Dutch, British, and French global influence increasingly crumbled in the face of local anti-colonial and nationalist movements.

Great Britain was forced to grant independence to India, Pakistan, Burma, and Ceylon. The British also faced increased hostility in Egypt, and by 1952 its sympathetic monarchy was overthrown and the British military ejected. The Dutch were forced to grant independence to Indonesia and the French struggled through a decade-long loss of influence and political control across Indochina. Indigenous communist parties within all the colonial territories as well as in regions such as the Middle East, ostensibly independent but dominated largely by the British, were active and vocal in the widening rejection of foreign influence. European and increasingly American economic control was viewed in the same hostile fashion as overt colonial governance.

Given their ideological links to the Soviet Union, communist parties were viewed as controlled fronts for Russian political warfare, especially as they repeated the same messages and accusations that were coming out of both Moscow and the Cominform. That messaging was strident, aggressive, and ongoing, a constant stream of accusations against the imperial powers, highlighting their support by America and vigorously opposing any new era of American economic and military "imperialism." Even socialist parties opposing traditional regimes and long-established alliances became suspect, especially if they began to assert similar views.

The view within the Western nations and at the highest levels of the U.S. State Department was that the rapidly expanding international political chaos was based on the success of communist agitation, agitation enabled by powerful Soviet political action networks supporting aggressive local Communist Party revolutionary actions. Two official, highly classified reports prepared circa 1953-54 provide a comprehensive insight into the international Soviet threat as it was perceived at that point in time.

The first is known as the Jackson Committee Report, and more formally, *The President's Committee on International Information Activities, Report to the President.*[1] Initially classified as top-secret, the June 30, 1953 document was ordered at Eisenhower's direction to characterize the nature of current international relations in terms of national security, focusing on Soviet intentions. It was to include a study on American counterefforts, including overt and covert information, economic and political activities, and clandestine quasi-military operations.

The report reaffirmed the existing perception that the Soviet regime quite simply desired a communist world controlled by the Kremlin. It was a picture of a tightly orchestrated quest for global domination, with Russia relying on political and psychological warfare until such a time that it deemed it feasible to move to overt military action. Both the content and the actual language used in the Jackson Committee Report are important in giving us a historical perspective on the evolution of political warfare as conducted by both Russia and the United States.

From a distance of over sixty years, one of the first attitudes that emerges from the report is that the international situation was viewed strictly in terms of "us and them." The Soviets wanted world disorder leading to their total domination. The United States wanted simply to preserve the international order, picturing that order as being essentially a moral choice between freedom and totalitarianism. The report refers to the general objectives of the United States as being both a matter of "security" and a "just and peaceful world order," concluding with commentary and proposals to deal with the ongoing Soviet attempt to "undermine and destroy the non-communist world through political warfare." As part of its conclusion the Jackson Committee Report presents suggestions for "The United States Program for World Order."

What is clearly missing from the report is any detailed discussion of the cultural or ethnic factors that were major driving forces in the explosive postwar rejection of colonialism and economic imperialism. A total of two paragraphs and some four or five sentences make references to nationalism, racial discrimination, and colonial exploitation. And within those paragraphs equal weight is given to "loss of faith," loss of loyalty, and pure opportunism as causes for the expansion of international communism. Overall, the context of the international struggle is stated in terms of America's stand for freedom and democracy versus Soviet totalitarianism.

There is only limited mention of the success of indigenous communist parties in positioning themselves as leading national movements against imperialism, ethnic and racial discrimination, and economic domination. The Jackson Committee Report dialog tends to avoid detailed elaboration of any issues with the current "order," minimizing them as points of exposure in political warfare. Instead of relating such issues to specific counter-actions, they are simply listed as points of vulnerability, leading to the creation of discord and anarchy as preliminaries to communist moves to seize political power. The report also fails to fully acknowledge the major Soviet propaganda efforts focused on countering the established colonial and economic imperialism of the Western powers with "fraternal" offers of technology and aid, intended strictly to support independence and self-determination.

That Soviet approach is seen in one of Premier Nikita Khrushchev's addresses, specifically targeting the newly independent nations of Asia and Africa: "Today they no longer need to go begging for up-to-date equipment to their former oppressors. They can get it in the socialist countries, without assuming any political or military commitments." Such offers were quite well received by the leaders of newly independent nations, many of whom had come into power with popular appeals to the belief that their own resources and economies had essentially been plundered by their former colonial rulers.[2]

To some extent, Khrushchev's promises were followed up with Russian action. In Africa, steel mills, sawmills, airports, roads, hotels, hospitals and even polytechnic schools were built. Russian investments in Cuba would become massive, enough to damage the overall economy of the Soviet Union. A report to the Central Committee in 1964 documented some six thousand overseas projects in developing nations.[3] The cost to the Russians had been enormous, creating a level of internal complaint that Khrushchev had gotten carried away with his promises.

But there is no doubt that Khrushchev's message had resonated internationally, and it was constantly repeated in Soviet propaganda as well as by Khrushchev himself. In a later speech at the United Nations, he praised the heroic leaders who had led the struggle for independence in India, Indonesia, the Middle East, and Africa. He also rebuked the Western powers for their ongoing efforts to continue the economic exploitation of those nations despite their new political independence. Russia also became a sponsor of a United Nations "Declaration on the Granting of Independence to Colonial Countries and Peoples" which strongly denounced colonialism in all forms.[4] The abstention of the United States and other Western nations only served to support the Soviet anti-colonial propaganda messaging.

The United States increasingly found itself with a serious image problem in regard to this messaging. While it actively and openly supported certain independence movements and established diplomatic relations with the new nations, it was still militarily involved with longtime allies such as Britain and France. Both were only grudgingly abandoning their political empires and most definitely trying to retain their global economic reach—initially driven by the dire state of their own domestic economies immediately following World War II. This American image problem, and the advantage it provided for the extension of Soviet influence globally, is only minimally remarked on in most of the official American national security reports and commentary of the early 1950s. The vast majority of the commentary is on the ideological threat of international communism and the strengths of the Soviet covert political action networks.

The Eisenhower administration's ongoing entanglement with the French efforts to maintain its influence in Southeast Asia, with the British efforts to maintain control over oil supplies in the Middle East, and its own general antipathy towards agrarian reform in Latin America raised considerable skepticism among third-world and newly independent nations around the globe. Postwar American economic and cultural dominance also aroused considerable local opposition, both culturally and in a popular sense that the smaller nations' resources were being "plundered"—a favorite Soviet propaganda term. Washington tended to blame international chaos on the reach of Russian covert operations within indigenous communist parties, largely ignoring the very simple and effective Soviet propaganda message on postwar "capitalist economic imperialism."

In most of the developing world it proved quite easy not just for local communist parties but for local nationalists and antigovernment movements of any stripe to adopt the "economic imperialism" mantra, casting existing regimes as tools of foreign economic powers. While the postcolonial political map had changed, propaganda touting its replacement by capitalist economic colonialism proved quite effective in opening Soviet approaches to new regimes around the globe.[5] When combined with the appeal of a populist/socialist political platform, the promotion of agrarian reform, and calls for the nationalizing of key industries (previously dominated by foreign businesses) the energetic Soviet outreach to former colonial nations and to developing nations was often well received. Russia moved openly to establish economic and military support for exactly the same new regimes and governments that Americans saw as threats to international political and economic stability. And with only a few exceptions, Russian support was straightforward. Mutual trade pacts were signed, diplomatic agreements completed, weapons shipments initiated and, as necessary, Russian military advisors appeared in-country.

Instead of focusing on the fundamental image and credibility problems of America's ongoing association with colonialism (politically or economically), or the legacy of imperial attitudes of racial superiority, the Jackson Committee Report concentrated on the Soviet Union's "impressive political warfare capabilities," and in particular its ability to leverage worldwide "communist apparatus" and national Communist parties. Those were seen as the major mechanisms for political infiltration, for the penetration of governments, and for the preparation for violent revolution. The legal participation of Communist Parties in national political activities was seen as a special threat, exposing any government to a forceful political takeover, as had occurred in Czechoslovakia. Somewhat strangely, the report did not mention that communists had been very unsuccessful in working with nationalist parties across the Middle East and Africa. Even in Latin America, Soviet and Communist Party propaganda had focused primarily on simply "fomenting hatred" based on the history of American political and military interventions—the legacy of gunboat diplomacy.

Overall, the Jackson Committee Report failed to address the simple realities that the colonial powers had been hugely weakened, both economically and militarily, in the recent war, and that local populations had been brought together by a common opposition to Japanese or German occupation forces. Ethnic, cultural, and religious differences were being overridden by a common desire to oppose any outside interference in local affairs, whether they were invaders like the Axis nations or agents of imperial powers. In retrospect it appears all too easy to simply blame postwar instability on what appeared to be a virtually unstoppable communist movement, and one that could do anything—from compromising the absolutely best-guarded U.S. military secrets to toppling a series of governments around the world, which had been in place in some instances for centuries.

It is true that communist ideology was a visible element of the political chaos developing across the imperial territories, but beginning with the Truman administration there was little to no American appreciation of the equal or greater impact of anti-colonialism, nationalism, and the simple rejection of Western cultural dominance. The reality was that the rapid collapse of the existing colonial empires was rooted not in an all-powerful world communist ideological explosion but rather in what was a unique opportunity for nationalist and even local ethnic movements.

For decades the United States would hold to this original fear of an existential communist ideological threat, with only brief respite under President Kennedy, whose worldview had grown to understand and even accept the value of neutrality among the developing nations. Upon entering office Kennedy had immediately became entangled in a series of covert projects already underway during the Eisenhower years. By 1963 he had begun to move towards a foreign policy that would improve relations with neutral nations such as India, even secretly establishing a back-channel communication with Fidel Castro with the goal of moving Cuba out of the Soviet bloc and into a neutral relationship.[6] However, his assassination forestalled any real change in such matters and over the following decades American foreign policies would continue to be driven by the fundamental error of interpreting regime change in the developing world as driven almost entirely by successful Russian political action operations.

In 1953, there simply was no acceptance of neutrality as a viable position; there were two blocs, East and West, and any nation not in the right one—or appearing to be open to Soviet economic or political influence—was a potential threat. The overall impression gained from the Jackson Committee Report is that the Soviet threat had placed the United States in the position of defending the established world order—order, stability, and peace were good and desirable. Change was dangerous, and any political change which involved socialism or neutrality, such as with India, was a change for the worse. Beyond that perception, recent history had demonstrated that any government which allowed legal participation by a Communist Party was seriously exposed, and the ascension of any leader who established economic or military ties to Russia or its satellite nations represented an imminent threat, with the implicit risk of taking that government directly into the Soviet political bloc.

The concluding remarks of the Jackson Committee Report are also quite interesting in the context of certain new directions in American political warfare that were about to emerge. The report specifically described political warfare as an instrument of national policy. It recommended a political action approach of clearly "demonstrating to others their self-interest in decisions which the United States wishes them to make." The negative possibilities of not heeding such national "self-interest" were to be specifically presented to those who "have the power of decision." Simply translated—be with us or suffer the consequences. It was an expression of pragmatism clearly consistent with practices expressed by Machiavelli.

The second report which allows us to look inside the Eisenhower administration's worldview was held even more securely. The Doolittle panel of 1954's *The Report on the Covert Activities of the Central Intelligence Agency* expresses the same general worldview as to the communist threat.[7] However, its characterization of the threat and in particular the nature of the American response is far stronger, far more urgent, and far more dark.

Surprisingly, while the report of the Doolittle panel makes extensive recommendations related to the Central Intelligence Agency and clandestine activities, those recommendations are primarily of a management nature and are methodically stated. Areas dealt with include organization and interagency coordination, personnel criteria and recruiting, issues of improved security, and an endorsement of a strong counterintelligence/counterespionage program. There are no specific recommendations for increasing paramilitary activities for clandestine military action or for more radical actions such as regime change projects, much less for tactics such as assassination.

Yet the wording used to introduce the report is dramatic and suggests actions of a far stronger nature. The Soviets are referred to as an "implacable enemy," with the United States being engaged in a life or death struggle with "no rules." The actions that must be taken to counter the Soviet moves towards world domination will have to go beyond "acceptable norms of human behavior," and "long-standing American concepts of fair play must be reconsidered."

The Doolittle Report's introduction ends with a call for subverting, sabotaging, and destroying the nation's enemy, specifically "Soviet Russia." While actual recommendations for implementing such practices do not appear in the report, clearly the panel was thinking of actions far beyond routine political action, propaganda, and psychological warfare. In short, circa 1953-54 the view of those advising President Eisenhower, and of senior officers in his administration such as Secretary of State Dulles, was that the United States was already fully engaged in political warfare with the Soviet Union. The nature of that warfare justified what would eventually become known as "preemptive defense," a turn from thoughts of "containing" regimes and nations which entangled themselves with the Soviets to actions that would either ensure such political movements never came into power—or remove them if they did.

Regime change would become standard practice for America during the Cold War, and it would consistently involve the United States in covert, deniable actions. In such actions the first step would normally be political warfare, as had been successful in Italy. However, if that proved futile and socialist/communist-leaning regimes came into power, there would be no hesitance to move to paramilitary action with aggressive political and economic subversion, sabotage, guerilla action, surrogate insurgencies, and on occasion political assassination.

While not explicitly stated in the early Eisenhower years, an anecdotal remark attributed to Secretary of State Henry Kissinger during a Nixon White House policy discussion related to elections in Chile, concisely sums up the highest-level attitudes of those who would be making the decisions on when and where the United States would be forced to engage in political warfare: "I don't see why we need to stand by and watch a country go communist due to the irresponsibility of its people. The issues are much too important for the Chilean voters to be left to decide for themselves."[8]

During the Eisenhower administration, Secretary of State Dulles continually reinforced the perception that the ongoing global political change was the result of an extensive, extraordinarily capable, and totally ruthless Russian intelligence network, which had the demonstrated capability of subverting virtually any government through the use of political action and psychological warfare. His position supported the view that Russia had an "unprecedented capacity" to advance its influence, with or without military action. Even worse, Soviet covert actions were supremely dangerous because Russian agents operated not only underground and outside the law, but outside accepted American moral standards—beyond even the most basic norms of human conduct.

With this view of what amounted to an undeclared state of war with the Soviet Union, there was virtually unanimous agreement among the senior leadership of the nation that it was necessary to ensure that CIA clandestine operations personnel had total freedom of action. That involved removing virtually all normal legal restraints, including those relating to various international neutrality agreements as well as those relating to actual criminal acts under U.S. statutes. Many of those exemptions were addressed by the legal code which was put into place to support the National Security Act of 1947.

Intelligence and clandestine national security activities are carried out under U.S. Legal Code Title 50 statutes, which cover both covert intelligence and operational missions outside the normal activities of the military services. The military operates under Title 10 statutes and its personnel are constrained by the legal requirements of the

United States Code of Military Justice (UCMJ). In practical terms this means that CIA personnel in the clandestine services, including those involved in political, psychological, and paramilitary operations, are not necessarily subject to standard civil legal constraints (to the extent that they are complying with sanctioned missions) nor to the restrictions of the UCMJ. At times personnel involved in CIA operations have also been protected by very special and very secret agreements ("memorandums of understanding") between the CIA and the Justice Department. Those agreements have allowed CIA officers to work with assets and surrogates whom they knew to be violating a number of U.S. laws, ranging from murder to weapons and drug smuggling.[9]

Over time, as more and more regular military personnel were detached for duty to CIA operations, and as regular military units were assigned to covert national security missions, considerable debate has arisen as to the conflict between Title 50 and Title 10 authorities in terms of personnel protections and congressional oversight.[10] Those concerns are outside our political warfare focus, but they do illustrate the consequences of the decision to "go darker," to operate where there are "no rules ... beyond the acceptable norms of human behavior."

The net result of the studies, the dialogue, the focus on "us versus them," and "freedom and democracy versus totalitarianism" combined with a lack of recognition of the fundamental nature of the factors driving postwar international political changes (nationalism, ethno-nationalism, anti-colonialism, economic independence) led the United States to assume a role of political spoiler. Beginning with deniable political and hybrid warfare projects started during the Eisenhower administration, the nation moved into some four decades of disruption, destabilization, and actual regime change against governments which appeared to be moving their nations in the direction of Soviet influence, nationalist policies, and the appearance of communist-oriented governance. Governments that established trade and military agreements with the Soviet Union or Warsaw Pact nations, regimes that nationalized industries and natural resources, and nations that moved into extensive agrarian reform were viewed as potential threats to world order and quite possibly beachheads in the Soviet quest for world domination.

Of course, foreign regime change activities were in direct conflict with America's own officially expressed international policies of non-interference and political self-determination. They also involved actions that were illegal under both U.S. laws and international agreements. The regime change operations examined in the following chapters were only made possible with the passage of a series of very special pieces of national security legislation during the years 1947-50. The most fundamental authorization for such deniable, covert activities had come in 1948, in the form of the previously mentioned National Security Council Directive 10/2. That directive was initially issued to support containment operations against the Soviet Union, primarily by the Office of Special Projects (later the Office of Policy Coordination). However, it also provided authorization for covert and deniable operations by the OPC's successor, the Central Intelligence Agency. As with the National Security Act of 1947, the National Security Council directives of the early Cold War years continue as precedent and legal justification for deniable activities today.

In short, covert operations were and are authorized with the understanding that they are "all activities" conducted or sponsored by the United States against foreign states considered to be hostile, and they are planned and executed so that no American government responsibility will be evident to unauthorized persons—so that the government can plausibly deny them. Plausible deniability is the heart and core of all such activities, which are allowed to include propaganda, economic warfare, and "preventive" direct action including sabotage, demolition and evacuation, subversion including assistance to underground resistance and guerilla groups, and support to any indigenous anti-communist elements. The only restriction is that any related military operations may not include armed action by "recognized" military forces of the United States.[11]

Over the period of only a few years in the mid-1950s, the United States moved from the basic, "traditional" practices of political action to something much more dark and violent—a combination of subversion and psychological warfare with actual combat by deniable paramilitary and surrogate forces. The following chapters refer to such operations as hybrid warfare. Such operations would be tasked to the Psychological and Paramilitary Operations staff of the CIA's clandestine service. Those specialists would conduct full-scale psychological warfare and combine it with paramilitary support (sometimes on a large scale) for insurgencies and revolutions intended to bring about regime change. Officially, many of the projects would begin with the stated intent of being relatively bloodless, but in almost all instances accepted the need for violence. And in no case would there be serious consideration of the long-term human consequences of enforced regime change for the states targeted in such projects.

The official direction and attitudes supporting such regime change operations are perhaps best understood by quoting one discussion on tactics that occurred during the regime change project PBSUCCESS to oust the government of President Jacobo Árbenz in Guatemala in 1954. At the time of that discussion, CIA field officers were very involved with both an exile military force and volunteers from a neighboring country. Both groups were constantly pressing for an aggressive assassination program targeting political parties and leaders inside Guatemala, including the democratically elected Árbenz. The CIA team leader requested the authority to proceed with developing a specific plan for sabotage and assassinations. While no specific written approval was given (an extended study of other regime change projects shows no such approvals were ever put in writing), the team leader did relay the instructions that he had received from Washington. They were simple, and explicit: "Arbenz must go, how does not matter."[12]

Chapter Six:
Hybrid Warfare

Along with the Italian and Iranian political action operations, regime change in Guatemala was viewed in Washington, DC as one of the earliest and most successful early CIA projects. The two operations did a great deal to solidify the reputation of the Agency, and to make its clandestine operations group a credible option for President Eisenhower. As a career soldier, Eisenhower had initially tended to prefer overt solutions for foreign relations challenges—international alliances, military aid, the establishment of in-country military assistance groups for training and planning support, and, if necessary, actual force deployment.

Yet events prove that over time he also became a great believer in covert operations. If Secretary of State John Foster Dulles could not come up with an international solution and the United States was forced to go it alone, Eisenhower more and more frequently allowed projects to be handed over to Dulles's brother Allen at the CIA. Surprisingly, when tallies are made, throughout the Cold War and beyond, President Eisenhower elected to employ covert action far more frequently than his successors, seconded only by President Ronald Reagan. In contrast, President George H. W. Bush, a former director of the CIA, would engage in foreign intervention in terms of conventional warfare, using the uniformed American military.

The Guatemala project appears to have been especially convincing for Eisenhower. Following the operation, the CIA director took several of the Agency's clandestine personnel to meet with and receive personal congratulations from the president. But while Guatemala is important for the impact it made on Eisenhower and the trend towards covert action that it solidified, it is also important as the first large-scale example of hybrid political warfare. It was the first major move into extended paramilitary operations, intended not just to nudge a regime out of power, but to crush its ideological foundations and replace them with a fully acceptable government, one that would be sure to reject any further taint of Soviet influence.

In this century, the term hybrid warfare is generally reserved to describe a combination of new tools and tactics which are used in active military combat between armed forces. In this study of political warfare, it is used to differentiate operations which include not only the standard political warfare practices of propaganda, psychological warfare, and covert political action but extend to the use of ostensibly deniable military surrogates and intimidation with regular military forces. PBSUCCESS was the hybrid warfare project that ultimately resulted in regime change in Guatemala in 1954. But that's not where it all started. It began with an abortive first effort, project PBFORTUNE, in 1952 at the end of the Truman administration. Unlike Iran, where the British had been the dominant economic and political influence, Guatemala was historically within the American sphere of influence, essentially claimed by the Monroe Doctrine of 1823. That rejection of European intrusion had certainly not prevented a level of American economic hegemony—as well as gunboat diplomacy—from developing across Latin America.

In 1950 a populist, nationalist movement swept the Guatemalan elections and put Jacobo Árbenz into office as president. His agrarian reform platform was of great concern to American business in the country, particularly to the United Fruit Company, which was a major economic power in the region. United Fruit had powerful connections in Washington, but within Latin America it also established a very supportive relationship with the CIA, allowing use of its vessels for covert shipments, and company employment as cover for CIA field officers. While United Fruit's CIA connections were indeed considerable, it may well have been most important that one of its employees, Thomas Corcoran, had direct access to policy makers in Washington, DC. It was noted earlier that Corcoran had been active in covert activities in China during the FDR administration, with the American Special Air Unit effort. Following the war he had become legal counsel for United Fruit.

With extensive business connections inside Guatemala, Corcoran was able to serve as an important source of information on political factions within the country, as well as on the emerging reform measures of the Árbenz regime. There is no doubt that Corcoran was a conduit to both the CIA and later directly to President Eisenhower in regard to commercial and political affairs in Guatemala. Corcoran's own personal concerns over a growing communist influence in that nation—as well as the negative impact of Árbenz's populist/socialist agenda on American business interests—are clearly documented.[1] [2]

The State Department was initially cautious about taking special action against Guatemala, viewing it as an overreaction. In fact, State likened any American intervention as being "the spectacle of the elephant shaking with alarm before the mouse."[3] It preferred the standard foreign policy approach of shaping a positive relationship though persuasion and cooperative assistance. Defense assistance pacts were already in place with neighboring states, including El Salvador, Nicaragua, and Honduras. The standard carrot-and-stick approach, offering American economic development cooperation to buffer any need for Guatemala to turn to the Soviet bloc, while establishing the safeguard of buffer zones around it through military assistance to neighboring states, was the State Department's preference during the last years of the Truman presidency.

As would become common during the Cold War, the CIA was far more concerned about Árbenz's regime not simply as a spawning ground for ideological change in the region but specifically as a beachhead for further Soviet bloc economic and even military penetration into Latin America. CIA Director Walter Bedell Smith began lobbying for sanctioned covert political action, with propaganda and monetary support for anti-communist factions—specifically the Catholic Church hierarchy, large landowners, and business interests—as well as a search for anti-communist leaders and factions within the Guatemalan Army. The goal would be to establish an active political alliance to oppose Árbenz's social and economic reform efforts. As mentioned earlier, that approach would become a standard one for American political action during the Cold War, pitting the United States squarely against change and on the side of the traditional political structure—the same structure that had lost in the elections which put Árbenz into the presidency.

In addition to the concerns of both the CIA and American businesses operating in Guatemala, President Somoza of Nicaragua provided a regional voice for action against the Árbenz government. It was a difficult call to resist, given the history of the United States in Central America, a history that had essentially established Nicaragua as the lynchpin of American influence in the region. As early as 1835 a contingent of U.S. Marines had been landed in the country to protect the personal business investments of Cornelius Vanderbilt. Not surprisingly, Vanderbilt's business dispute with the Nicaraguan government was settled on Vanderbilt's terms. A year later the U.S. ambassador to Nicaragua had protested to Washington that he had been personally insulted. The American response was first to shell a Nicaraguan port and then put ashore a Marine landing party to burn the remains of the town. During that period Marines were sent to assert American will on some eleven different occasions.[4]

More recently, in 1927, some six thousand U.S. Marines were deployed to crush a popular revolution against a pro-American regime. Even then there was little hesitancy to assert the American position. Under-Secretary of State Robert Olds was quite clear on that point, stating that Central America had always understood that governments recognized by the United States stayed in power, and those which were not were destined to fall. To that point, a Marine "peace-keeping" force remained in Nicaragua for a number of years, withdrawing only in 1933 after fully training and installing an internal security force, one totally loyal to the ruling Somoza family. The Marine liaison to the National Guard became its commander and the Nicaraguan National Guard kept the family in power over some forty-two years. Over time the National Guard itself evolved to control most of the public services within the country, including radio and telegraph networks, the railroads, postal services, immigration, and even the internal revenue service.

With the support of the National Guard, strong economic and social ties to the United States, and the benefit of major export of raw materials to the Allies during World War II, the Somoza family and Nicaragua became even more closely aligned with the United States and became by far its dominant trading partner. For decades the Somoza family, and Nicaragua as a nation, never failed to aggressively support American interests or to assist in pushing back against any new government in the region which might appear to threaten American influence.

It was the personal urging from President Anastasio Somoza in 1952 that helped move the United States intervention in Guatemala from covert political action to the next level of ostensibly deniable but fully obvious hybrid warfare. In April 1952, during a visit to Washington DC, Somoza circulated the proposal that if given weapons and support from the United States, he would be happy to work with an ex-patriot Guatemalan military officer, Carlos Castillo Armas, to militarily oust the Árbenz regime. Armas had received training at Fort Leavenworth, Kansas; had served on the Guatemalan Army General Staff; and was a fervent and aggressive anti-communist. He was also very politically connected to the established, conservative political factions in Guatemala.

President Truman, not quite as averse to CIA cloak-and-dagger work as he would later maintain, reportedly suggested to CIA Director Smith that the Armas option should be considered. An officer was dispatched to explore the possibility of Nicaragua serving as a third-party partner for such an operation. With Truman's approval, the CIA opened a formal covert program, designated PBFORTUNE, to address the deniable military option.[5] Armas was initially supplied with $225,000 to begin organizing the military element of what would become an invasion of Guatemala by surrogate forces funded by the United States. Both Nicaragua and Honduras would serve as bases to assemble, support, and launch military operations. In the meantime, the official, public American relationship with Guatemala remained one of neutrality and non-intervention as related to that nation's national politics.

The Guatemala intervention was seminal in terms of American political warfare, offering the most dramatic examples of where the fear of the communist ideological menace was taking the nation even before the Jackson and Doolittle Reports were prepared. PBFORTUNE was dramatically different, even in its earliest stages, from the political action in Italy or Iran. There was no organized insurgency within Guatemala, there were no rebel forces engaged against the Árbenz regime. There was only limited establishment opposition to certain of his measures and extensive popular support for them. The Guatemala operation also illustrates the extent to which surrogate forces would drive the actual practices used, both in Guatemala and for decades on through the Cold War.

Perhaps the most dramatic example of new and darker practices would be the fact that a CIA historical study documents that one of the contemplated tactics was assassination. Months before formal project approval, the CIA Directorate of Plans had officially compiled a "hit list" including names of communists obtained from a Guatemalan Army list provided by Armas. The list was described as showing the "top flight communists whom the new government would desire to eliminate immediately in the event of a successful anti-communist coup."[6]

Of course such eliminations would be done by the surrogate military forces and the new regime, not by American CIA or paramilitary officers, but the creation of such a list demonstrates a turn to the same sorts of practices that the Soviets and their Communist Party surrogates had used in Eastern Europe. Pragmatically, it ensured the removal of all possible vestiges of the regimes being replaced. The Doolittle study would speak to turning to practices previously considered immoral and out-of-bounds for America. However, two years before its report was handed to the president, CIA planning staff were already working under a new concept of undeclared political warfare. Such blacklists would become a standard practice in other covert warfare projects, perhaps most notably in regard to the Cuban JMARC project in the early 1960s.

During the fall of 1952, Armas had begun to prepare special "K" groups whose mission was to kill all of Árbenz's political and military leaders. Locations of their homes and offices were mapped for such actions. CIA project officers were aware of the planning and asked headquarters to review the list as well as another list of those to be locked up post-coup. Ultimately the initial planning was developed into a "disposal" list of individuals to be "executed." As forwarded to CIA headquarters, it included some fifty-eight Category 1 targets for elimination and another seventy-four Category 2 Guatemalans to be imprisoned or exiled.[7]

These blacklists would be an element of the Guatemala planning that would carry on throughout the life of the project, to the ultimate success of the coup. Different terms would be used for the practice—"elimination," "neutralization," and "execution." The intent remained the same and such actions were of course to be completely deniable, carried out by surrogate forces. One aspect of the planning called for exiled Nicaraguan soldiers as well as soldiers from Honduras and El Salvador to be infiltrated in civilian dress to assassinate leading Guatemalan "communists" prior to the actual entry of uniformed "revolutionary" forces.[8]

It is also noteworthy that while such practices show up throughout the CIA project planning memoranda and even in the CIA's own history, there is always a caution to separate such actions from CIA or even American personnel. And no headquarters directives or even acknowledgements go into the record authorizing such actions.[9] The rules of the practice are quite clear. The CIA might provide intelligence and planning support for eliminations, even help in preparing lists. It might go as far as developing training manuals on assassination and teaching the tactics. But surrogates are on record as initiating the dialogues, making the proposals, and of course being the ones to carry out the eliminations. The practice was structured with its own deniability. Indeed, decades later when investigated by Congress on the subject of foreign assassinations, the response was always quite clear: no orders were ever given to surrogates to carry out such things, and certainly no CIA personnel were ever directly involved in assassinations or executions.

Unfortunately for the initial PBFORTUNE project, with planning for deniable paramilitary action well underway, the son of General Somoza happened to be in a meeting in Panama with the American U.S. assistant secretary of state for inter-American affairs. During casual conversation the son inquired whether or not the "machinery" promised by his father "was on the way." This seems to have produced considerable discussion. A report of the remarks was sent to Secretary of State Dean Acheson and President Truman. Apparently Acheson, who had grudgingly accepted the covert military project in the first place, made a convincing case that the operation had been compromised and was becoming a diplomatic and foreign policy risk. Within days, the CIA's PBFORTUNE project was suspended with an order from the president.[10]

But shortly a new president would be in office. The Eisenhower administration would have a new secretary of state and a new director of the CIA, and the calls for drastic political action would surge. The era of "whatever it takes" was beginning. It is also fair to say that the calls for action from commercial interests were continuing. Documents show that Thomas Corcoran was in direct contact with both the CIA and Eisenhower, carrying the message that Árbenz and his agrarian reform initiative had to go. By the fall of 1953, Árbenz had moved to expropriate even more of the United Fruit Company land holdings and, worse yet, had legalized the Guatemalan Communist Party. Both moves triggered the worst possible fears of potential Soviet influence in Central America.

Corcoran was particularly close to J. C. King, the CIA officer whose jurisdiction was the Western Hemisphere division.[11] In later years, even CIA officers directly involved in the eventual regime change in Guatemala expressed the view that it was Corcoran's access to Eisenhower, rather than their feedback or that of the CIA, which had convinced the new administration to launch a second covert operation.[12] The depth of the relationship between United Fruit and the CIA is quite clear; in some of the earliest planning documents there are calls from CIA officers to use United Fruit shipping for covertly moving military supplies and for company commercial employment as covers for the clandestine field personnel assigned to the project.

Congress was also politically sensitive to the new red menace, vocally so in public session and behind the scenes in close touch with the senior officers of the CIA, encouraging them to take an aggressive stance against the communists in Guatemala. Senator Alexander Wiley,

Republican of Wisconsin, had encouraged Allen Dulles to go public in announcing shipments of Soviet client state weapons to Guatemala as "part of the master plan of World Communism." Senator George Smathers, Democrat of Florida, consistently used similar language, warning that "the Politburo of Guatemala" was "taking orders from Moscow" and that the arrival of a cargo ship with armaments "was concrete evidence of Soviet intervention."[13]

When word was received that Guatemala had purchased surplus equipment from an Eastern Bloc nation and that a Soviet satellite nation cargo ship was on the way to Central America, new CIA Director Allen Dulles asserted that with those new weapons, Árbenz could "roll down and seize the Panama Canal."[14] Factually the story was a bit less sensational. The CIA bribed a Guatemalan military officer who examined the shipment and informed them that the cargo ship *Alfhem* had carried a mix of virtually unusable Czech weapons including heavy cannons designed for railcar mounting, antitank guns, and a large quantity of vintage WWII German and British weapons—most of which were rusted and nonworking.[15]

In a study titled "Congress, the CIA, and Guatemala, 1954: Sterilizing a 'Red Infection,'" David M. Barrett reveals that American intervention in Guatemala was widely supported and that Congress had indeed demanded that the Eisenhower administration do "whatever it took to stop the commies."[16] And over the course of several months, by 1954 the CIA Guatemala operation had reemerged, with most of the same players, the same plans, and much the same logistics as PBFORTUNE. Only the name had changed; regime change in Guatemala would occur under the auspices of PBSUCCESS and the project was funded with a $3 million working budget.

With State Department endorsement the project's official objective was to "remove covertly, and without bloodshed if possible, the menace of the present Communist-controlled government of Guatemala."[17] Political maneuvering, psychological warfare, and intimidation were initially proposed to pressure the Árbenz government from power. It would be left to the new regime, led by Armas, to "roll up" communists and their collaborators following the departure of Árbenz. Such roll ups are often bloody and often come with regime change. Eliminations, neutralizations, and imprisonments were common in Eastern European nations immediately following the end of World War II, carried out by local Communist parties and with the Soviet internal security forces providing support as needed. But during most of the Cold War, Russia was generally invited in by new regimes. By the time Russian diplomats and economic advisers arrived, the human carnage was largely over.

In Guatemala and elsewhere, concern for the human consequences of regime change projects was not discussed in operational planning. The CIA was simply directed to make it happen. On the other hand, American corporations were alerted to the projects and given advance notice to prepare their own plans. Documents reveal that Western Hemisphere Division CIA Chief J. C. King conducted a number of confidential meetings shortly before the actual start of the secret military effort against the Árbenz government. Those meetings included directors of several American companies with major financial investments in Guatemala whose businesses involved significant importing and exporting. The list of companies being briefed included W. R. Grace and Company, Standard Oil of New Jersey, American Coffee Corporation, and others unnamed in the documents. The briefings are described in notes as an "approach to heads of American companies for covert action."[18]

In the meetings, senior CIA officers were quite explicit that the Guatemala project was urgent and that the CIA was under extreme political pressure to perform.[19] Both King and CIA Deputy Director General Charles P. Cabell were quite explicit in the briefings: "General Cabell stated we not only have a full green light to go ahead, but a bayonet prodding our back to get going."[20]

Extensive detail on the associated military and paramilitary activities of PBSUCCESS is available in other books, including *Shadow Warfare: The History of America's Undeclared Wars,* by the author and Stuart Wexler. From a purely military perspective, Armas was supplied with an extensive quantity of military weapons, ammunition, and supplies, shipped covertly out of the Army's Raritan Arsenal in New Jersey. The first shipment involved over 60,000 pounds of material, providing Armas's force of only 200 recruits with 750,000 rounds of rifle and pistol ammunition, 600 pounds of high explosive and armor piercing anti-tank shells, and 2,200 hand grenades. Provisions were made for a second shipment of over 900,000 rounds of ammunition out of New Orleans. It appears that the CIA planners had little doubt the effort would require combat and bloodshed.[21] Surprisingly, it would not—most likely due to the fact that the psychological warfare program was aided and abetted by a large U.S. Navy task force immediately offshore. The task force made its presence felt with a blockade of foreign shipping, including cargo carriers from America's closest allies, and one totally unauthorized, but highly visible, bombing mission.

The psychological warfare and political action elements of PBSUCCESS are especially educational, quite different from the propaganda and political influence campaigns we explored in the Italian and Iranian actions. To a large extent it can only be described as a "fear" program, specifically targeting the senior members in the Árbenz government as well as key socialist and Communist Party leaders. As noted earlier, political assassination was discussed from the very beginning of the CIA's involvement in PBFORTUNE. It had been proposed by Armas, described as an accepted practice in project discussions, and clearly covered in training for Armas's personnel. In fact the CIA paramilitary trainers had specifically prepared what can only be described as an assassination manual. Titled *A Study of Assassinations*, it was drafted early in 1952 and contains background on the planning, use, and justification of political assassination. It features an in-depth study of techniques and commentary on devices and strategies ranging from bare hands, accidents, the use of drugs, edged weapons, various firearms, and explosives. In addition, some twenty-plus known political assassinations are listed and outlined. The document has the appearance of a training guide in that it contains detailed instructions and advice in regard to various assassination techniques.[22]

In reviewing the PBSUCCESS psychological warfare activities, we find murder threats a key element. In one instance, mourning cards were mailed to top communist leaders, mentioning purges and executions of communists around the world, and hinting at the "forthcoming doom" of the addressees. Death-threat letters were also sent to top Guatemalan communists. These actions, part of the program's "Nerve War against Individuals" included sending wooden coffins, hangman's nooses, and phony bombs to the targeted individuals. Beyond that, the targets were treated to slogans such as "Here Lives a Spy" and "You have only 5 days" painted on their houses.[23]

As mentioned earlier, Armas's group routinely pushed for the violent disposal of senior communist leaders. In one instance PBSUCCESS headquarters pushed back against endorsing immediate murders while offering mixed messages, including remarking that the idea was not a good one for the present time, since it might touch off violent reprisals. Then the responses noted that a CIA field officer might wish "to study the suggestion for utility now or in the future." In March 1954, a meeting at PBSUCCESS headquarters was held to consider the murder of fifteen to twenty of the top Guatemalan leaders by "Trujillo's trained pistoleros."[24] The record indicates that the idea for select assassinations was actually endorsed by CIA Deputy Director of Plans Richard M. Bissell Jr., with concurrence from the State Department representative to the meeting. Another meeting attendee stated that "such elimination was part of the plan and could be done," objecting only to murders at that particular time.

Overall psychological fear tactics targeted regime leadership, not with the objective of changing the overall popular perception of the Árbenz government or swaying the political balance (as in Italy or Iran), but specifically with the intent of destabilizing it and pressuring it out of power—and hopefully out of the country. Beyond radio broadcasts (from pirate CIA stations outside Guatemalan borders), targeted leafleting drops (with aircraft loaned by President Somoza and flown by CIA contract pilots), scare tactics, and rumor campaigns, the intimidation campaign received powerful support from the deployment of a major American naval force. In early June, the U.S. Navy had implemented, with both ships and submarines, the centuries-old blockade practice of stopping and boarding commercial vessels headed for Guatemala, supposedly in search of weapons shipments from the Soviet bloc.

The naval operation, designated "Operation Hardrock Baker," was directed to use force in its blockade, even if foreign ships were damaged. The blockade included the boarding of foreign flagged transports in international waters as well as suspect vessels destined for Guatemala. Arguably illegal under international law, the aggressive measures might well have produced incidents with foreign powers—including America's own allies—had it continued for any extended period. In fact, the Dutch government lodged a formal protest after one of its flagged vessels was boarded while at San Juan, Puerto Rico.[25] Although not part of the blockade, a CIA field officer acting on his own directed one of the Nicaraguan aircraft flown by CIA contract pilots to bomb a British commercial transport, the Springfiord, suspected of carrying weapons.[26] The field officer reportedly acted at the urging of General Somoza rather than with any orders from the CIA chain of command. The incident was internally condemned but reportedly helped convince Árbenz that the United States was prepared to engage in open military action against him.

During the blockade even British and French ships were challenged, stopped, and inspected. There is no record that weapons were found during any of the boarding actions, and the boarding of allied ships clearly was done for effect and psychological impact within Guatemala rather than on Great Britain, France, or the Netherlands. Even more aggressively, a force of five amphibious assault ships and an antisubmarine (helicopter-equipped) aircraft carrier were deployed off the Guatemalan coast. The landing assault ships were backed with a full Marine battalion-level landing force. The landing force appears to have been a major factor in convincing Árbenz not to act militarily against the U.S.-backed insurgents—doing so would have clearly invited massive American military action against his forces. Rumors were reportedly rampant within Guatemala that the Marines would support Armas, and Árbenz also assumed that the fear of U.S. forces would encourage his army commanders to strike a deal with the rebels.

In reality PBSUCCESS involved little actual military action other than strafing and bombing of select targets by the small CIA air force, attacks staged more for psychological effect than as part of any coordinated military effort. On June 16, 1954, CIA-backed armed Guatemalan exiles entered remote border areas from Honduras, advancing tentatively and having difficulty overcoming even the resistance from local police forces and citizens. As one of the CIA officers described it, the "invasion" consisted of several trucks crossing the border without opposition. Carlos Castillo Armas was out front in a battered station wagon.

The rebel forces were divided into four groups, entering at five separate points on the border to give the image of a massive effort, yet numbering less than five hundred men in total. That approach was also consciously selected in order to prevent the effort from being aborted due to the destruction of the entire force. Some ten saboteurs were sent to blow up selected bridges and cut telegraph lines. A conscious effort was also made to avoid engagement with the Guatemalan Army. The invasion was actually more of a psychological device than a serious military effort to match the much larger regular Guatemalan military forces.

Armas's forces moved quite slowly and in their first battle, 122 rebels were defeated by some 33 Guatemalan soldiers. Only twenty-eight of Armas's troops escaped being killed or captured. In another attack on a heavily defended port city, the local police chief used dockworkers in opposition and the majority of the rebels were killed or captured, with the few remaining fleeing back to Honduras. Inside three days, two of the four rebel groups had been neutralized. Amazingly, at that point Árbenz reportedly ordered his military to allow the remaining Armas forces to advance, apparently due to a concern that if they appeared totally defeated, the American military would intervene.

Without doubt the combination of opposing forces actually within the country, the bombing and strafing, and a large American task force immediately offshore intimidated Árbenz, who was never known as a forceful, military-style leader. His own rise to power had been through politics rather than via armed rebellion. At that point he clearly panicked, first suspending civil liberties and then ordering an electrical blackout of the capital, which was not under any type of imminent threat. His failure to dispatch troops against Armas's small forces, much less to take any part in military action against them, further undermined the confidence of the Guatemalan Army.

Within twenty-four hours, Árbenz broadcast a resignation speech, fled to the Mexican Embassy with several hundred supporters, and shortly afterwards departed the country. Armas and his troops were flown from their remote location to a landing field outside the Guatemalan capital, which they entered in a victory parade. Psychological warfare and massive intimidation had won the day; PBSUCCESS would become the model for some three decades of American hybrid warfare. It would also prove to be a flawed model. Other projects modeled from it would fail repeatedly, most publicly and embarrassingly at Cuba's Bay of Pigs in 1961.

As to consequences, beyond establishing a flawed model that somehow assumed a life of its own—and emerged once again this century in actions by the Russian Federation—the Guatemala operation proved to be just as obvious to the nations in Latin America as the Iran coup had been in the Middle East. Deniable, yes. Covert, yes. Brutally obvious, also yes. The lack of widespread bloodshed was simply due to the quick resignation of Árbenz and his immediate departure from the country along with most of his supporters. That flight had occurred well before Armas moved any forces into the capital.

In subsequent years, political assassination indeed became a major fact of Guatemalan life. Armas assumed dictatorial power and his regime moved to stay in place by organizing what came to be called "death squads"—a political warfare practice that would blight Latin American nations for decades. Studies conducted by human rights groups suggest that during the next four decades, from 1954 to 1994, more than 140,000 Guatemalans were either killed or "disappeared."[27]

1958: INDONESIA

In 1954, PBSUCCESS established a set of hybrid warfare practices the United States would repeatedly turn to throughout the Cold War. The successes of those practices would be limited, their failures sometimes little known. But at other times, as in the years of actions against Cuba, they would prove hugely embarrassing. The combination of psychological warfare, surrogate military support, and overt Navy intimidation worked in Guatemala. To illustrate how easily the same set of practices could prove fruitless, we move around the globe to another CIA operation in Indonesia in 1958.

The American political warfare intervention in Indonesia during 1957-58 had a great many similarities to PBSUCCESS in Guatemala and a number of differences. It also illustrates the steps by which what was initially conceived as a political action campaign evolved into a significant covert military effort involving not only U.S. Navy ships, submarines, and aircraft but a deniable CIA air force supported out of the U.S. Air Force's Clark Air Base in the Philippines. The similarities and differences in practices are educational, but the Indonesian intervention also reveals a good deal about how the combination of American personnel (CIA political action officers, CIA covert paramilitary staff, and uniformed American military) worked together in covert operations. In the end the major difference was that the Indonesian operations ultimately failed, poisoning American foreign relations in the region for an extended period.

The covert intervention in Indonesia also provides us with a second introduction to the types of American hybrid warfare that would be carried out consistently around the globe during the Cold War, from Tibet to Laos, from Cuba to Chile, from the Congo and Angola to Afghanistan. The details of all those operations are not our story here, however a full appreciation of the practices involved will help in the recognition of hybrid warfare in other times and other places, most especially in contemporary events. The Indonesian experience also reinforces how important it is to appreciate the American foreign relations Cold War worldview, which began under Truman, solidified under Eisenhower, and continued through President Reagan. The accuracy of that description can be judged by the detailed internal policy dialogues now available in hundreds of pages of official documents related to American intervention in Indonesia—including transcripts of the National Security Council discussions involving the statements and positions of President Eisenhower, Secretary of State John Foster Dulles, and CIA Director Allen Dulles. Those dialogues provide clear and personally revealing insights into their thinking and decision-making process. That material is the basis for much of the following exploration. Readers are encouraged to review the full body of work, and particularly meaningful documents from the cited releases, along with other sources.[28]

As a nation, Indonesia is a consolidation of a great many ethnic and religious groups spread across several large islands and many smaller ones in the Indonesian archipelago. The archipelago as a whole had been a possession of the Dutch Empire through World War II and contained immense mineral and oil reserves, many still under the commercial control of Western companies, with Americans heavily involved in oil production. Sukarno, the first democratically elected president of Indonesia, was a populist, a nationalist, and a neutral as willing to visit and talk with the Soviets as with the United States. He had been elected in 1945 with support from the Communist Party of Indonesia, the PKI. The openly communist PKI had actually carried the voting majority areas on Java, the largest Indonesian island.

President Sukarno proved as annoying to Washington, DC as had the leaders of Iran and Guatemala. His reliance on the PKI was seen as a distinct threat, and the theme that runs throughout many of the National Security Council discussions on Indonesia is quite familiar. If Indonesia went communist, the U.S. would likely be forced into overt military intervention, and in a "domino effect" other nations in the region could easily be overwhelmed by Communist Party takeovers. The same language can be found in regard to Italy in 1948, and to both Iran and Guatemala in 1953-54. The domino-effect fear would become most popularly expressed later, in the 1960s, in regard to Vietnam and Southeast Asia, but in reality it had been a stock fear for well over a decade.

As early as 1954, CIA Deputy Director of Plans Frank Wisner, head of CIA clandestine operations, was encouraging Alfred Ulmer Jr., the newly appointed chief of the Agency's Far Eastern Division, to "hold Sukarno's feet to the fire."[29] At that point in time there were no NSC directives and no executive-level postion related to initiating any actual political warfare programs against Sukarno. However, every American diplomatic mission (as well as every Russian mission) contained its own political action officers, under cover as diplomatic staff.

Embassy-level missions normally contained actual CIA stations, with a variety of personnel all operating under diplomatic cover. Smaller consulates and offices sometimes had only a political officer or a handful of officers regionally assigned to them out of a major station, with the officers circulating among the outposts.

Paramilitary specialists were assigned in a similar fashion. However, if actual covert military operations developed, separate and special field facilities were established for them, usually facilities with adjacent airfields. In PBSUCCESS the hybrid warfare staff operated out of Nicaragua and Honduras. During this same period the CIA operated covert military missions into Tibet, first out of a facility/airfield located in Pakistan and later in India. By 1958, when political action against Sukarno turned to hybrid warfare, the Philippines and in particular Clark Air Base would serve as the staging point for the CIA covert air campaign in Indonesia.

But all that came later. First it was standard political action, with CIA officers covertly using their business and military contacts and in many instances long-established personal social networks to prospect for points of weaknesses in Sukarno's regime. They specifically searched for individuals who might serve as agents of influence to destabilize his governance to the point at which economic and military aid from the United States would move him away from the Soviets. Such a move would hopefully stop Sukarno from seeking further support from the PKI portion of his political base.

Given that Sukarno had been popularly elected, in a post-colonial, ethnically and religiously diverse nation, it was easy to find potential opposition. But it soon became clear that any meaningful destabilization of his regime was going to have to come from regional divisions within the Indonesian military forces. In Iran the CIA had turned to a politically ambitious general inside the country; in Guatemala the CIA had found a politically ambitious expatriate general in Nicaragua; in Indonesia various political action officers would recruit a variety of politically ambitious Indonesian Army officers from points across the archipelago.

By August 1957 the possibility that Sukarno might actually place Indonesian Communist Party members in government positions was the familiar fuel for a National Security directive outlining a two-phase political warfare strategy in Indonesia. On the main island of Java, the CIA would covertly attempt to recruit anti-communist military officers who might stage a coup against Sukarno. Overtly, the United States would maintain economic aid to Indonesia, continuing positive diplomatic relations in Jakarta, the nation's capital. In the outer islands, including the large island of Sumatra, CIA political action officers would locate and support regional insurgencies and anti-Sukarno parties in an effort to reduce central government control. That pragmatic, but bipolar, American foreign policy was officially endorsed by President Eisenhower as of September 23, 1957.[30] The Joint Chiefs of Staff were also advised that should a communist regime truly come to power in Jakarta, the United States would move to full military support of revolutionary forces across the archipelago, essentially the same military planning guidance given to the American military in regard to Italy in 1948 and Iran in 1954.

Given that the search for opposition factions had been well under way for almost a year, support for insurgent military factions moved quite quickly. During 1958 the story of the various insurgencies on some half-dozen islands outside of Java and the support provided to them is more than a little complex. Some factions were primarily interested in assistance with establishing independent revenue sources (which primarily involved seaborne smuggling of copra) while others wanted weapons, not just small weapons but boats, aircraft, and artillery including anti-aircraft weaponry. Heavier weapons were needed for any serious insurrection since the Indonesian Army was equipped with air transport for paratroop operations, vessels for seaborne troop movements, and an air force consisting of both light bombers and fighters.[31]

Experienced CIA officers were deployed into the Indonesian operation from Singapore, from Washington, and from Taipei on Formosa. By November 1957 the first major shipment of weapons and ammunition was delivered to rebellious forces on Sumatra by Operation HAIK ("HA" being the CIA cryptonym for Indonesia). Deliveries involved a U.S. Navy submarine, the USS *Bluegill*, and barges towed by the USS *Thomaston*, a landing ship. Sailing out of Subic Bay in the Philippines, the *Thomaston*'s barges carried small arms and equipment for as many as eight thousand fighters.[32] As in Guatemala, the CIA would be supplying materials far beyond the capacity of the actual insurgent forces on the ground.

During the next several months various insurgent factions operated independently on Sumatra, Sulawesi, Halmahera, and other outer islands, sometimes coordinating their political efforts to offer threats, demands, and ultimatums to the central government. In February of 1958 there was a declaration of an independent government, designated the Revolutionary Government of the Republic of Indonesia (PRRI), with its own cabinet. During that same period Sukarno and the elected government in Jakarta conducted a number of reasonably well-orchestrated joint military operations against each of the factions involved in the rebellion. Throughout those months the CIA consistently overstated both the size of the insurgencies and the capabilities of the various factions. It also repeatedly offered the opinion, endorsed by Secretary of State John Foster Dulles, that if the revolution failed, Indonesia would inevitably go communist.[33] Secretary Dulles also pointed out that the insurgency on Sumatra provided an ideal cover for higher-risk covert operations and that the situation demanded the United States commit itself to "substantial risks." It was this assessment that would drive the next major steps in American hybrid warfare, including the creation of a U.S.-operated insurgent air force.

Throughout the winter of 1957 and into the spring of 1958 covert military shipments into Indonesia had continued, primarily by chartered air transports flying out of the Philippines. In addition, the insurgents had established commercial relations with the Republic of China and began to purchase not only weapons but aircraft. China would ultimately provide both pilots and a military operations team of its own, flying its own attack missions against Indonesian government forces. Taipei also sent large shipments of weapons to Sumatra by freighter.[34]

By March 1958 the CIA and the Navy were upping the ante with Operation Hance, delivering a massive shipment of weapons by sea in towed barges and by large-scale air transport shipments. The shipments were particularly important as the Jakarta government had begun a series of offensive military operations, with plans for a major action against the insurgent PRRI on Sumatra. Initially those operations included plans to bomb key oil refineries on the island. American ownership and personnel were involved in those oil operations, and the Indonesian government preemptively advised the American ambassador of the pending attacks in order that precautions could be taken to protect American citizens. The resulting series of discussions, as revealed in the State Department history, provide an illustration of how tightly American political warfare was coupled between the Department of State and the CIA. The U.S. Navy also offered its cooperation in an overt defensive action to protect the refineries, going so far as to begin assembling Task Force 57 and sending two destroyers to Singapore with a cruiser and an aircraft carrier scheduled to follow.

The Navy offer of direct military involvement was ultimately declined. There is some reason to believe that the pending attack was viewed as an actual opportunity in some quarters. The record of a highly pragmatic conversation between Secretary of State Dulles and Allen Dulles reveals that the CIA Director opposed the involvement of the U.S. Navy in delivering a "bloody nose" to the Indonesian government offensive. Allen Dulles felt that such an Indonesian attack, and the probable consequences—including damage to American properties and casualties among American employees—would offer the U.S. the opportunity to "yell and scream" about it, providing leverage against Sukarno. It appears that Secretary Dulles concurred with that assessment.[35]

It is also clear that in Indonesia the American ambassador was as equally involved in the overall political action as had been the ambassador in Iran during TPAJAX. The records of his conversations with the Sukarno regime illustrate the extent to which a dual carrot-and-stick approach was being followed. That strategy involved ostensibly normal, friendly relations with the Jakarta government in conjunction with escalating covert American military action to support the various insurgencies. It also included yet another example of confidential diplomatic information being leaked to the press to frustrate the targeted regime's own efforts.

On March 7, the Indonesian foreign minister lodged a complaint in regard to newspaper reporting of comments by a Department of State spokesperson opposing the refinery bombing mission. The Indonesian military was "furious" over the compromise of its plans and the government was irate about such a "breach of confidence."[36] Subsequently the government attack plans were altered, however the military asked that the diplomatic communication regarding any delay or changes should not be given to the press due to concern over its being seen as too easily influenced by foreign pressure. In the end, a combination of government parachute troops and seaborne landings secured the oil complex areas without bombing or destroying them; insurgent resistance had proved minimal, despite Director Dulles's earlier praise for the abilities of the insurgent forces on Sumatra.

By March there was increasing concern in Washington that not only would the insurgency and the PRRI not overthrow the Sukarno regime, but that it was beginning to crumble to the point of not even being a viable threat, much less a tool of political leverage. Increasingly successful military actions by Indonesian forces had to be blocked and short of overt Navy action, the only answer was air power to oppose further government moves against the PRRI. And the PRRI group on Sulawesi, already operating two C-54 transports supplied by Taiwan, was definitely interested in attack aircraft, for defense but also to carry the fight against forces being deployed by the Indonesian government.

Officially announced on March 8, 1958, the new PRRI air group was designated as the Revolutionary Air Force, more commonly referred to as the AUREV. Ostensibly it was purely Indonesian, headed by officers formerly with the Indonesian Air Force. In reality and operationally, it was all CIA—organized and supported with logistics out of the Philippines, using CIA-recruited pilots and supplied from Clark Air Base. In short, it was another and more logistically ambitious version of covert CIA air operations over Guatemala. The attack aircraft included P-51 Mustang fighters and B-26 Invader attack bombers, stripped of their former U.S. Air Force markings and sanitized as having been purchased on the commercial, postwar resale market. Eventually, Taiwan adapted a C-54 transport aircraft for bombing operations. Air operations by the AUREV involved strafing and bombing attacks carried out independently by CIA pilots and ROC air crews.

The first AUREV attacks on April 13, 1958 struck government airfields and military camps on Sulawesi. However, in terms of the larger insurgency across the archipelago, such strikes had relatively little impact. During April the government conducted a number of successful military operations, regaining territory and moving to broaden central government authority and control. Also during April, a number of incidents involving the recovery of American supplied weapons and materials as well as direct observations of air supply drops had made the American involvement obvious to the Indonesian military. That story was on the verge of expanding into the international press.[37] Increasing visibility of covert American involvement appeared likely to force the Indonesian government into formal protests. Given the increasing stress on the insurgency itself, there was high-level State Department and NSC discussion of options ranging from official United States recognition of the PRRI as a legitimate government to the provision of overt military American support. The key question now was whether it was time to switch sides to Jakarta, cultivating anti-communist regime elements and essentially abandoning the insurgency.

A good deal of the Washington dialogue revolved around the importance of the insurgency on Sumatra, which was under immediate central government military pressure in new attacks. With its mineral, oil, and other natural resources, Sumatra was key to the economic independence of any confederation of outer islands beyond the Sukarno regime in Java. If Sumatra fell to the central government, the odds of destabilizing the Sukarno regime would decrease significantly. And beginning on April 16, in a series of coordinated attacks, central government forces effectively eliminated the insurgency on Sumatra in a matter of some two weeks. The only remaining American hope was to sustain the anti-government groups on islands to the east of Java, primarily on Sulawesi, and the only tool available for that was the new CIA covert air unit.

At this distance in time it is hard to appreciate the extended exchanges in Washington, DC, the failure to face reality, and the fact that the hybrid warfare project in Indonesia had indeed failed with the fall of Sumatra. In reading the transcripts and memoranda related to the ongoing discussion, the failure seems largely to be the result of Allen Dulles's convincing Secretary of State Dulles not to abandon the CIA effort, to simply give it more time. Although never openly stated, it may have been that the CIA director was holding out in the hope that broadening the new air strikes to include commercial vessels and freighters might be sufficient to affect Indonesia economically. Intimidation had proved effective in Guatemala, both the CIA and Republic of China aircraft had successfully flown attacks against Indonesian government bases and patrol ships. CIA Director Dulles seemed to be maintaining there was still a chance for the CIA to assist the insurgency in gaining some degree of leverage in Indonesia.

As of May 1, 1958, AUREV was directed to begin attacking commercial shipping, the hope being that foreign operators would get the message and pull their ships out of the Indonesian trade zone. Oil installations and pipelines were also to be targeted, further damaging government revenues. The first air strikes were dramatically successful—the *Flying Lark* (Panamanian registry), *Aquela* (Italian) and *Armonia* (Greek) were sunk. In addition, the British-flagged tanker *San Flaviano* was sunk, another tanker attacked, and oil pipelines inside port facilities were destroyed. Economic warfare had most definitely begun.[38] The immediate result was that commercial ships operating out of Singapore were ordered to avoid Indonesian waters, and within days Dutch-operated vessels received the same instructions.

During May the Sukarno government registered diplomatic protests against foreign air attacks, specifically against involvement of the ROC and in regard to Clark Air Base's support for the air campaign. Meanwhile attacks against both Indonesian forces and commercial shipping seriously escalated. The Indonesians had considerable proof of American involvement but actively tried to plead their case with U.S. diplomats rather than through the press. In return, American diplomats continued to respond with what can only be described as blatant untruths: "…the U.S. did not desire the fragmentation of Indonesia… shocked surprise that Clark Field could have been involved…hard to believe…U.S. had no control over bombings by rebels. . .there is nothing that we can do to stop them."[39]

Indeed, nothing was done to stop the air strikes, although in response to new government military operations, attention turned to attacks on Indonesian invasion forces and the bases supporting them. While individual strikes were successful, the small CIA and ROC contingents faced growing opposition from anti-aircraft fire and from fighters of the Indonesian Air Force. The tide had simply turned against the insurgencies across the archipelago; factionalism, independent commands, and colonels with their own agendas had not been able

CREATING CHAOS

to maintain a broad-based and coordinated military initiative. Equally importantly, unlike in Iran and Guatemala, Sukarno had never panicked and his regime's senior commanders had ultimately remained loyal—or at least opposed to the colonels leading the independence movements on the various islands. There had been no military coup on Java.

On May 15, the U.S. Embassy in Jakarta advised Washington that its dialogues with Sukarno's representatives had produced encouraging remarks about his willingness to move against PKI Communist Party influence, especially within the government's military. The Embassy offered the opinion that it appeared to be time to wind down support for the rebels and shift attention to fostering positive relationships with Sukarno. The language of the communication implies a quid pro quo, with the United States acting to bring about a "cessation" of foreign support to the rebels and increasing economic and development support while the government of Indonesia moves to minimize communist influence.[40]

An objective reading of the communications suggests that the proposal for a quid pro quo was essentially a diplomatic expedient to soften the actual failure of the campaign against Sukarno. The American Embassy reasserted its call for a policy shift on May 18, declaring that "the moment has arrived" to demonstrate American goodwill towards the Sukarno regime. That "moment" was also evident in the extent to which insurgent bombing raids had aroused intense public opposition, along with continually increasing suspicion of foreign sponsorship.

On that same day, yet another air strike provided the Indonesian government with such solid proof that the United States was directly involved with attacks, that there was no real choice but to accept the path proposed by the U.S. Embassy. One of the CIA contract pilots had been shot down during an attack on Indonesian military transport ships. Given the frequent air attacks, the government flotilla had been extensively equipped with anti-aircraft guns, and fire from multiple boats had downed the attacking B-26. The pilot was recovered from the sea, alive and with extensive documentation on his person. Of course, standard practice was for the pilots to fly "sterile," with no documentation at all, but in this instance Allen Pope had carried his flight log which recorded all his previous attack flights—as well as his identity card, his military separation papers, and a copy of his secret orders assigning him to the CIA covert air project. Later his friends would speculate that Pope was very much aware of what had happened to CIA pilots who had been captured in China, and the fate of some of them.[41] Pope's paperwork was simply the final addition to a considerable list of evidence the Indonesian government forces had collected, including shipping labels on captured pallets of weapons showing transshipment from Taiwan via Clark Air Base.[42]

On May 20, 1958, American foreign relations with Indonesia dramatically reversed course. A telegram went out from CIA Director Allen Dulles, routed through Clark Air Base to CIA paramilitary units working with the insurgents; the orders were simple, cease field operations immediately and withdraw to the Philippines.[43] That same day Secretary of State John Foster Dulles issued a public statement describing the Indonesian conflict strictly as an internal matter, affirming that there should no foreign interference with that nation's affairs. By May 22, Indonesia and the United States had concluded an agreement for the immediate sale of thirty-five thousand tons of rice, with highly favorable remarks from President Sukarno during the trade agreement signing. Within a week, a government military delegation had arrived in Hawaii, receiving a warm welcome. A cable from the chief of U.S. forces in the Pacific described the visit as an effort "to get our relationship back with the right forces in Indonesia."[44]

Chapter Seven:
Active Measures

I t is a reality of foreign relations that adversary states—and even major allied powers—conduct certain intelligence activities on an ongoing and routine basis. As an example, virtually every major state performs covert human and technical intelligence collections that generate information intended to help its leaders determine other nations' plans, military capabilities, and internal political maneuverings. As with the other covert practices we have explored, officially such things do not happen. However, on occasion they surface in the media. During the 1960s a handful of American defections exposed the fact that the National Security Agency was monitoring not only Soviet and Warsaw Bloc military communications but also diplomatic and commercial traffic from targets designated as ALLO (all other countries) and ROW (rest of world) transmitted on international leased carriers. The primary monitoring station for this was in Kirknewton, Scotland. The monitoring teams worked off "watch lists" designating targets by name, company, and even by commodity; the lists were provided by the CIA, the FBI, and the DEA.[1]

Such activities continued following the end of the Cold War, driven by threats of terrorism and by the never-ending war on drug smuggling. Following the attacks on America in 2001, global jihadi activity and suspicions of terror cells in nations around the world—including possible covert support from cliques within certain national govern-ments—drove the practice of technical intelligence collections to new heights. And in 2013 CIA contractor Edward Snowden obtained and disclosed classified documents revealing details of advanced intercept activities around the globe, not by the United States alone but also by the United Kingdom.[2]

Such revelations have not been limited to the activities of the United States and its allies. Russian political officers have also provided extensive details on Russian intercept activities, including major pro-grams conducted from within Russian consulates in New York City and San Francisco. Sergei Tretyakov, first secretary at Russia's mission in New York, defected in 2000 and provided extensive details on active measures carried out by Russia inside the United States. He described the construction of a highly advanced and secure technical facility on the eighth floor of the Russian Permanent Mission to the United Nations.[3] That floor was actually floated on heavy springs so that no surface touched the adjacent walls, thereby preventing acoustic cou-pling. The walls were made of metal, and white noise was coupled into them to provide an electronic barrier. There were no windows within what the Russians called "the submarine." Personnel from several dif-ferent groups used the technical assets within the facility, including those from Line OT (technical operations) and Line RP (radio inter-ception). The facility was also equipped for secure, encrypted trans-mission of information developed by Line X (science and technology), and the largest group within the Russian mission, Line PR (political intelligence).

At that time the Russian diplomatic mission to the United States actually operated out of several different facilities in the New York area—the Permanent Mission to the United Nations on Sixty-Seventh Street, the Russian Consulate, the Russian residential compound in the Bronx (in the Riverdale community), and two estates on Long Island, one at Glen Cove and one in Oyster Bay. Tretyakov related that the

Bronx compound had proved especially useful as it was located on a steep hill, one of the tallest points in the city. An extensive antenna array (concealed under wooden covers) was installed on the residency roof; similar arrays were installed on the roof of the Permanent Mission facility. Each facility maintained a listening post with not only intercept capabilities but in support of a surveillance system designated "Post Impulse," which allowed extensive monitoring of "police broadcasts, cell phone calls, and other electronic communications not only in Manhattan but over some forty miles of New York, Long Island, and New Jersey."[4]

Of course, active measures are not unique to either Russia or the United States. One of the classic twentieth-century examples comes from a combination of covert intelligence collection and sophisticated political shaping during World War I. In January 1917 the British obtained a politically provocative message, the so-called Zimmermann Telegram, from German Foreign Minister Arthur Zimmermann to the German diplomatic mission in Mexico. At the time Germany had no means of directly communicating with Mexico. But with the United States still neutral, the U.S. State Department had offered Germany the use of its diplomatic telegraphic network to send what were agreed to be routine but encrypted diplomatic communications. The American network required that messages routed from Europe go through lines in London. British intelligence had begun to tap into the American diplomatic communications network early in the war, with special attention to encoded messages and especially to German communications.

There is no doubt that such covert intelligence collection is an age-old practice. It is a matter of record that in the 1600s, with the establishment of the British Royal Mail service, the government of Oliver Cromwell routinely monitored, opened, and re-mailed postal items from suspected conspirators. In more contemporary times the British General Postal Office (GPO) Special Investigations unit monitored

British mail at sorting offices, intercepting and photographing items of interest before sending them onwards. The photographs were forwarded to MI5.[5] During the Cold War both the FBI and CIA[6] used U.S. Post Office resources to intercept and open mail from communist countries as well as mail going to Russian diplomatic offices in the United States.[7] In addition, during the 1960s the CIA operated its own mail monitoring and opening program, targeting anti-Vietnam war protesters.[8]

When such activities do become known there is always public angst, official protests are made, apologies are issued, and certain activities may be suspended—for a time. Machiavelli would have been amused; as he pragmatically observed, no ruler and hence no state can turn a blind eye to potential threats or challenges and survive over the long-term. To paraphrase one of his key observations: it is necessary for a prince wishing to hold his own to know how to do wrong and to make use of it according to necessity. Like it or not, that observation remains as accurate as it was centuries ago when he first expressed it.

Covert intelligence collection, whether it be human as in the days of the Great Game or technical (electronic, signals, cyber) as has become increasingly common in contemporary times. It remains a key element in supporting and enabling political warfare, though it in itself is not our focus. Instead it is simply one aspect of a broader series of ongoing practices referred to under the general title of "active measures." The term has traditionally been associated with Russian political warfare, however its practices are really quite generic, common in the political warfare of all major powers. With that understanding, the term will be used for both Russian and American activities involving intelligence collection, the identification and manipulation of agents of influence, news manipulation, disinformation, propaganda, counterfeiting official documents, and in more contemporary times, information and social media warfare using the global internet.

Zimmermann's telegram destined for Mexico was copied and turned over to British code specialists who deciphered it and recovered a truly sensational message. The Germans were using a back channel into the Mexican government, with the intent of dramatically shaping both Mexican foreign policy and ultimately military action. If the United States chose to enter the war against Germany, Mexico would be encouraged to join the German alliance. Mexico would then be encouraged to attack America. With a German victory, it would receive several U.S. states, specifically Texas, New Mexico, and Arizona.[9]

The intercept and decoding of the telegram offered a huge opportunity for helping move America into the war on the side of Great Britain, but revealing it would also have exposed not only the ability of British intelligence to break German diplomatic code but its tapping into the American diplomatic telegraphic network. To avoid this, the British used intelligence assets within the United States to obtain a copy of the telegram as it had been retransmitted from Washington, DC to Mexico City. It was then offered to American diplomatic contacts as having been obtained in Mexico City.

After thorough American review the telegram was made available to the press, presented as having been intercepted and decoded by U.S. Intelligence. By March 1, 1917, the full text was printed in papers across the nation and the public response immediately began to turn the United States from neutrality towards war.[10]

In a very real sense, the full body of active measures practices appears to be virtually ageless, ongoing today and far different from the special, relatively short-lived political warfare projects explored in proceeding chapters. Active measures are often built off constant, routine, and quite prosaic work by certain staff personnel assigned to virtually every diplomatic mission. Those activities range from relatively benign diplomatic relationships to the more challenging work of developing and cultivating potential agents of influence—from academics and journalists to individuals capable of influencing a nation's foreign policies. In their most negative form, active measures include covert actions intended to fragment domestic political parties; to create racial, religious, or ethnic strife; and to disrupt established military and political alliances. Active measures are routinely supported from within a given nation's diplomatic mission, whether it be a United Nations mission, a foreign embassy facility, a consulate, or even a residency.

As early as 1959 the Russian intelligence service (KGB) established its independent "Department D" to conduct disinformation activities, with the authority to utilize technical, military, and scientific resources as needed. The department's director, Ivan Agayants, personally involved himself in certain missions, participating in a number of foreign disinformation programs around the globe, from Sweden to Pakistan and on to Indonesia.[11] Active measures involving anti-American disinformation were standard Soviet practice during the Cold War. One of the earliest known examples comes from 1966, when a Turkish senator came forward with documents purporting to show American plans to eliminate certain Turkish military officers and intervene with covert political action in support of the regime in power, the Justice Party. One letter purported to be a communication with the military attaché to the American diplomatic mission.

Upon closer inspection it was found that the initials in the letters did indeed match certain American diplomatic staff. Both Turkish political figures and military leadership readily accepted the documents, rushing to harshly condemn American intervention as fact. Ultimately, American personnel used inconsistencies and mistakes in the letters to support a formal Turkish government acceptance of the official American denial. However the public and, most important, many in the Turkish military remained increasingly suspicious of the CIA.

Soviet active measures using planted disinformation including false news stories crafted with a combination of true and false content, faked documents, and even manipulated academic studies surged during the 1960s, reaching an activity level almost on par with Russian espionage operations. Operations tapered off during the early 1970s but reached their highest levels during the Reagan administration in the early 1980s.[12] In 1981, well over one hundred Soviet diplomats were expelled from Spain, Canada, and six other countries. Pakistan alone expelled one hundred.[13] Studies report an estimated ten thousand total Soviet bloc disinformation operations during the Cold War era. While the success of such operations appears to have been marginal in the United States, despite the KGB's own internal claims, it had far more impact within the developing nations.

The reason for regional Soviet success lay in the fact that America's own covert political and hybrid warfare had sensitized the Middle East and Latin America to CIA political intervention. In that context, it was relatively easy for the KGB to focus the press in those regions on claims of CIA abuses—sometimes very real and at other times largely fictional. KGB central records reveal that some 250 active measures operations targeted CIA activities in third world countries by 1974. A number were performed with Soviet deniability, simply by using affiliated Soviet bloc intelligence services such as the Czechoslovak State Security Service (StB).[14] Following the collapse of the Soviet Union, one of the StB's senior officers, Ladislav Bittman, related information on several projects undertaken for the KGB, observing that: "Anti-American propaganda campaigns are easy to carry out. A single press article containing facts of a 'new American conspiracy' may be sufficient. Other papers become interested, the public is shocked, and governments in developing countries have a fresh opportunity to clamor against the imperialists while demonstrators hasten to break American embassy windows."[15]

The activities of the StB are educational not only for the operations themselves, but because they illustrate the fact that while active measures are generally ongoing and relatively limited, some of them can escalate into major actions, on the order of the American political warfare campaigns discussed previously. The Soviets had a full understanding of that risk and turned to their own intelligence surrogates to isolate themselves from the political interventions. In terms of leaving fingerprints, Russian active measures campaigns were and are often conducted more covertly than American political and hybrid warfare. That did not mean that their major interventions proved any more successful over the long-term.

A Soviet/StB active measures campaign in Indonesia circa 1964 illustrates that point particularly well.[16] The basic tools used were quite familiar ones, including forged documents and planted news (well-crafted disinformation). We have already seen American political warfare at work in Indonesia in the late 1950s, an effort, which although deniable, revealed itself in a number of ways. The end result was a legacy of ongoing suspicions of the CIA and American covert political meddling. In this Indonesian instance, the StB used an agent of influence (an Indonesian diplomat, acquired through sexual entanglement) to bring a series of faked documents to the attention of President Sukarno. The papers contained discussions of either his assassination or an overt invasion of certain islands in the archipelago by British and American forces (something actually discussed at NSC levels in 1957-58). Given prior experience it was no surprise Surkarno took the documents seriously.

The documents were also leaked to the Indonesian media by reporters acting as paid agents of influence, and Radio Moscow conducted a number of international broadcasts supporting the disinformation campaign. The resulting mob actions, widespread anti-American protests, and overall emotional response were far beyond expectations, generating a huge amount of political instability and raising the level of religious and racial hatred already in existence across Indonesia. Various factions including the PKI, by then one of the largest communist parties in the world with an estimated three million supporters, became increasingly involved in a power struggle for control of the nation's government and policies.

The following year a group of junior officers staged a coup in Indonesia. Declaring themselves the 30 September Movement, they stated that they were opposed to American influence within the military high command and had acted to preempt a U.S.-sponsored "generals coup," in the process murdering six general officers. In retaliation, a group of anti-communist generals took control of the Army.[17] State Department documents and CIA situation reports show no signs that the United States had anticipated any imminent political action in Indonesia, and initial speculation was that it might actually have been a political move by Sukarno. The American high-level discussions of the Indonesian chaos were largely in terms of the possible need to evacuate Americans, and there were remarks that the situation appeared to be hopeless.[18]

The coup proved to be short-lived but provoked an extreme amount of violence throughout the archipelago. Over the next year the Indonesian Army and anti-communist militias conducted what can only be described as a campaign of extinction against the PKI across Java. Estimates place the death toll at between half a million to a million Indonesians in Java, Sumatra, and Bali.[19] In the years since, there has been considerable discussion of American support for the Indonesian anti-communist campaign, largely based in the known, well-established American/Indonesian military contacts that had been encouraged following the abortive American political warfare projects of 1957-58.

It is now documented that an American political officer within the Jakarta embassy shared lists of PKI leadership and senior PKI cadre names that had been compiled from domestic Indonesian PKI media articles. The preparation of such lists (of both suspected opponents and supporters in a given regime) is actually a part of routine active measures work. Political officers in the American embassy had routinely compiled and reported the names of PKI leaders and cadre to CIA headquarters, and it was that ongoing activity that had generated the list. The ultimate result of mass killings, political chaos, and Sukarno's failure to cope with the situation was the end of the Sukarno regime. In following years Indonesia came under autocratic rule under new President Suharto, who led a regime that became rigorously repressive and anti-communist. This was certainly not the result that the Soviet/ StB anti-American influence disinformation campaign of 1964 had anticipated.

The disastrous end-result of the Soviet active measures campaign in Indonesia failed to change KGB practices any more than the failure of American hybrid warfare in Indonesia had changed CIA practices. In 1968, using a now familiar tactic, the KGB initiated a disinformation project in India. It began with the creation of a fake document, a letter ostensibly written to the Bombay *Free Press Journal* by Gordon Goldstein, who was with the U.S. Office of Navy Research. The signature and letterhead had been taken from an earlier invitation sent by Goldstein to an international distribution list.[20] It is routine practice for active measures personnel to collect such materials on a regular basis, thereby creating an inventory available should a new project come into being or an opportunity arise.

The letter was supposed to represent an official American assurance that India was not at risk in respect to the bacteriological weapons stored and prepared for use in Thailand and Vietnam. The United States was deeply involved in combat in the region and had conducted chemical spraying with Agent Orange in pursuit of targeted deforestation. Operation Ranch Hand involved more than twenty million gallons of herbicides used over Vietnam, Cambodia, and Laos from 1962 until 1971.[21] That provided a basis of fact, enough to construct an effective disinformation campaign. The letter was picked up from the Bombay paper and carried by the *Times* of London—while Radio

Moscow was broadcasting stories that the letter was confirmation of rumors of epidemics in Vietnam caused by American chemical warfare. In the end, the disinformation simply became stated as fact, with an article in the Indian weekly *Blitz* featuring a "U.S. Admits Biological and Nuclear Warfare" headline.

There is little doubt that Soviet active measures were consistently practiced throughout the Cold War. They often produced highly negative public perceptions of the United States and CIA "meddling" in Iran, Turkey, and India. In other instances, the activities failed rather dramatically, resulting in Soviet diplomatic personnel being expelled from their posts. A brief review of Cold War-era expulsions includes:[22]

> 1970-71: Republic of the Congo expels all Soviet diplomats for encouraging student unrest.[23]

> 1971: Mexico withdraws its ambassador from Moscow and expels five Soviet diplomatic staff, including the chargé d'affaires, in reaction to its security force's discovery that Russia had been actively involved in recruiting, developing, and supporting a cadre of revolutionary leaders and "shock brigades." The goal of the project was first to covertly escalate violence associated with student demonstrations. Beyond that the revolutionary groups had cached weapons and created a guerilla network with the intent of a violent revolutionary overthrow of the government.[24]

> 1978: Canada expels thirteen Soviets for efforts to bribe a number of Royal Canadian Mounted Police.

> 1979: Costa Rica expels two Soviet diplomats for efforts to organize a general nationwide strike.

> 1979: Liberia expels three Soviet diplomats for inciting riots.

1980: Spain expels two Soviet diplomats for clandestine contacts with outlawed terrorist and revolutionary groups, followed by two more expulsions for attempts to influence press stories and for monitoring weapons shipments.

1980: Pakistan expels dozens of Soviet diplomats for engaging in "subversive and illicit propaganda activities."

1981: Malaysia expels three Soviet diplomats for efforts to recruit the political secretary of the deputy prime minister.

1981: Egypt expels seven Soviet diplomats—including the Russian ambassador—for inciting religious strife and riots between Coptic Christian and Muslim fundamentalists. Seventy people were killed in the rioting.

1983: France expels forty-seven Soviet diplomats for a variety of political action and espionage activities.

Generally speaking, Soviet active measures, including the recruitment of agents of influence within the media and government, were most effective outside the United States and Canada. Due to intensive Cold War security measures, the American sensitivity to communism, and the FBI's ongoing focus on communist influence, the recruiting of high-level American media and political contacts as political assets proved to be quite difficult. There of course was successful recruiting for espionage purposes, but recruiting for political and media influence is another thing entirely. The sheer Cold War paranoia over potential communist association was a considerable barrier to Soviet contacts. In addition, there were very few areas of Russian-American trade. Business contacts have always been among the most common venues for recruiting assets.

In that regard, America most definitely held the advantage of cultivating foreign assets developed through trade and business connections. Of course, the higher the level of contact, the easier it is to obtain some amount of leverage on national politics and particularly national policy. One of the most successful examples of American Cold War-era active measures can be found in the CIA's activities in Mexico. CIA political action there during the 1960s is especially educational in that it allows considerable insight into how CIA stations operated from within inside U.S. diplomatic missions. It also provides an example of how truly effective the development of high-level agents of influence—acting quite voluntarily in regard to common national interests—can be, especially if such relationships are maintained over an extended period of time.

During much of the Cold War, the CIA's station in Mexico City was its largest foreign presence in the Western Hemisphere, second in size only to the Berlin station in Germany, although both were later eclipsed by the Saigon station during the Vietnam conflict. Normally the CIA's most experienced staff served in either Berlin or Mexico City, rotated only to headquarters or to special operations such as Guatemala or later to Vietnam. One of the things that made active measures in Mexico City exceptionally effective was that Chief of Station Winston "Win" M. Scott was there for an exceptionally lengthy tour, some thirteen years. One of the reasons for that lengthy tenure was Scott's wartime background in OSS counter-intelligence. Mexico City in Latin America (as with Berlin in Europe) represented the front line between American and Soviet covert activities.

CIA practice in Mexico City, as elsewhere, was to insert its basic active measures operations within the American diplomatic mission. As previously mentioned, that was and remains standard practice for Russia and virtually all major nations who have organized intelligence services. Diplomatic covers are routine and, in Mexico, Winston Scott's official title was first secretary of the United States Embassy. As we move into contemporary events, it will be important to keep in mind that diplomatic staff of any mission almost certainly have strong intelligence ties and many embassy and consulate personnel have either received special intelligence training or are actually intelligence agency staff.

At times there are also separate groups operating in-country, but great efforts are made to isolate them for operational security, especially since their work routinely involves illegal activities. In addition, such clandestine personnel serve as cut-outs for embassy political officers operating under diplomatic cover. Given its front-line status, Mexico City not only had the standard CIA station within the diplomatic mission but separate operations for both intelligence collection and a variety of special missions targeting Cuba and Latin American nations with political and military connections to Cuba. Personnel deployed for those particular missions were run out of an independent operation detached from but supported by the primary Cuba project station (JMWAVE) in Miami, Florida.

A considerable amount of detail in regard to the Mexico City station has been cleared and released by the CIA; the primary document containing that information is the 247-page CIA historical record of the station.[25] The American diplomatic mission in Mexico City was located in a rather common multistory building, with a coffee shop on the building's ground floor. The station had been moved at Scott's request to the top floor to maximize security. The CIA's primary mission in Mexico was to fight the growth of communist political influence, which largely meant establishing a supportive relationship with the ruling Institutional Revolutionary Party (PRI), itself declaredly anti-communist. While anti-communism offered a point of joint interests, the history of American intervention across Latin America meant that no governing regime could be seen by the public to be subservient to American interests.

Given that sort of sensitivity, the American ambassador to Mexico constantly faced the issue of diplomatic relations being tainted by other

CIA activities, including support for operations against Cuba. Having diplomatic relations with Mexico, Cuba enjoyed a good deal of popular support among the Mexican public. While it has been shown that American ambassadors and the State Department sometimes worked closely on joint operations, in Mexico Win Scott and Ambassador Robert Hill pursued their own missions, virtually independent of each other. Hill made it clear that he had little patience for intelligence work and that he would bear no responsibility for CIA station practices.[26] Those practices involved a huge political action program, opposing communist influence within Mexico but also conducting aggressive political action and intelligence collection work of all types against both the Cuban and Soviet missions in Mexico.[27]

The CIA station in Mexico City was headed by Scott as station chief. His staff included a deputy chief, eleven case officers, two intelligence analysts, a photographer, two translators, and a variety of other administrative and clerical staff. Beyond political action (a major personal focus for Scott) the station also covertly employed a number of Mexican nationals for intelligence collection and had an extensive and supportive relationship with the Direccíon Federal de Seguridad (DFS), Mexico's federal police force. As a result, the Mexico station produced the most productive wiretaps of any CIA facility.

Scott's success in recruiting agents of influence was notable compared to the virtual lack of influence developed by the American ambassador, who spoke no Spanish, appeared to have more of an interest in American politics than those of Mexico, and primarily socialized with other diplomats and ambassadors. In contrast, Scott leveraged CIA intelligence collection data in his outreach to Mexican political figures, providing them with information of value to their own political needs, on occasion with payments made directly to them, but, most importantly, with money and information to be channeled to their own social and political networks. Scott's social circle, including both American and Mexican political and business figures, was extensive and he worked it constantly. Scott's biographer Jefferson Morley describes the reality of Mexico City in the words of a State Department employee: "As Win worked his contacts and built his nets he became the go-to-guy. The Mexicans called the CIA station the real embassy."[28]

Scott's efforts certainly were helped by the fact that new President Adolfo López Mateos was an active CIA asset (with his own crypt designation of LITENSOR). Mateos was a highly adept politician, with a great need to know what opposing parties and opposing politicians were doing, especially those on the left side of the political spectrum. He also had a great need to know what certain foreign governments, including the Soviet Union, Cuba, and other Latin American countries, were working towards in Mexico—both in terms of domestic Mexican affairs and in using Mexico as a nexus for operations throughout the region. The CIA had the opportunity to be a valuable resource to Mateos, providing political and commercial intelligence while doing so in a deniable fashion. Win Scott offered the resources of the CIA station in trade for both influence and support. In that respect the relationship is classic in terms of mutual benefit, the key to recruiting individuals at the policy level of government. Scott and the CIA station were providing intelligence in trade for introductions and access to individuals who could not only enable collections work but who were shaping the domestic and foreign policies of their nation.

Scott's reach went well beyond President Mateos, who was so sufficiently impressed that he brought Minister of Government Gustavo Diaz Ordaz into the relationship. Both would become personally and socially connected to Win Scott, but the individual he assigned for actual covert operational contact was George Munro,[29] who had been an assistant legal attaché (a standard cover for FBI personnel attached to American diplomatic missions) for over a decade, giving him an impressive level of insight into life in Mexico City. He knew the public, stylish side of the city but importantly its less lawful elements as well. Munro had become a close personal friend of Scott, who had recruited him for work at the CIA station. In combination, the two men developed what became known as the LITEMPO intelligence collections network.

LITEMPO included Mateos and Díaz Ordaz as well as a variety of paid agents and assets associated with the Mexican president's office, including senior officers within the DFS. A supportive relationship with the federal police, which operated under the Ministry of the Interior, was especially important because it focused on both domestic political investigations and the control of foreigners. The only downside to the DFS connection was that any joint activities exposed the CIA to the fact that many DFS agents were known to be quite corrupt.[30]

A working relationship with the DFS proved to be exceptionally useful to the CIA, not just shielding covert intelligence collection but actually enabling one of its most technically sophisticated projects, LIENVOY, the centralized phone tapping and recording of dozens of telephone lines via a telephone company switching center. Even before Scott's arrival the CIA station had developed the extensive wiretapping effort LIFEAT, implemented beginning in 1947. The system used "outside taps" placed on junction boxes of telephone cables serving targeted homes and residences as well as a few diplomatic facilities. The taps were placed by a local telephone company employee, who was recruited by the CIA and under the control of a case officer. The case officer also used a home shop to repair and maintain the equipment, and conducted training for the listening-post operators. By the time of Scott's arrival up to twenty-four lines were being monitored from posts in adjacent homes. Monitoring, taping, and limited transcription were completed at the listening posts, using local Mexican nationals as paid employees, under the supervision of two CIA case officers.[31] The listening-post staff involved some twenty-one field workers averaging seven years of service each.[32]

LIFEAT was complemented by LIEMPTY, a photographic effort which maintained camera surveillance of vehicle and pedestrian entrances at the Soviet and Cuban diplomatic facilities. With LIFIRE, a separate covert operation with Mexican security services, the CIA was allowed to review commercial airline passenger lists and photograph passports of intelligence targets, especially Cubans traveling into or through Mexico and Americans traveling to and from Cuba. CIA station contract field teams performed mobile surveillance primarily focused on tracking the movement of Soviet operatives, but as required they would follow arriving airline passengers to their hotels. In addition, the CIA station conducted LIBIGHT, a massive mail-intercept collections effort. Covert mail collection alone involved some twenty-two employees.[33]

While the field wiretapping effort was significant and well organized, taps at diplomatic facilities were always a risky operation and at times were discovered and compromised. Scott's answer to that was brilliant and highly unconventional. With support from President Mateos and access to the DFS, the CIA carried out one of the most ambitious foreign collections projects of the period, using a commercial telephone exchange to establish a centralized phone tapping and recording system. The cable tap was set up with the help of government officials and the cooperation of a telephone company executive.[34] Some thirty lines were tapped and fed by cable from the telephone central office collection point to an intercept center equipped with a bank of reel-to-reel tape recorders. The equipment was able to capture the dialed telephone number for outgoing calls as well as the voice on the call; incoming calls only recorded the voice. The project was designated as LIENVOY and the collections focused on a number of foreign embassy and consulate facilities. Transcriptions were shared with the DFS, the CIA, and to some extent with the FBI. The intercepted information revealed by the monitoring of foreign embassy traffic was of such consequence to Mexican diplomacy and commercial activity that President Mateos himself reviewed at least some of the transcripts.[35]

Such a large-scale operation had an element of risk, both to the CIA and to Mateos's government. Security was provided for the intercept center, but it was clearly understood that it might need to be abandoned at any time, which is why the completely independent LIFEAT effort was maintained and the collections from the two sources were totally compartmentalized. In his extensive research on the CIA intelligence collection activities in Mexico City, Bill Simpich has been unable to identify the exact location of the central office intercept center but determined that it was in a residential neighborhood and that Mexican Army officers were responsible for the installation.[36] Work at the center involved ten Mexican personnel with four monitors who prepared daily transcripts as well as summaries of what had not been transcribed from each set of tapes. The calls from the Cuban and Soviet embassies were transcribed daily and special measures were taken for all calls made in English; CIA station contract employees did the translation for calls in Russian.[37] Because much of the daily operation was handled in the intercept center, essentially a Mexican operation, only a single CIA officer was assigned to act as liaison to the LIENVOY project, although Win Scott was very much in charge of the overall audio-surveillance program involving both LIENVOY and LIFEAT.

An appreciation of the scope of the twin Mexico City wiretap programs, in terms of both sophistication and coverage, helps illustrate the depth of the personal relationship that developed between Win Scott and senior leaders of the Mexican government. In terms of American intelligence production, the information produced by the programs was immense, up to 30 percent of the total take was determined to be of significant enough value to go into CIA case files. Annually the station used the information to prepare some 150 memoranda for the State Department and another 75 for the FBI.[38]

As far as the Mateos regime was concerned, the audio intercepts provided an invaluable source of real-time information on their political rivals, in particular those leftists in the labor movements and socialist parties. Some 20 percent of the LIENVOY material came directly from the lines of Vicente Lombardo Toledano, the head of the Popular Socialist Party (PPS) and a leader in the world trade-union movement. The personal lines of former Mexican President Lázaro Cárdenas also received considerable attention as did the telephone lines of the Movimiento Liberación Nacional (MLN). A federation of leftist parties as well as workers and peasant organizations, the MLN was most certainly a vocal opponent of the Mateos regime—it advocated for a reduction in the power of the presidency. Beyond that, taps on the lines of both Cuban diplomatic personnel and even Guatemala's former President Juan José Arévelo provided valuable insight into the most active topics of regional political discussion.

Given Scott's access to the governing regime, there was no need to meddle in Mexican elections. However, the station did turn to standard active measures practices in planting propaganda and disinformation intended to undermine opposition to government policies. LIEVICT surreptitiously supplied funding to an anti-communist Catholic student group; its president routinely met with an assigned CIA political officer. A related program, LILISP, almost entirely paid for a Catholic Church publication, which routinely published anti-communist articles as well as ones on the negatives of land reform, the dangers of Castro's agrarian reform policies, and similar topics.

Scott's influence with and access to Mateos not only enabled a virtually unique level of covert intelligence production within Mexico, it also gave Scott direct access to the regime's plans and positions on topics such as agrarian reform and nationalization, allowing the United States an advance view into issues that could be used to separate Mexico from the policies of the new Castro government in Cuba.[39] Those sorts of political insights were uniquely available through Scott and the CIA station within the American diplomatic mission, not through the American ambassador or the normal diplomatic contacts of the American Embassy. Beyond that, at times Scott's influence made possible Mexican support of covert operations totally at odds with the official Mexican position of neutrality in relation to Cuba. In one example, LITEMPO assets were used to arrange the shipment of Mexican fuel to be used by the ships of the Cuban exile brigade that landed at the Bay of Pigs.[40]

When examined in detail it becomes clear that the practices of active measures are consistent, conceptually simple, and routinely applied via intelligence officers placed under cover of each nation's diplomatic missions. The identification and manipulation of agents of influence, covert intelligence collection, and the planting of disinformation and propaganda (if necessary supported by the counterfeiting of official documents) are all standard practices. In comparing the Soviet experience with that of the United States, it becomes obvious that Russian practices worked particularly well in nations which had already been sensitized to American political intervention. Experienced Soviet political action officers became particularly adept at taking advantage of pre-existing bias and mistrust, targeting propaganda to take advantage of ethnic, racial, and religious regimes. In contrast, American officers enjoyed considerable success with governing regimes with strong economic connections, especially with governments facing populist or factional movements. In such cases the ability of the CIA to collect and share valuable information was viewed positively rather than as a threat.

The practices themselves did not change, it became simply a matter of whether at a given point in time the Soviets or Americans were working to sustain governments or to undermine them. Depending on circumstances, and the orientation of a particular regime, the KGB and the CIA quite easily worked either for or against governing regimes. That sort of flexibility in political warfare reveals a level of pragmatism that Machiavelli would easily recognize and no doubt fully appreciate.

Chapter Eight:
Privatization

Through some three decades of the Cold War, the general pattern of American political warfare developed around decisions to covertly intervene against change that appeared to increase Soviet global, political, and military reach. If that meant sustaining an anti-communist regime, political action and active measures of all types were brought into play. If a new and suspect regime came to power, whether by democratic election or political coup, much more aggressive, but still deniable, covert measures were used, including military intimidation and full-fledged hybrid warfare using surrogate forces.

By the end of the 1970s, the CIA had become heavily involved in paramilitary operations of all types, still using its standard practices of deniability, but with increasingly less success. In 1979 it became embroiled in two new major operations, each of which would effectively shatter the standard practices then in use, opening the door to new forms of operational covers and funding practices including the first major use of non-governmental organizations (NGOs).

The first of those missions would be against the new government in Nicaragua that replaced the longtime, intensely pro-American Somoza regime, which had proposed and supported America's first major hybrid warfare operation in Guatemala. The second would be far different; it would be in response to what was itself a total change in Soviet political action practices—the use of overt military force and the Red Army to install and support a client government. That action had been taken against an already strongly pro-Soviet regime in Kabul, Afghanistan, but one that had become too ideologically aggressive. Placing communist principles and practices above those of the Muslim religion, the regime raised concerns over Soviet intentions and undermined Soviet foreign relations initiatives across southwest Asia and the Middle East.

Initially the American responses to both Nicaragua and Afghanistan involved classic Cold War political warfare. However, in Nicaragua, the CIA hybrid warfare project eventually became quite public and also quite visible to the U.S. Congress, which had already been shocked by the revelation of massive CIA-led covert warfare in Laos. In the years following the American military involvement across Southeast Asia, there was less tolerance of another massive political intervention, especially one that appeared to be failing yet again. Covert warfare in Nicaragua led the administration of President Ronald Reagan into direct conflict with Congress. The result would be the privatization of American political warfare, something that would have highly negative consequences during the 1980s and decades later in the twenty-first century.

America became involved in political action against Nicaragua following the ouster of the pro-U.S. Somoza government, which had been in place for decades. The new government in Managua came into power through a popular revolt, its leaders had been part of the Sandinista National Liberation Front. The Sandinista regime's political agenda included land reform, unionization, nationalization of certain types of properties, and diplomatic non-alignment in foreign affairs. As seen previously, it was just the sort of agenda that made America's leaders extremely nervous. The fact that President Daniel Ortega had close personal ties to Cuba—including being trained in guerilla warfare there—elevated concerns even further. Ortega adamantly rejected the history of America's previous military interventions in Nicaragua and its lengthy political involvement with the Somoza government, and he increasingly turned to Cuba for both economic and military support.

This combination of factors virtually guaranteed that the Sandinista regime and Nicaragua would be perceived by American leadership as a launching point for replicating the Cuban revolutionary (and anti-American) movement throughout Central America. In response, President Jimmy Carter moved not towards an immediate political warfare program against the Sandinista regime, but to increased military aid to neighboring nations. Carter's decision was a "holding the line" move, focused on sustaining friendly neighboring governments rather than regime change in Nicaragua. The Pentagon was directed to develop a major counter-insurgency program for Nicaragua's neighbor El Salvador. Three hundred Salvadorian Army officers went to Panama for special training, military advisors were dispatched, and helicopters were provided to the Salvadorian forces. A special program was even organized to protect El Salvador's annual coffee harvest (Operation Golden Harvest).[1]

By the late fall of 1980, aerial photography revealed shipments of weapons going into El Salvador from Nicaragua and within a few weeks there was an abortive insurgency, intended to replace the established, pro-American government. The attempt was quickly crushed, ultra-right Salvadorian death squads had already taken a toll on those who might have joined the revolution. By the end of 1980 over eight thousand people had been killed, the majority by deniable but government-supported paramilitary groups obviously supported by the Salvadorian regime. Even with the abortive insurgency in El Salvador, Carter did not move to immediately initiate a regime change operation against the Sandinista government. However, he did approve almost $6 million in lethal (as compared to humanitarian) aid to El Salvador in January 1981.

It would be the Reagan administration and its new policy of "pushing back" that would move directly against the Nicaraguan government, first with the standard hybrid warfare practices and later with something entirely different, a public political warfare campaign involving private entities—non-governmental organizations—and using humanitarian aid as a cover for providing financial and logistical support for surrogate military operations. With that drastic change in political warfare practice, the Reagan administration did not simply move outside the accepted practices box—it threw away the box. The full consequences of that decision would only become clear over two decades later.

As with President Eisenhower and John Foster Dulles, President Reagan's decisions on how to act against the perceived threat of international communism were heavily influenced by his Secretary of State Alexander Haig. Reagan's appointment of Haig was a strong indication that the administration would be resetting American foreign relations priorities to the familiar Cold War playbook, focusing on the Soviet bloc as the major national security issue for the United States. And from his earliest days as secretary, Haig adamantly asserted the view that the Sandinista regime was nothing less than a Cuban (and hence Soviet) surrogate, willing and able to export communist revolution throughout Central America.

Haig's initial proposals for dealing with that threat included blockades, military interdiction of the supply lines from Cuba through Nicaragua to El Salvador, and massive escalation in military assistance to El Salvador—more than the entire allocation for Latin America and the Caribbean that year. At Haig's urging, President Reagan committed $20 million without congressional approval. The first move was to send a team of fifty-six American military advisors to train special rapid-response Salvadorian army battalions. Reagan also advised Congress that he had authorized the CIA to initiate both covert political and paramilitary operations to sever supply routes into Nicaragua and El Salvador.[2]

Most significantly, he issued a classified National Security Directive for building an army of some 1,500 anti-Sandinista rebels. The authorized size of that rebel army would in the thousands by the end of 1983.[3]

It was going to be classic American hybrid warfare, with economic and propaganda elements but with a heavy shift to sabotage and ground combat inside Nicaragua, virtually a repeat of the CIA operations against Cuba in the early 1960s. The CIA began sending large amounts of money directly to exiled Nicaraguan political figures, and training camps were again established in Florida. In the spring of 1981, there were even media tours of the camps, with coverage in both the *New York Times* and *Washington Post*—including the fact that Green Berets and former Vietnam veterans were serving as trainers for the insurgent military force. By 1982 an estimated 800 to 1,200 volunteers were reported to be training inside the United States.[4]

In contrast to its initial recruiting successes, the CIA's anti-Sandinista media campaign proved considerably more challenging. The image of the anti-Sandinista military forces, ultimately referred to as Contras, suffered from the fact that their combat units were led by former leaders of the Somoza-regime's National Guard, infamous for its corruption and brutal public security activities. One unit, the Rattlesnake Battalion, had been so violent that the identification of its troops and leaders within the Contras proved highly negative, generating humanitarian concerns from all quarters. Even worse, as Contra expeditions into Nicaragua began, one of the most visible and assertive Contra field officers conducted press interviews in which he referred to himself as Commander Suicide. He also adopted the practice of continuously bragging about the murders and atrocities that his two-thousand-man force was committing.[5]

For the most part, the first year of hybrid warfare against the Sandinista regime appears quite similar to the CIA's operations against Cuba. However, after Cuba, Vietnam, and the disclosure of highly secret, full-scale CIA-led deniable surrogate warfare in Laos, Congress was less than committed to a repeat of efforts that had ended as hugely costly, highly visible failures. In December 1982, a rider was attached to the new CIA appropriations bill. Known as the Boland Amendment, it denied money for "the purpose of overthrowing the government of Nicaragua or for provoking a military exchange between Nicaragua and Honduras." The funding bill itself set a cap of $24 million for Contra aid in the 1983 fiscal year.[6] Essentially, Congress was attempting to move the CIA out of hybrid warfare and paramilitary action against Nicaragua. That proved to be a constraint President Reagan, his secretary of state, and the National Security Council would refuse to accept. An NSC memorandum of July 1983 asserted that "State does not believe the Boland Amendment constrains covert U.S. activities in Nicaragua to a serious degree."[7]

Acting in accordance with its own interpretation, the Reagan administration continued economic pressure and the CIA continued support for an expanding paramilitary effort. During 1983, thousands of CIA-backed insurgents mounted a major intrusion into northern Nicaragua, attacking towns and villages with the goal of consolidating a liberated zone where a "provisional government" could be established. The premise, as it had been at Cuba's Bay of Pigs, was that the liberated region would allow the United States to recognize a provisional Contra government. However, previous brutal incursions into that region by Contra forces had already alienated the locals and there was no popular uprising to support such an enclave. Operation Dark Moon was met with a series of aggressive central government counterattacks and in the end the Sandinista Popular Army drove the Contra forces back across the Honduran border to their staging areas.[8]

The overall U.S. intelligence community evaluated the CIA effort and produced an estimate of the situation (later leaked to the *Washington Post*) which concluded that "there are no circumstances under which a force of U.S.-backed rebels can achieve a military or political victory over the leftist Sandinista government."[9] In response, the CIA proposed an escalation of its operations with a broader covert military commitment, directly involving American military personnel. President Reagan agreed and in October 1983 signed another national security directive that allowed American personnel to conduct "harassment" military actions, including attacks on infrastructure targets such as bridges, ports, refineries, and oil pipelines. With presidential approval, CIA helicopters provided "suppression fire" against defensive weapons installations opposing the attacks.

Attack aircraft were also introduced into the operations, obtained by having been declared U.S. military surplus and sold through a CIA-created commercial cover company. Other CIA companies modified the aircraft and still others leased them for use or simply sold them to El Salvador, to be transferred to CIA contract employees. Companies around the United States participated, including Summit Aviation, a California company called Armairco and its East Coast branch, Shenandoah Airleasing.[10] Later estimates deemed that some $12 million in military equipment was transferred to the Nicaragua project through the same process.[11]

There was nothing at all new in any of this, standard CIA practices were being used, and there were accounting and tracking systems in place to monitor all of it. By the 1980s such practices had been in place for over three decades. The same was true for the standard deniability practices for detaching and assigning American military personnel and dealing with their deaths during operations. And there were American deaths. First, a CIA helicopter went down in an aerial attack against a Nicaraguan military installation killing two "freelancers." Another incident resulted in the death of a helicopter pilot who strayed over Nicaraguan airspace. Two SEALS died in accidents, and four other Americans were killed and six injured, including Green Beret special operations personnel.

In the face of those American losses the CIA began recruiting contract personnel from El Salvador, Honduras, Chile, Argentina,

Ecuador, and Bolivia. Referred to as "unilaterally controlled Latino assets" (UCLA), their missions were to target ports, refineries, oil pipelines, boats, and bridges. It was a major escalation of military action and covert economic warfare against the Sandinista regime. In reality even the use of "Latino assets" did little to fool the international press or even Congress. Major American involvement was obvious in an increasing number of highly visible attacks carried out using specialized high-speed attack boats equipped with mortars and machine guns, mother ships for attack boats (equipped with helicopter pads), frogman raids, and bombing and rocket attacks from aircraft and helicopters. BBC journalists even managed to locate, interview, and film two documentaries involving UCLA team leaders.[12]

Yet even with the new weapons and seasoned, well-trained combatants, the CIA was simply not having any significant impact on the Sandinista regime other than forcing it to begin spending on new military equipment of its own, purchased from Cuba and the Soviet Union. In something akin to desperation, the CIA made the decision to massively escalate American economic warfare by covertly mining major Nicaraguan harbors on both its Atlantic and Pacific coasts. The CIA dispatched boat teams that used special equipment to place canister mines (developed in conjunction with the U.S. Naval Weapons Center) and directed the Contra military to claim responsibility, broadcasting its own international warnings. This was hybrid warfare intimidation at its most obvious, the only thing lacking was a U.S. Navy carrier attack group with Marine landing elements.

During the first week of April 1984, some dozen commercial vessels from six different countries were damaged by the mines, seamen were injured, and two Nicaraguans killed. The Soviet Union, which had one of its ships damaged and crew injured, formally protested, but the Reagan administration deferred all blame to the Contras. In the end it was obvious to the world that the United States had been behind the mines, and the Reagan administration was forced to fall back on legalities, claiming the harbor mining as a "legitimate means of interrupting the flow of arms destined for infiltration…or to disrupt the flow of military and other materials essential to the attackers' overall aggressive effort."[13]

Given the lack of any actual Sandinista attacks on anyone other than the Contra forces crossing its borders, that response gained no international traction. Even America's European allies were outraged. France offered a minesweeper to Nicaragua. Congress was especially embarrassed given that its own effort to rein in the CIA had clearly failed. Senator Barry Goldwater, chairman of the Intelligence Committee, went on record stating that the harbor mining was a flagrant violation of international law, declaring it an actual "act of war" with no conceivable explanation. Senator Daniel Patrick Moynihan, Committee vice-chairman, resigned in protest.

Other than public comments, the initial congressional response was limited at best. In April 1984, the Senate overwhelmingly passed legislation opposing the use of federal monies for mining Nicaraguan harbors. This was reported by the media as a "rebuke" to President Reagan.[14] However, Congress did not pass any additional resolutions constraining administration military action, nor did it cease major annual budget allocations for humanitarian aid, which continued to go through the same Nicaraguan exile groups that were supporting the Contra fighting forces. That in itself was a significant step outside the box of standard practices. In previous years American humanitarian and international development agencies had indeed been used as covers for CIA personnel and even for CIA assets, but funneling large amounts of money, not to mention supplies, directly to private groups primarily involved in paramilitary operations was something new. It was also something that would increasingly grow out of control since exile political leaders of the groups managed to take personal financial control over a good deal of the "humanitarian" funding.

The initial decision to route large amounts of money directly to Nicaraguan exile groups, rather than keeping it under direct CIA control, would be the beginning of a serious contamination of the overall concept of American NGOs—nonprofit, voluntary citizens groups organized primarily for humanitarian aid, economic development, or environmental action. NGOs are ostensibly independent of control by any particular government, but often request and accept government funds. NGO military contamination would become far worse during the second phase of American political warfare against the Sandinista regime, to the degree that virtually all aspects of the hybrid warfare campaign were moved out of CIA control and essentially privatized in terms of funding, logistics, and military operations.

This move was forced by further exposure of American military involvement with operations inside Nicaragua during 1984. The highly public exposure forced Congress to accept that it was being essentially ignored by both the president and the CIA. Senator Moynihan called it a "crisis of confidence" with the Reagan administration. Senator Joe Biden described the continuing secret warfare in Nicaragua as a "charade," where a presidential finding for covert action was being manipulated into operations far beyond its stated intents and purposes.[15] In response Congress passed legislation declaring a moratorium and specifically forbid either direct or indirect support for military operations against Nicaragua by any U.S. "intelligence agency." Furthermore, Congress authorized only humanitarian aid to the Contras, placing what it felt to be a new box around Reagan administration efforts in Nicaragua.

Being placed in any box was not at all satisfactory to Reagan, Haig, or CIA Director William Casey. Their solution was to move totally outside the box (and beyond congressional authority) with a series of activities ultimately known as the Iran-Contra affair and scandal. The full story of that 1984-86 effort is well beyond our scope here, but its impact on American political warfare practice most definitely proved to be seminal in many regards, particularly in effectively moving highly organized political warfare into the private sector.

The second—non-CIA—phase of Reagan's Nicaraguan regime change operation was directed from an administration level by National Security Advisor Robert McFarlane (who was succeeded by Admiral John Poindexter). Operational control was assigned to Lieutenant Colonel Oliver North, the deputy director for political-military affairs. Given that the effort would have to be conducted totally outside normal CIA logistics as well as financial and accounting systems, it obviously had to be exponentially deniable, protected not only from public but congressional scrutiny. Distance had to be established between the Contra humanitarian aid which Congress had funded and the very lethal military operations that would become part of North's efforts. Contra military activities inside Nicaragua would still be visible, but they would have to be conducted without any obvious CIA or U.S. support. Ironically, the Kennedy Administration had attempted a somewhat similar, highly deniable program against Cuba, begun in 1963 and designated as AMWORLD.[16] However that program, which had proved to be yet another total failure, had at least been funded and operated under standard CIA practices and controls. North's program would have none of that support, none of the accounting controls, and virtually no system of checks and balances.

Small Contra supporter-owned grocery stores and businesses in Miami were used as purchasing and supply fronts. Those business were simply handed tens of millions of dollars in both humanitarian and military aid, with virtually no detailed accounting and absolutely no independent financial control. A series of offshore banks, separate from those routinely used in the long-established CIA dark money network, were created and used for weapons and military supply purchases.

At one point North's chief Contra liaison reported that one of the main Contra leaders was selling American dollars on the black foreign exchange market for a thirty-seven percent profit. Other Contra leaders, and Honduran generals, floated money from bank to bank in Miami, the Caymans, and the Antilles by marking-up purchase orders and skimming substantial profits off weapons sales for the Contra forces. A number of those same banks would eventually be investigated for concealing and laundering money for drug shipments facilitated by Contra leaders (and their associates) and carried from Columbia into the Caribbean and the United States.[17] In terms strictly of the congressionally-authorized humanitarian aid, the Government Accounting Office (GAO) would estimate that some $4 million had simply gone missing.

In addition to such financial diversions, North's military logistics operations also contaminated the regular humanitarian supply efforts. Non-lethal supplies were funded by Congress and purchased by the State Department's Humanitarian Assistance Office (NHAO). The NHAO then contracted air shipments to Nicaraguan refugees in El Salvador. However, North privately arranged for those same aircraft to be reloaded with very lethal cargo and flown into Contra military camps in Honduras. The piggybacking of military shipments on what were supposed to be strictly humanitarian aid flights was facilitated by the fact that many of the pilots, cargo handlers, and maintenance crews had previously worked for the CIA contractor Air America in Southeast Asia. North also purchased and leased transport aircraft from a former CIA proprietary, Southern Air Transport, which had become independent in 1973 but continued to do contract work for the CIA and its associated company, Corporate Air Services.[18]

From North's view the mixing of humanitarian and lethal shipments on a single aircraft saved a considerable amount of money; he was simply billed for the short final delivery flight to the Contra bases.[19] The ultimate result was that many people, including those involved with the legal humanitarian aid shipments, assumed they were still working for the CIA and that the continued Contra military actions were CIA-sanctioned and official U.S. policy. It became extremely difficult to separate North's autonomous programs from those formerly conducted by the CIA itself. Distance and degrees of separation were further complicated by the exceedingly complex funding of the ongoing military effort.

It is now known that the vast majority of those funds secretly came from foreign government sources. Robert McFarlane would eventually estimate contributions from Saudi Arabia to have been some $31 million, with another $10 million coming from the Kingdom of Brunei. Those contributions went into a Swiss bank account set up by one of North's associates. Non-CIA cover companies such as the Stanford Technology Group used the money for military purchases and shipments. Ultimately, funds were generated by the sale of American missile systems to Iran, in an exceptionally risky arrangement that ended with the exposure of those involved in what became known as the Iran-Contra scandal.

But that was all behind the scenes. As far as the American public was supposed to know, the Contra military effort and the goal of regime change in Nicaragua had been handed over to the private sector, to patriotic citizens and groups dedicated to an ideological struggle against the spread of Soviet (and Cuban) influence. It would be non-government organizations which would carry out a new form of political warfare against the Sandinista regime in Managua. Those organizations would raise the necessary funds to support an ongoing Contra military effort and President Reagan joined in the fundraising effort, repeatedly and very publicly endorsing the groups and their efforts. It was a form of military "democracy initiative," carried out by NGOs but with presidential endorsement.

Of course, such a highly public program required new organizations and foundations to be created, a national campaign for public donations, and an outreach to private anti-communist organizations to join in with both contributions and volunteers. In addition, the Nicaraguan Democratic Force (the FDN) conducted its own humanitarian fundraising, although that effort reportedly brought in less than a thousand dollars. Some of the most visible public participation involved the fundraising and promotional activities of retired Army Major General John K. Singlaub, a career officer whose experience included wartime service with the OSS in both Europe and China, acting as CIA deputy chief in Korea during the Korean War, and becoming commander of the Joint Unconventional Warfare Task Force (MACV-SOG) during the Vietnam war.

Singlaub's social network included an extensive range of contacts with ultra-conservative political figures and activist anti-communists. In 1981, he organized a meeting that created an American chapter of the World Anti-Communist League. The League was largely a Republic of China effort, established to push back against Communist China and Communism in general. The former CIA chief of station in Taiwan, Ray Cline, had helped found and build the group after communist takeover on the mainland. The new American chapter— The United States Council for World Freedom—was extremely well connected within both the American intelligence community and the military. Its vice-president had formerly served as the head of the Defense Intelligence Agency, and other officers included the former Marine commander in Vietnam, as well as retired Air Force and Army colonels.[20] Objectively it appeared to be a non-governmental organization with very much the look and feel of the Reagan administration.

The United States Council for World Freedom, assisted and supported by the League, became the public voice of the pro-Contra, anti-Sandinista movement. And as far as the public was concerned, President Reagan was totally behind their efforts, meeting with Contra leaders, with Nicaraguan refugees, and appearing in White House photo sessions with an "I'm a Contra too" pin on his lapel. It would have been hard to imagine that the American government was not really involved in supporting the ongoing Contra military operations, despite official denials. And of course, it was.

As for the Council for World Freedom, it certainly did raise some money and it most definitely became involved in funding the Contra military. In a gesture of support its initial efforts were funded with a $20,000 loan from Taiwan, and Singlaub continued to use it to promote the Contra message. Its 1984 international conference was held in San Diego, attended by President Reagan and a host of global anti-communist figures, including a number of South American military dictators. Perhaps the best known and most infamous was Alfredo Stroessner, president of Paraguay. At that point in time, Stroessner had officially governed the nation for more than two decades under a state of siege (i.e., virtual martial law), with all civil liberties and even public meetings suspended.

During the 1984 League meeting, the organization committed itself to becoming more operational, declaring it would supply materials and personnel to "liberation forces" in the field. It acted quickly to do just that. Within months the first of a series of DC-3 supply flights were flown into a Contra base camp in Honduras.[21] By 1985, with the congressional ban on CIA involvement with Contra military action in effect, the League would become even more active in supply efforts and in general fundraising. To facilitate fundraising in the United States, the Council for World Freedom applied for tax-exempt status. Following initial denial by the Los Angeles IRS office, an appeal was approved at IRS headquarters and wealthy conservative donors began to line up to contribute.[22] Texan Ellen Garwood put in $65,000 towards purchase of a Contra helicopter and Singlaub brought in a $10 million donation from the government of Taiwan.[23] Singlaub also volunteered his personal services to North in assisting with European purchases of weapons for the Contras. He was involved with at least one $5 million arms buy, but his name was well known and his profile was apparently a bit high for such activity, producing an undesirable level of noise within the international weapons-trafficking community.

The highly public effort to bring in private organizations, groups, and individuals also led to considerable confusion on the ground on the Nicaraguan border. Anti-communist mercenary and weapons-enthusiast magazines such as *Eagle* and *Soldier of Fortune* featured an ongoing series of supportive articles about volunteers joining the Contra military campaign. *Soldier of Fortune* even sent some of its own staff to Contra camps to conduct training, and it published and promoted articles covering volunteers going into combat with the Contras in the jungles of Nicaragua. The magazine also started the El Salvador/Nicaragua Defense Fund to support Contra operations.

Some private paramilitary groups had joined in the effort to overthrow the Sandinista government even while the CIA was officially running the regime change project. One of the most vocal was the Civilian Material Assistance group headed by Tom Posey, who had started his own effort to collect money and send volunteers to the Contras as early as 1983. Posey described his volunteers as "missionary-mercenaries," reporting that three were in Contra camps by January 1984.

In 1985 Posey claimed that his group had taken in $5 million and was sending fifty soldiers per month to serve as Contra trainers and military advisors. Posey's earliest fundraising had actually been through pickle jars in general stores, but by 1985 he had attracted financial backers such as a wealthy Texas oil man who hoped to receive title to small islands off Nicaragua after a Contra victory.[24] Posey, who provided security at World Anti-Communist League conferences, and Singlaub reached out to other paramilitary groups, ranging from a "Recondo" (reconnaissance/commando) mercenary training school in Dolomite, Alabama to the Cuban exile Brigade 2506 in Miami.

The net result of it all was that by 1986 numbers of private individuals began to show up along the Nicaraguan borders, many armed and appearing to be acting covertly. None admitted to any clear chain of command, nor did they appear to have any sort of common oversight. Some served as trainers, others as medical support, and yet others as mechanics and pilots. At the same time, North's activities continued to send in large amounts of money, weapons, and supplies to the Contra units, with transportation and logistics facilitated by private contractors, mostly former CIA employees or assets. Such activities also had no obvious chain of command. North's aides and liaison personnel operated covertly as if they were actually undercover CIA officers, and in some instances received support from CIA station chiefs in the region. No matter how many official denials were given, virtually everyone assumed that U.S. government connections were behind it all.

The Reagan administration effort to move outside standard covert practices and involve NGOs as a cover for distancing itself from deniable political warfare in Nicaragua had precedent in some aspects. At one point, some of those involved in the Iran-Contra scandal raised the defense that decades earlier President Roosevelt had secretly used non-government entities and "creative" funding in his effort to establish the Chinese Special Air Unit. Following World War II the Soviets had used the Cominform to sponsor and manipulate a number of NGOs with global reach. Those included the World Peace Council, the World Federation of Democratic Youth, World Federation of Scientific Workers, the International Union of Students, the International Order of Journalists, and the International Association of Democratic Lawyers. All were ostensibly independent and highly democratic, but while Soviet political officers did use these NGOs for recruiting agents of influence, for propaganda, and on occasion for espionage, there is no evidence that they served as operational covers for paramilitary or hybrid warfare projects.

The United States had most definitely turned to non-governmental organizations in its containment efforts in Eastern Europe. The creation of the National Committee for a Free Europe (NCFE) and its Crusade for Freedom produced donations of two to three million dollars annually through the early 1950s and it also served as a cover for large amounts of government money channeled into propaganda as psychological warfare programs. In some respects the use of the Crusade for Freedom during the Truman administration and the Reagan era turn to the World Freedom League appear similar. In both cases NGOs were used as fundraising covers and for ideological messaging purposes. Prominent American businessmen, lawyers, and philanthropists (including Allen Dulles) had joined to promote the NCFE just as a variety of prominent military and intelligence figures (including President Reagan) had joined in to endorse the Contra fundraising effort.

However, a deeper look reveals just how strikingly different the second phase of the Contra effort had become in terms of operational practices. As compared to the containment effort in Eastern Europe, it had none of the wartime expertise that the OSS personnel had brought to the OPC or the CIA during the Truman years. It also had none of the security, administrative, or operational controls that the established intelligence groups developed for Cold War era operations. Perhaps most strikingly, it had virtually no financial controls; huge amounts of money were solicited from foreign nations and dumped into the hands of Contra political leaders, many with reputations for extensive corruption while part of the Somoza government.

While the Crusade for Freedom served as a public financial cover, it was directly organized and controlled by the CIA, as were its propaganda projects. In contrast, the World Freedom League was more than simply a cover. It was a part of a totally independent international entity with financial ties to the Republic of China and its own Nicaraguan field operations, involving not only air transport but a wide variety of military and non-military volunteers on the ground in border regions and even in-country with Contra military units. The result was that by the final years of the Nicaraguan regime change initiative, it had become almost impossible to differentiate the players in Central America.

In response to congressional attempts at oversight and control, the Reagan administration had essentially privatized political warfare. At the same time, around the globe in Afghanistan, it was not only privatizing surrogate warfare, it was putting U.S. intervention totally under the control of a combination of foreign governments and a very different type of NGO—an organization not with an ideological agenda but a very radical religious one.

The initial American moves against Soviet regime change in Afghanistan had come during the Carter administration. Secretary of State Zbigniew Brzezinski had taken a very pragmatic view of the matter: if possible, the Soviets should be forced to withdraw their troops, but if that did not work the occupation should be as costly for them as possible. The CIA officer assigned to lead the Afghanistan mission described his assignment in similar terms, "…just go out there and kill the Soviets, and take care of the Pakistanis and make them do whatever you need them to do."[25]

As with Nicaragua, the Reagan position would be much more aggressive than that of Carter. The Soviets needed to leave Afghanistan, and a strong anti-Russian Afghan government needed to be in place. That meant locating and supporting an insurgent force strong enough to essentially defeat the modern Soviet military. Such a force did exist; it was native, and it was deeply hostile to the Russians, not because of ideology but because of religion. That insurgency already had an active base of support just across the Afghan border, in Pakistan.

The Pakistanis held inherent credibility and control with certain of the Afghan rebel groups due to their shared Muslim religion. Pakistan viewed the Russian presence in Afghanistan as an existential threat, not ethnically but simply because the Russians were communist (which meant agnostic) infidels. The Afghan regime the Russians had ousted had already proved the danger of having communists in control—it had actively tried to suppress many aspects of Islam. As a nation state, Pakistan itself had been expressly created on a religious foundation. To that end its current leader, Muhammed Zia ul-Haq, had already orchestrated the creation of hundreds of *madrasas* (religious schools) along the Afghan border. The schools were organized and operated with the intent of embedding a very rigid concept of Islam among its young male students. Zia's goal was to establish a shield of thousands of Islamic fighters willing to accept martyrdom to defend Pakistan from any challenge from its west. It would be Zia, and insistence on total control of the anti-Soviet insurgency in Afghanistan, that would come to totally dominate the first years of the Reagan administration's regime change operation in southwest Asia. George P. Shultz, secretary of state under Reagan after Alexander Haig, clearly expressed what would become a total American dependence on Zia: "We must remember that without Zia's support, the Afghan resistance, key to making the Soviets pay a heavy price for their Afghan adventure, is effectively dead."[26]

Congressional action had led to the Reagan administration's attempt to distance itself from regime change operations against Nicaragua, officially removing the CIA from field operations and replacing it with a very small National Security staff and a host of private actors and surrogates. The result was a major loss of operational control, security, and financial accountability. Decisions in regard to Afghanistan would result in an exponentially greater loss of control over political warfare across southwest Asia, but that would be the least of the consequences to follow.

The agreement with Pakistan and its intelligence services (ISI) removed the CIA from all field operations in Afghanistan. CIA officers were simply not permitted by the Pakistanis to make any direct contact with the *mujahedeen* fighters. Instead, the ISI made the decisions on which insurgent groups would receive weapons, supplies, and money, and handled all transportation logistics. The CIA simply provided hundreds of Toyota pickup trucks. Pakistan organized all mujahedeen training camps, conducted weapons and tactical training, and controlled virtually all intelligence coming out of the contested areas. The ISI was given total responsibility for delivering all weapons and all payments to the Afghan insurgents; doing so gave Pakistan the ability to select groups and leaders that matched its own national interests and geopolitical goals. That change in historical CIA practices was fundamental, and it meant that aid and support to the surrogate guerilla forces was going to be channeled by the ISI almost entirely to extremely fundamentalist religious groups of fighters. Later attempts by CIA officers to involve themselves within Afghanistan proved quite dangerous, the insurgent groups favored by the Pakistanis viewed them as foreign infidels—much the same as the Russian invaders they were already fighting.

Initially simply passing money to the Pakistanis seemed highly efficient, albeit extremely expensive. Supplying the Afghan insurgency cost America close to $30 million in 1981, and that escalated to almost $200 million by 1984. From a distance it looked like an amazingly effective and highly deniable approach. In 1981 alone the Soviets had lost over four thousand military personnel and some five hundred vehicles of various types. By 1984 none of the Soviet-held regions were safe from attack and the CIA had helped procure deniable Chinese rockets, which allowed the insurgents to conduct long-range and very deadly bombardments. Pakistan had even sent the ISI, disguised as mujahedeen fighters, into Afghanistan; they carried out attacks on the main Soviet airbase at Bagram, destroying twenty-two Soviet aircraft.[27]

In addition, as with the second phase of the Contra effort, certain Arab regimes stepped forward with substantial donations to the fight. Conservative Muslim nations such as Pakistan and Saudi Arabia—with aggressive, fundamentalist religious factions—viewed the Soviet presence in Afghanistan as an existential religious threat. To them it was a simple matter of religion and basic belief systems, culture rather than just politics. The insurgency in Afghanistan was not political warfare— the drive to replace the Soviet Afghan regime was *jihad*. In such a view, the United States truly had no place, its influence needed to be heavily moderated and its personnel were not welcome within the insurgency itself.

The reality of Pakistani and Saudi involvement was certainly not initially clear to the Reagan White House. The administration almost totally failed to grasp the extent to which the insurgency was truly turning into Islamic jihad, driven by increasing amounts of Saudi money and escalating participation by private, fundamentalist religious groups within that nation. The number of Arab "volunteers" going into Afghanistan exploded in the mid-1980s with the support of enormous "charitable donations" from fundamentalist Saudi princes, wealthy families, and religious leaders.[28] The Saudis were quite concerned that their aid and funds went to the "correct" jihadi groups within Afghanistan. To help ensure that, key leaders and commanders were invited to the annual pilgrimage to Mecca. While there they were courted and connected to the most fundamentalist Saudi religious factions and madrasas. While in Saudi Arabia they were also given large donations by wealthy, private Saudi citizens. One of the key figures in this process was an individual who would become well known to the United States in later years—a wealthy young Saudi fundamentalist named Osama bin Laden.

To ensure that his own donations went to the proper insurgent groups, bin Laden personally traveled to Pakistan to meet with Afghan commanders.[29] Later, the International Islamic University in Islamabad, Pakistan, would become a focal point through which donations could be routed via Abdullah Yusuf Azzam, a Muslim Brotherhood scholar and fundraiser from Palestine who had relocated there. Azzam became quite close to bin Laden and used him as his own bridge into Saudi Arabia, for recruits and donations.[30] From that point on, and for the next two to three years, something on the order of $25 million per month of private Saudi and other Arab money flowed into the jihadi militaries in and around the Pakistan's border regions.

As the "Arabization" of the Afghan jihad increased, other insurgent factions began to complain about what the Pakistanis and Saudis were doing, which was essentially isolating and marginalizing traditional

Afghan factions and rebel groups including Afghan nationalists, monarchists, and Muslims who were not necessarily jihadi fundamentalists. The CIA station in Pakistan became aware of those complaints, some were passed back to headquarters but many were not. CIA political officers in the field and at headquarters were hesitant to point out problems with an operation that increasingly appeared to be a success, not only embarrassing Soviet leadership but having bloody and morale-destroying impact on the overall Soviet military. In retrospect, it appears that to some extent the Pakistanis failed to appreciate, or admit, the degree to which their own effort to push back the Soviets in Afghanistan had been hijacked by jihadi fundamentalist involvement from Saudi Arabia.[31]

The result of privatization in both Nicaragua and Afghanistan was that the CIA was losing operational control of political warfare around the globe. Some of its officers were not satisfied with being forced out of field operations, especially in Afghanistan. As early as 1985 the Agency pushed for more direct involvement, and President Reagan signed off on a new national security directive, NSDD-166, "U.S. Policy, Programs and Strategy in Afghanistan." With that endorsement the CIA moved once again to insert itself into direct contact with the Afghan insurgency, both for intelligence collection on combat operations and to report back on Pakistani activities inside Afghanistan.

It was a move that was far too late. By that point in time it was becoming clear that sending in covert CIA officers simply was not an option. In one incident a CIA team, escorted by a Pakistani officer, crossed over into Afghanistan and encountered a roadblock manned by Arab Islamic fighters. The escort was accosted, a shouting match ensued, and the Saudi jihadists declared that the Americans were "infidels with no business in Afghanistan." Only after hiding behind a jeep, an extensive dialogue and a reluctant agreement by the Saudi fighters were the Americans able to escape.[32]

CIA field personnel were going to have to be not only deniable as American operatives in the larger sense but also able to distance themselves from the CIA in terms of concealing themselves and their activities from the Pakistani ISI. In order to accomplish that the CIA began to recruit, in a somewhat similar vein to the recruiting of "unilateral Latino assets" in Nicaragua, volunteers from the ranks of freelance journalists and photographers. Most were European, eager for action in spite of the risks, and willing to go into the field with concealed communications equipment. Part of their mission was to confirm or deny the extent to which the ISI was playing favorites, controlling money and materials to freeze out traditional groups not part of the radical Islamic jihad movement, which would ultimately style itself as the Taliban.

However, at the same time the new "unilaterals" were beginning their intelligence collections, the CIA was escalating its own support efforts, shipping not only Stinger anti-aircraft missiles through Pakistan but adding the types of night-vision equipment, long-range sniper weapons, and explosives training that would later become a constant factor in jihadi terror attacks. The Russians in Afghanistan proved simply to be the first targets for such weapons. In fact, the tools and level of monetary support being sent via Pakistan were beyond virtually any level of surrogate warfare support previously seen, other than possibly in Laos. Towards the end of the campaign the CIA was even working on delivering captured Soviet tanks into eastern Afghanistan.

By the end of 1987 unilateral field assets were actively relaying reports from several Afghan insurgent groups that they were being not only harassed but actually displaced by thousands of new Arab jihadi volunteers. These new fighters were fundamentalist Wahhabi, the majority trained in Saudi or Pakistani madrasas. They accused local Afghans of being ignorant of the Koran and of violating Wahhabi religious practices, which they of course viewed as the only true Islamic practices. All who did not follow those practices, including other

Muslims, were regarded as infidels. The new fighters had even begun desecrating Afghan graves.

Curses had been exchanged, fire fights had erupted, and the insurgency was beginning to fragment over the issue of religion. In retrospect the seeds for the future division of Afghanistan between a jihadi-supported Taliban and its nationalist opponents had been planted by the Pakistani and Saudi creation of a jihadi force, with a great number of its volunteers coming from outside Afghanistan. The volunteers were not only from Saudi and the Gulf states but out of madrasas spread across North Africa. Their goal was the establishment of an Afghan religious state where Sharia, the enforcement of the moral and religious Islamic codes they considered proper, would be public law. Afghanistan would become a very specific type of religious nation.

Perhaps not surprisingly, with the continual bloodbath the Soviets were experiencing, a number of CIA officers preferred to largely ignore the negative reports coming out of Afghanistan as simply being unreliable. The new assets on the ground were written off as unsophisticated, unprofessional, and perhaps too excitable.[33] After all, the Soviets continued to take heavy losses. The American ground-to-air Stinger missiles had neutralized much of the effectiveness of Russian close air support and a noted lack of enthusiasm for Afghanistan was apparent in remarks from the new Soviet leader, Mikhail Gorbachev. In fact, by 1989 a Russian withdrawal was underway, leaving the communist regime in Kabul on its own and with little chance of long-term survival. It appeared that handing off the war to Pakistan had been a brilliant move. Indeed, some officers within the CIA would still hold to that view even after the jihadi terror attacks on America in September 2001.

In the years following the attacks of 9/11, the United States committed itself to an ongoing series of large-scale military operations across the Middle East and ultimately around the globe. It assumed the former Soviet role in Afghanistan, moved into major conventional warfare in Iraq, and immersed itself in nation-building in southwest

Asia. Its commitment to fighting terror groups around the globe led to an ongoing state of virtual, low-profile warfare, a form of shadow warfare integrating CIA intelligence collection and political action with overt military assistance and Joint Special Operations Command military operations.

The first decade of the twenty-first century would witness a major role reversal in American political warfare, moving it into overt military action, increasingly integrating CIA and military operations. In turn, by the end of the twentieth century the Soviet Union had fragmented and the ideological threat of the red menace largely faded away. There was even a belief that, with the end of the Cold War, deniable political and hybrid warfare was ending, some felt forever. Yet the practices of active measures quietly continued, an apparently integral part of for- eign relations among major powers. While active measures may seem to diminish during periods lacking active confrontations, they remain in place to some extent in what might be termed a housekeeping mode.

Chapter Nine:
Role Reversals

From the earliest post-World War II containment operations in Eastern Europe, through an extended series of ongoing global regime change projects, American covert political warfare had been conducted as an effort to check the expansion of the Soviet Union's political and military influence. In terms of ideology and public emotion it was justified as a response to the existential threat of worldwide communism. In retrospect, it appears to have been fundamentally an attempt to maintain the prewar status quo, which included the political and economic hegemony of the former global imperial powers, including the United States.

Hegemony involves many things, its synonyms include influence, dominion, leadership, authority, power, and control—all imply some level of sovereignty. Communism, nationalism, socialism, anti-colonialism, and even neutrality in foreign relations were all perceived as threats to the status quo and traditional Western sovereignty. At first that seems a radical and wild-eyed statement, however it is hard to avoid given our exploration of the actual American political warfare operations conducted during the Cold War era. The triggers for those operations are expressed and cited in transcripts of National Security Council meetings, in State Department communications, and in remarks by both presidents and national security advisors, and they are quite consistent.

A foreign regime that moved towards policies of land and agrarian reform, nationalized certain segments of its economy, endorsed trade and agricultural unions, expanded its voting population, engaged in openly populist politics, and even considered making communist parties legal for organizing or voting purposes was tagged as a potential threat. It did not matter if the regime had been democratically elected, and neutrality in foreign policy was viewed as highly suspect. Economic trade pacts or military assistance from not just Russia but any Eastern Bloc nation was virtually the last straw.

It is hard to avoid the conclusion that the driving factor in American policy was maintaining the prewar status quo, that Western sovereignty and territoriality were not in play, and that it was not simply a matter of democracy versus communism. The verbiage involved in assessing regime threats often reflected a territorial view, expressing both political and physical hegemony—suspect regimes had to be acted against to prevent "beachheads" and the fear of a domino effect; this was expressed long before Vietnam, originally in regard to Italy, Iran, and then Guatemala.

During the Cold War era, American political warfare was fundamentally a matter of either sustaining pro-American regimes or pushing back against any change that would lead to pro-Soviet governments. In contrast the Soviet Union enthusiastically endorsed coups and revolutions and followed along as they occurred. What America viewed as triggers—anti-colonialism, nationalism, ethnic and racial independence movements, land reform movements, and of course socialist and communist parties—were all seen in Moscow as Soviet opportunities and supported through propaganda and political action practices. Postwar regime change appeared to favor Russia's geopolitical interests and elections, and change was a good thing.

This Soviet push/American pushback model drove political warfare by the KGB and CIA for decades. And then in a matter of only a few years that model shattered. It began in Berlin on November 9,

1989. That night crowds simply began taking down the Berlin Wall, with no response from the East German regime and no Soviet intervention. The result was that in less than a year Germany had reunified. Popular action and change had suddenly become not an opportunity but a threat to the Soviet Union. In Poland in 1989, a new popular movement Solidarity gained sufficient political leverage to force truly open elections involving anti-communist political parties. Much the same happened in Hungary, with competitive elections that same year. Suddenly revolution and regime change were no longer viewed in Moscow as being Russian opportunities.

Eastern Bloc states that did not move to open elections saw increased violence, from Czechoslovakia to Romania. The Baltic states of Estonia, Latvia, and Lithuania demanded increased independence. There was little immediate Soviet response and no military intervention, unlike previous revolts against Moscow's dominance. By 1990 popular movements collapsed decades-old Soviet political satellite regimes. Ultimately a series of increasingly open democratic elections confirmed the end of Soviet political dominance in Eastern Europe, through the Baltic nations and across Russia's southern borders. The result was a fragmentation of the Russian territorial sovereignty Stalin had forced into place so quickly at the end of World War II.

An abortive coup in August 1991 failed to replace Soviet leader Mikhail Gorbachev with a regime that would have very likely responded militarily to the increasing fragmentation of the Soviet Union. By the end of 1991, Gorbachev had resigned and the Union of Soviet Socialist Republics effectively dissolved. It appeared that the Cold War was largely over, demonstrated by the response of the George H. W. Bush administration in pledging $4.5 billion to support economic reform in what by 1991 was officially the new, albeit smaller Russian Federation of politically affiliated states. The Bush administration offered both credit and technical assistance, embarking on negotiations for a major reduction in nuclear weapons held by both nations. In addition, a number of restrictive measures were lifted in regard to the diplomatic and foreign relations personnel allowed to serve in each country.

The full story of the end of the Cold War and the new relationship between the United States and the Russian Federation as one century ended and another began is obviously beyond our political warfare focus. Instead we will turn to its effects on the intelligence services of each country and to the active measures which never fully disappear in foreign relations between major powers. Following the Soviet collapse, changes in the CIA were primarily driven by a demand for increased intelligence support for both conventional warfare and special military operations including counter-terrorism activities. The shift to more intelligence work and less clandestine political warfare can be seen in a dramatic reduction of CIA spending on covert operations, which represented only about five percent of annual expenditures during the Bush administration.[1]

The major shift in CIA activities from political warfare to a focus on counter-terrorism began in 1993 when President Bill Clinton was faced with the bombing of the World Trade Center in New York City. At the time of that attack, America's intelligence services had most recently been involved in supporting conventional warfare in the Middle East as well as the traditional practices of collecting intelligence on foreign states. They had not focused on the emerging non-state terror threat, which had evolved around a type of privatized NGO infrastructure developed during the jihad in Afghanistan. The jihadi support infrastructure involved totally new types of financial fronts and covers which were largely unknown to both the CIA and the FBI, entities such as the Afghan Services Bureau, affiliated with charities declared to be supporting Arab combatants in the Afghan warfare.[2]

We now know that Osama bin Laden and his new al-Qaeda organization had become proficient in operating globally within both charitable and commercial covers. Several ostensibly charitable and humanitarian Saudi citizen–funded entities such as the al-Haramain

Foundation were used by al-Qaeda for highly compartmentalized dissemination of money and personnel for new jihadi operations far beyond Afghanistan.[3] Unfortunately as of even the mid-1990s that was largely a revelation for American intelligence. The Reagan era trend towards privatization of covert political warfare and its approach to regime change in Afghanistan had bred NGOs of a type never envisioned, and entities completely outside the traditional Cold War-era intelligence collections reach of either the CIA or FBI.

The Clinton administration was faced with the fact that the jihadi groups had not previously been designated as a primary intelligence target. It took considerable time to come to grips with the extent to which bin Laden and his various fronts (charitable, commercial, and financial) were actually recruiting and directing a multinational force. People familiar with the events of the period relate that initially bin Laden was viewed simply as "a radicalized rich kid, playing at terrorism by sending checks to terrorist groups." Even the CIA initially opposed the idea that there was such an organization as al-Qaeda.[4]

The earliest warning of this new form of international threat had appeared during the regional war between Bosnia and Serbia in 1992. At that time the CIA began to track significant numbers of Arabs, many former Afghan mujahedeen, showing up in Bosnia. Most significantly they were not appearing as individual volunteers but rather as fully organized brigades, officially attached to the Bosnian Army but operating almost solely on their own. They were highly experienced, highly aggressive, and agonizingly brutal. And they came with a support organization of financial, commercial, and charity groups—the exact infrastructure that had developed in Pakistan to support the Arab fighters introduced into the Afghan war against the Soviets.

By 1996 President Clinton and his National Security Council had begun to prioritize the non-state terror threat. The CIA was specifically directed to increase its focus on Osama bin Laden. A virtual station was implemented inside the Agency, totally focused on bin Laden.

The CIA was tasked with producing sufficient field intelligence for a comprehensive plan of attack on al-Qaeda. Clinton authorized broad-based covert action against both bin Laden and al-Qaeda. That tasking included something else, something sensational. For the first time since the Eisenhower years, a president directed not just covert action, but authorized and granted the CIA the authority to either capture or kill a political target—Osama bin Laden.[5] The CIA as a whole was increasingly becoming "operationalized," still working covertly and in the shadows but in support of what were in reality military missions. That trend escalated dramatically following the terror attacks on New York and Washington, DC in 2001.

After 9/11, new President George W. Bush ordered direct military action against al-Qaeda, bin Laden, and anyone allied with the attack on America. Indeed, one of Bush's first directives authorized the CIA to hunt, and if capture was not feasible, kill figures from al-Qaeda and its associated groups and organizations. During 2002 a target list was prepared; those on the list were referred to as "high-value targets" and the Bush executive directive gave the CIA blanket authority to act without obtaining specific presidential approval for each individual action.[6]

In part that shift had to do with the CIA's ability to collect and analyze intelligence on a non-state enemy, one that proved itself capable of adapting virtually all the standard covers and financial fronts traditionally used in covert political warfare. It was an enemy operating from within nations across Arabia, Africa, even the western Pacific. In response a new model of CIA operations emerged. Throughout the Cold War the CIA had carried out hybrid political warfare on its own, utilizing paramilitary officers, detached military personnel, and indigenous surrogates. Now roles were going to be reversed, it would be the CIA which would be integrated within military operations, supporting officially acknowledged but low-profile activities of Joint Special Operations Command.

Defense Secretary Donald Rumsfeld was a prime mover in reshaping the role of the CIA and in advancing the concept of the Joint

Special Operations Command (JSOC) during the Bush administration. In September 2003, he issued an order establishing JSOC as the principal U.S. counter-terrorism force. In addition, he drafted an order, known as the "Al Qaeda Network Exord," for President Bush. That executive order included a preauthorized list of some fifteen countries where actions could be conducted.[7] Not all the nations on the list were going to welcome American anti-terrorist military activities. On occasion, military counter-terrorism operations against "non-state enemies" were going to have to be conducted inside hostile territories, within nations where the regimes in power either would not grant approval or might well use force to oppose American intrusion. There would also be major risks of compromising such operations by even raising the possibility of such an operation with the nation's leaders and its intelligence community. Deniability was no longer the issue, operating inside potentially hostile foreign territory, without official permission—referred to as "denied area operations"—was the new concern.

An obvious example of denied area operations is found in the Obama Administration mission into Pakistan in 2011, conducted by SEAL Team Six (the U.S. Naval Special Warfare Development Group, or DEVGRU). That operation resulted in the death of Osama bin Laden. The mission was built around information gathered by the CIA, planned at CIA headquarters, and authorized under the legal statutes related to the 1947 National Security Act, which granted the CIA the right to conduct certain covert activities which would be outside normal boundaries for the U.S. military. The bin Laden operation illustrates the extent to which the CIA and American Special Forces have been integrated early in this century, from the highest levels of the Pentagon down to actual field operations. For legal purposes it was described as "a complete incorporation of JSOC into a C.I.A. operation."[8] From another perspective, it simply acknowledged what had become a full merger of the CIA and the uniformed military into a new type of American warfare.

The last decade of the twentieth century and the first decade of the twenty-first saw the emergence of an entirely new threat to America, taking its military and political action response in an entirely different direction, and bringing the CIA into a wholly new venue of operations. The Cold War was past, the CIA's attentions were no longer focused on Russia or the Russian threat. On the other hand, the Bush administration did open the century with a new ideological/political initiative of its own. It was described as the Freedom Agenda and was global in scope.

That new initiative had the stated intent of enabling democracy as a weapon against terrorism: "the spread of freedom as the great alternative to terrorists' ideology of hatred because expanding liberty and democracy will help defeat extremism and protect the American people."[9] While it was largely oriented towards the Middle East and Africa, it was global in concept and endorsed the promotion of open elections in other areas, including among the newly independent, former Soviet republics. As part of the initiative the Bush administration moved to support and help fund a number of international and non-governmental organizations with aims of spreading both freedom and democracy. American funding was made available to efforts in support of "democracy worldwide."[10]

At the time it seemed to be all good. Few voices were raised in opposition. Within a decade, there would be serious and totally unanticipated consequences, which set the stage for a major Russian political action reversal—and what some began to term a second Cold War. This will be examined in detail, but first we need to take a closer look at Russian intelligence activities during the 1990s and into the new century. As noted previously, certain forms of political warfare never totally disappear. In this instance, Russian intelligence services—under new names and guises—most definitely did continue active measures campaigns, both regionally and against the United States. In doing so they began to take advantage of certain avenues and opportunities that were almost entirely new, avenues only available to a financially powerful state which possessed the power of both economic coercion and "investment potential."

With the collapse of the Soviet Union, its largest political entity, the Russian Republic, was reconstituted as the new Russian Federation. As a nation, Russia entered a period of intense political and economic stress during much of the 1990s. Its military was in considerable disarray, and its economy moved into a period of instability as price controls were lifted and a free market emerged. In a move to private ownership of businesses and even real estate, its public was forced to deal with the pressure of a hyper-inflated currency. By 1992 Russia was facing inflation on the order of 2,500 percent and posting a negative economic growth of over fourteen percent. The Russian public was reeling, the government was desperately in pursuit of economic stability and, as with virtually every other facet of the Russian system, its intelligence service was also experiencing a restructuring.

The KGB's largest department, the Ministry of Security, was first re-designated as the Federal Counterintelligence Service (FSK) and later the Federal Security Service (FSB). Much of its role remained constant, however new threats focused it on domestic and regional concerns. The Russian Federation increasingly faced security challenges from certain of its own semi-autonomous areas, areas with their own ethnic and religious histories in which Russians were generally minorities. Demands for increased autonomy and independence were sometimes negotiated successfully—and sometimes not. In the mid-1990s a secession effort by the self-declared Chechen Republic of Ichkeria turned into a full-fledged war with the Russian federal government. Russian military units suffered heavily during early efforts to establish territorial control in the mountains of Chechnya.[11]

Ultimately the Russian federal government deployed massive military force and the Chechen capital of Grozny was hit with major air strikes and intense artillery bombardment. Civilian casualties were heavy and virtually all the buildings in Grozny were destroyed, including hospitals. There were extensive protests from humanitarian NGOs operating in the region, and the ultimate legacy of the Russian victory was an ongoing series of ethnic and later radical Islamic terror attacks, including attacks into the Russian Republic itself. In order to deal with that threat the FSB was assigned an aggressive counter-terror-ism mission. Later, in 2003, the FSB was also assigned the responsibil-ity for foreign collections of electronic intelligence.[12]

The directorate of the KGB, which had previously conducted its foreign intelligence operations, was re-designated as the Foreign Intelligence Service of the Russian Federation (the SVR RF). It was the SVR that carried on with the personnel and methods the KGB had conducted overseas, including the political warfare practices known as active measures. Section A of the KGB had been designated as the active measures organization. With the re-designation of the SVR, Section A was renamed: it would be the Section for Assistance Operations. In practical terms that meant carrying out the same KGB practices but referring to them as efforts to "assist" the perception of the Russian Federation within targeted foreign governments.

The re-designation had come about in the early 1990s, during a period of the most positive American relations with the new Russian government. The CIA reportedly requested that active measures against the United States cease. In response, active measures did indeed cease, but in name only. They were now "assistance measures."[13] In actually carrying out active measures in foreign nations, the SVR was supported by a disinformation group within the FSB; that group combined largely objective factual information with propaganda-related material, placing it into the correct context and targeting its use. In 1999 the head of the FSB's Center for Public Communications publicly described the FSB's role in supporting "assistance programs," exposing what had previously been a new and confidential term for a very old KGB practice.[14]

Earlier, in the chapter on Russian and American active measures, we reviewed details of the Russian foreign mission in New York City during the period of 1995-2000, demonstrating that for all practical purposes the KGB's Cold War-era practices had largely been carried on without any substantive change by the new Russian Federation. Moving forward to the present, we find that as recently as 2015 three Russians were the subject of a complaint by the Federal Bureau of Intelligence. That complaint followed a prosecution in 2010, in which Russian agents had attempted to "infiltrate the upper levels of U.S. business and government."

United States Attorney for the Southern District of New York Preet Bharara stated that:

> Following our previous prosecution with the FBI of Russian spies, who were expelled from the United States in 2010 when their plan to infiltrate upper levels of U.S. business and government was revealed, the arrest of Evgeny Buryakov and the charges against him and his co-defendants make clear that—more than two decades after the presumptive end of the Cold War—Russian spies continue to seek to operate in our midst under cover of secrecy. Indeed, the presence of a Russian banker in New York would in itself hardly draw attention today, which is why these alleged spies may have thought Buryakov would blend in. What they could not do without drawing the attention of the FBI was engage in espionage. New York City may be more hospitable to Russian businessmen than during the Cold War, but my Office and the FBI remain vigilant to the illegal intelligence-gathering activities of "other nations."[15]

The specifics in the 2015 incident are especially helpful in understanding certain contemporary SVR practices. For example, one individual named in the complaint had entered the United States as a private citizen, an employee of a Russian bank with offices in New

York City. A second individual served as a trade representative of the Russian diplomatic mission in New York City, and a third as attaché to the Russian mission to the United Nations. It was the trade representative who performed the cut-out role of assigning tasking and reporting back to the SVR. Among the tasks assigned was the collection of information in regard to American sanctions and the development of alternative energy resources. This is a subject particularly important to Russia given its use of its own energy resources as economic tools in its European political warfare. Recruiting targets included individuals employed by major companies, including consultants as well as university students. The complaint also alleged exactly the types of cut-outs, clandestine meetings, covert document exchanges, coded communications, and other tradecraft that we have seen as historically standard intelligence methods used by both the KGB and CIA.

The FBI complaint detailed the close association between the SVR assets and Russian state-owned news organizations. One of the tasks assigned was to develop particular lines of questions, including ones about the New York Stock Exchange, which were to be used by Russian news agency reporters in attempts to collect "open source" intelligence. Perhaps most interesting was the tasking which directed contacts with the "representative of a wealthy investor" looking to develop casinos in Russia. That task was assigned to a Russian bank employee who apparently was charged to probe into areas far beyond the scope of his official work at the bank. Among those was an effort to collect documents from a source (actually an FBI informant) which would disclose information regarding American sanctions against Russia. It also needs to be noted that the Russian Bank employee was quite active on the internet, belonging to several groups which focused on finance.[16]

While the charges filed in 2015 might well have surprised the average American citizen, they do provide us with a good deal of information about the current operations of the SVR, much of it quite familiar in terms of practices. And within two years the American public was once again made aware that traditional Cold War-era Russian practices within the United States had never really ceased. In September 2017, reporters were quick to note and cover the fact that when Russian consulate personnel in San Francisco were ordered to leave their facility and apparently feared that it would be thoroughly searched, they began burning documents in the building's fireplace. The staff admitted the burnings were intentional, complaining that they feared that not only the consulate but the homes of some fourteen Russian staff were going to be searched. The U.S. State Department's response was simply that access to the building would only be with State Department permission. Rick Smith, formerly FBI head of counterintelligence in San Francisco, told the press that certainly the Russians had been conducting intelligence operations from the facility—as they had been doing for over fifty years.[17]

While confirming that there are still deep-cover intelligence assets placed within the United States, the 2015 FBI investigation also highlighted the fact that SVR assets are placed within Russian government missions, either as diplomatic staff or as trade officials representing the Russian Federation, entitled to diplomatic immunity. What was a change in Russian practices, although a standard for the CIA during the Cold War, was the use of individuals with regular jobs, in this instance involving contacts associated with financial activities and investments. That was a familiar "non-operational" American intelligence cover, which we have repeatedly encountered. In fact, it has been noted that senior CIA officers often had routine contact with corporate business officers, vetted them as assets, and exchanged information with them. Beyond that, American businesses provided both employment covers and at times actual operational support for CIA projects.

During the Cold War, there would have been considerable suspicion and even concern over contacts with "Russian businessmen." However, the communist system and state ownership naturally created a number of barriers for the KGB in trade and business outreach to Western Bloc nations. With the end of the Cold War, Russia's move to a type of capitalism (even if it was oligarchic rather than corporate) and the immense improvement in its economy during the 2000s, made it common to find Russian financial and investment activities in what was formerly thought of as "the West." The 2015 FBI filing notes that Russians working for private businesses today tend to receive little attention, and their activities simply do not rouse suspicions as they once would have. It also notes that this provides considerable new advantages for intelligence collection as well as access to individuals who would be regarded as good sources of political and economic intelligence.

Of course this was no real surprise for the FBI or the U.S. intelligence community, although it appears to have been for the public and a number of seemingly sophisticated Americans, including international business people, former government employees, and even former members of the military and intelligence communities. The growing risk of "entanglement" through business and investment contacts will be returned to, but first it is important to understand why the FBI was looking for precisely the type of active measures that appear in the 2015 incident. Furthermore, why was the broader intelligence community, including the NSA, monitoring Russian communications in search of clues to new channels of access to high-level political influence at levels far beyond those of the SVR activities in New York City?

One impetus for an expanded search for Russian influence developed as early as 2000, with the defection of the highest ranking SVR officer in the United States. The defector became a source for contemporary Russian practices and also brought documents providing a considerable level of insight into SVR operations inside the United States. Perhaps most significantly, he described a new type of active measures recruiting that involves practices specifically targeting both agents of influence and trusted contacts within the international business community, as well as among international consultants and journalists.

The SVR officer was able to offer those insights because he had been involved in one of the earliest recruiting projects targeting individuals beginning to do business in Russia, as early as 1994.[18] That was well before the Russian Federation developed the energy-based financial clout that now makes it broadly attractive to the international business community. However, it was an era when Western consultants began traveling to Russia to help it with the transition from a communist to a capitalist economy.

The target of this very early recruiting project was a Canadian, formerly an employee with the Canadian Centre for Arms Control and Disarmament, but then retired and working with a consulting firm in Ottawa. Initially the individual had simply been recruited as a voluntary intelligence informant, eventually turning into a paid asset. With Canadian intelligence still in a Cold War mode, the difficulty was in how to pay him; the solution was to offer him a consulting contract, working inside Russia. A shell company was created to serve as his employer, his consulting fees effectively laundered his espionage payments, and the employment gave him justification for frequent travel to Moscow—eliminating any problem with covert communications.

At the time the only problem with the new approach was that in those early days the SVR was restricted to foreign operations. Russian Federation President Boris Yeltsin actually had to sign off on an exception to support the arrangement inside Russia. In later years and contemporary times, that problem would be eliminated under a new arrangement whereby the FSB simply absorbed all operations within Russia (and covertly within certain of the former satellite nations) and the entire foreign intelligence community was placed directly under the control of a former lieutenant colonel in the KGB, President Vladimir Putin.[19]

That initial Russian commercial recruiting approach worked so well that the decision was made to create a major new project that could employ the Canadian asset long-term. Ostensibly the project was to develop desperately needed housing outside of Moscow. It was a special area of focus for Russian President Yeltsin and in his first meeting with former President Jimmy Carter, Yeltsin was promised an initial investment of $6 million from the United States. Other western nations and the World Bank stepped up and foreign funding was used to pay the new consulting company established by the Canadian asset.

The location of the housing project also allowed the Canadian's frequent travel to an area reasonably close to Moscow. In a standard practice perfected by the KGB in earlier years,[20] during several of the asset's visits an attractive translator was assigned to him. Compromising videotapes were prepared—should future leverage be necessary. This commercial approach succeeded extremely well and appeared to provide an excellent cover not only for paid agents but for a variety of other types of influential contacts including individuals well placed to shape American policies.

The new practice was designated as "business recruitment" and Section A, the "Section for Assistance Operations," determined it would help influence policies, particularly in light of how Westerners were beginning to take advantage of the new consulting and development opportunities (first funded by international monetary support).[21] People could now work for Russia without it appearing suspicious. People could now be paid by Russian firms without it being suspect. As Russia's economy rebounded beginning in the early 2000s and it suddenly emerged as an energy and financial power, a whole new set of Westerners wanted to do business with Russia, with Russian banks and investment firms, with Russian energy companies, and with its new class of capitalists—the Russian oligarchs.

The open Russian economy had become a valuable tool of the Russian intelligence community, and an increasingly broad range of American business contacts resulted. As events would show, the same tried and true practices of influence and entanglement would be attempted with a great many of those contacts. Congressional testimony of November 2017 suggested that efforts may have been made to compromise a very well-known American doing business in Moscow in 2013, a businessman who would become president of the United States in no more than three years.[22]

Active measures tend be a constant, and their clandestine practices remain fundamentally the same over decades and even centuries. It is always the context of foreign relations that drives and targets them at any given point in time. During the Cold War, American active measures were intended to maintain supportive regimes in power against revolutionary threats or to destabilize those that appeared to be open to doing business with the Soviet bloc of nations. In pursuing that mission, the United States was able to leverage the power of its economy and its global financial reach. As we saw in Mexico, CIA political officers were constantly on the lookout for mutually supportive relationships, where information or economic incentives could be offered in exchange for political and policy influence with the regime in power. Such soft active measures are a fundamental in foreign relations, it is often simply a matter of who—official diplomatic staff or deniable private sector assets—is playing point in carrying them out.

The first decade of the twenty-first century saw the emergence of this entirely new context for Russian active measures programs, especially those of the soft-influence form. In a total reversal of roles, the Russian Federation and Russian firms would acquire sufficient economic leverage to offer economic incentives and commercial opportunities to European nations and ultimately to business people in both Europe and the United States. In 1999, at the same time Vladimir Putin was appointed as premier of the Russian Federation, global oil prices began to rise significantly, and they would surge upwards during the following decade. By 2000, Russia showed its first budget surplus since the dissolution of the Soviet Union. The government instituted major tax reforms, moving personal tax rates up to thirteen percent as well as increasing the tax on oil and gas production. Land sales including agricultural land were also permitted. The resulting boom in tax revenues allowed the Russian government to pay off at least a portion of the foreign debt that it had incurred during the previous decade, ahead of schedule.[23]

By 2003, with oil holding at twenty-three dollars per barrel (twice the level of the 1990s), energy income made it possible for Russia to post a budget surplus and pay off the rest of its debts. Russian oil and gas exports not only saved the nation economically, but made it financially stable, giving it the type of economic clout it had lacked during the Cold War. By 2008, the price of oil had reached new heights, creating not only a class of wealthy oligarchs but opportunity for major foreign investment that for a time attracted both Europeans and Americans in search of capital. Such business relations provided a totally new venue for acquiring Russian political and policy influence.

As noted previously, the worldview and strategic perceptions of U.S. presidents were always critical in regard to directing political warfare. When all the discussions were done, it was the president of the United States, heavily influenced by the strategic concerns of the secretary of state or the national security advisor, who made the final decision and issued directives to the CIA. And regardless of where and how the CIA was instructed to conduct its missions, the one constant in American covert action was that the CIA always had to isolate the president from its missions and actions. Even if it all went bad and became public political warfare, it was not to be linked to any sitting president. This was an axiom Machiavelli would have well understood.

One of the major tactics for establishing such isolation, as well as deniability for the CIA itself, was the use of commercial and financial covers, either of the CIA's own creation or willingly provided to them through personal relationships with American business and financial leaders. We have seen that social network connections to financial and business leaders were used by President Roosevelt in his own turn to deniable actions, even before the start of World War II. Given that many of the CIA's first senior officers were also personally connected to the business, banking, and investment community, that practice became well established even in the earliest days of post-World War II covert operations. Such personal connections would come into play once again under the Reagan administration, with the virtual privatization of political and even hybrid warfare.

With that history and with Machiavelli's observations about rulers in mind, there is no reason to expect Russian leaders to behave any differently in regard to creating isolation and deniability for FSB commercial active measures and recruitment activities. Under communism, the KGB simply did not have access to the sorts of commercial and business covers most commonly used by the CIA. However, it would appear that as Russian economic commercial influence developed, both the SVB and the FSB were quite enthusiastic about availing themselves of new opportunities.

Long-established KGB entanglement tactics were efficiently and aggressively incorporated with the new practice of business recruitment. It is very possible that the new practice was encouraged by the fact that the president of the Russian Federation at the time of economic revival was a longtime KGB career officer, the former director of the FSB, and the head of the Kremlin Security Council. Yet in the beginning, foreign political action was not President Putin's primary concern. His first political action initiatives were domestic, and his first FSB intelligence initiatives were focused inside Russia and across its immediate borders.

Upon assuming the Russian presidency, Putin's gravest security concern was that foreign intelligence services, both European and American, had become quite adept at operating inside Russia under the cover of NGOs, specifically non-profit foundations pursuing humanitarian, charitable, and even environmental concerns. Putin was very aware of the privatization of American political warfare and the use (knowing or unknowing) of NGOs as covers for both intelligence collection and political action. As director of the FSB,

Putin had stated that the interests of the state demanded that the FSB devote its "steadfast" attention to the activities of NGOs. Later he would even claim that British charity group workers were "teaching Chechens to make bombs."[24] Putin directed that one of the primary missions of the FSB, as it had been for the KGB, was to monitor, investigate, and build dossiers on NGOs and private entities active anywhere in Russian territory. Both foreign and Russian NGOs were targeted. A Russian human rights NGO, the Moscow Helsinki Group, was charged with accepting money from British intelligence, and Putin publicly identified several British diplomats as spies, financially manipulating NGOs.[25]

The FSB was redefined as the senior Russian intelligence agency, with the specific responsibility of collecting information (specifically "operative information"/suggesting political action operations) and performing investigations both inside Russia and the "post-Soviet" states on its borders.[26] A new department, the Directorate of Operative Information, was established in 2004 and specifically assigned to focus on border states. Beginning in 2004, FSB political officers would become deeply involved with a series of public elections in the new republics surrounding the Russian Federation.[27]

At the same time, the FSB's domestic and foreign intelligence role was being expanded to foreign political action. A considerable number of senior KGB/FSB officers were either retiring, entering politics, or moving into very senior positions in Russian business, especially within the energy and financial communities. It has been estimated that over 75 percent of the top one thousand political figures in the Russian government had retired from the KGB or previously worked for the FSB or the GRU (Russian military intelligence).[28] Unlike the CIA, which had formed largely within the highest levels of the American business and political community, the post-Cold War Russian intelligence community had moved in the other direction, into business and politics. Those individuals now provided the FSB with access to the same types of social networking and the use of financial and commercial covers that the CIA had previously used—covers and cut-outs perfect for creating distance and deniability for active measures programs.

The full extent of the connections between the intelligence and business/financial networks that developed during the revival of a strong Russian national economy will likely never be revealed. Even after numerous congressional inquiries and records releases, we only have limited insight into the privatization of American intelligence operations that occurred decades ago. However, the extent to which intelligence/commercial linkages developed in the reinvigorated Russian economy can be illustrated with certain examples:

> Igor Sechin, formerly in military intelligence, became not only deputy Russian prime minister but chairman of Rosneft, the government-owned oil company.

> Sergei Ivanov, KGB foreign intelligence branch, also served as Russia's deputy prime minister.

> Vladimir Shults, FSB deputy director, moved to a leadership position in the Russian Academy of Sciences.

> Vladimir Yakunin, a former political intelligence officer assigned to New York, became head of Russian Railways, one of the world's largest rail networks.

> Yuri Zaostrovtsev, FSB head of economic security, was appointed head of Vnesheconombank, the Russian State Bank of Development and Foreign Economic Affairs. In 2010 the bank announced an agreement with the Export-Import Bank of the United States.

> General Alexander Perelygin, KGB technical services then deputy FSB Moscow chief, became an advisor to Moscow's mayor and a major figure in Russian real estate before being

appointed as deputy director of Norilsk Nickel, the world's largest nickel and palladium producer.[29]

Even younger but socially networked FSB officers moved into influential financial positions. Andrei Patrushev (whose father had served as FSB director from 1999 to 2008) followed three years of service in the FSB as an economic intelligence service officer with an appointment as a full-time advisor at Rosneft. In 2007, the twenty-seven-year-old was given a special award by President Putin for his service to the state.[30]

Under Putin, Russia's intelligence services have gained access—officially and via their personal networks—to the same types of economic and financial covers that the CIA enjoyed throughout the Cold War. Its senior officers are intelligent, experienced, and familiar with the CIA's practices, and they have moved to effectively incorporate new commercial opportunities and tools into their operational practices. The first foreign activities of the expanded and reenergized FSB would become evident in a series of new Russian political action initiatives, active measures directed towards Russia's immediate neighbors, former members of the Soviet Union. By 2004-05 journalists in neighboring countries began to publicly report on new FSB activities within their borders.[31] Those regions had always been considered strategic to Russian interests and even following the fragmentation of the Soviet Union the economic and social relationships with many had remained close. Formal political control no longer existed but there was still a very fundamental Russian desire for a degree of political and economic hegemony. Issues of Russian regional sovereignty had not truly vanished with the end of the Soviet Republic. The revival of the Russian economy allowed Moscow to return its attention to those geopolitical concerns, and sovereignty issues would reignite a new era of political warfare. But this time, Russia would become the champion of stability and the United States would be viewed as the existential threat, the covert sponsor of revolution and regime change.

Chapter Ten:
Sovereignty Issues

The Russian public and President Putin (elected to the Russian Federation presidency in 2000) both benefited from the major Russian economic turnaround in the first years of the new century. Government debts were paid off, budget surpluses became the norm, the consumer economy boomed, and along with it all, a new class of extremely wealthy capitalists emerged—the new oligarchs. Many, if not all, were tied to energy sales and capital investment. Yet in the midst of a new level of economic security, Russia had to face a series of major terror attacks. The separatist conflict in Chechnya, and Russia's response, had bred its own extreme, radical terrorist consequences.

In October 2002 a series of small diversionary attacks culminated in a horrendous hostage siege at the Dubrovka Theater in Moscow. The FSB responded to the incident with Special Forces and in the end fentanyl gas was used during a rescue attempt; 45 died and 850 were treated for serious side effects of the gas. Within two years, beginning in June 2004, a brutal series of separatist attacks were launched beyond Chechen borders against Russian government buildings and personnel in the North Caucasus. That summer two domestic Russian passenger flights out of Moscow were destroyed in mid-air by terrorist bombs. In Moscow itself, bombers carried out individual attacks targeting city and government officials. And in September, a large group of terrorists seized a school in the Russian federal republic of North Ossetia, almost immediately executing a dozen adults. The FSB organized security response evolved into a street battle that not only involved the school but much of the adjacent town of Beslan. When it was over an estimated 334 hostages, including 186 children, were dead.[1]

Given that the new terror attacks were coming across Russian borders from adjacent territories, Russian intelligence—primarily the FSB—was directed to look outwards, to identify threats and if at all possible to abort or interdict them before more incidents occurred inside Russia itself. President Putin described Russia as being under attack, effectively in a "state of war" and moved to exert tighter political control over the regional governments in the North Caucasus.[2]

The FSB's new 2004 foreign mandate was codified by the creation of the Directive of Operative Information. As mentioned in the previous chapter, "operative information" translates to political action and the result was that there was a significant increase in FSB officers traveling to and involving themselves in a good many of the new republics that had previously been members of the Soviet Union. It appears that at first the FSB political action was of the soft form, essentially reconnecting with individuals and parties known during the Soviet era who were essentially pro-Russia. In Moldavia, Deputy Director of the FSB Vyacheslav Ushakov (former head of the Directorate of Operations) was thought to have recruited a prominent local politician as an agent of influence.[3] Senior FSB officers traveled to a separatist region of Georgia (Abkhazia) in 2004 to contact and support a Moscow-oriented candidate. Apparently their presence was noted and reported on, and their candidate lost, undermining future intelligence collections in the area.[4]

In Belarus the FSB had been accused of trying to sway presidential elections as early as 2003.[5] That sort of political action, outside Russia's own borders, was confirmed in 2005 when the director of the FSB officially advised the Russian *Duma* (parliament) that the FSB had helped abort a plot against the pro-Moscow regime in Belarus.[6] The plot had ostensibly been organized by NGO actors, operating out of Bratislava, the Slovakian capital. The government of Belarus almost immediately confirmed the FSB announcement and its own intelligence services began a series of coordinated operations, which included Russia (FSB), Belarus (State Security Committee) and Kazakhstan (National Security Committee).[7]

The FSB also looked towards the new republics across Central Asia, adopting a modified set of practices focused on maintaining a level of political influence and supportive contacts with the security services of those nations. Many of the regimes in those new republics—still led by political strongmen from the Soviet era—faced political opposition from Islamist and anti-secular movements. Their response was typically the total suppression of dissent characteristic of Soviet rule. Those actions resulted in a number of their opponents fleeing across the border to the Russian Federation, creating ex-patriot communities which were deemed a threat by regimes in republics such as Kazakhstan, Uzbekistan, Azerbaijan and Turkmenistan.

In response, the security services of the regimes proceeded into Russia to covertly hunt down and either eliminate or kidnap those suspected of being political threats. In some instances the FSB directly assisted—capturing, arresting, and handing them over while publicly announcing the activities as counter-terrorism operations.[8] The FSB appears to have been particularly active, or at least particularly public, about its joint work with Uzbekistan. In 2008 an announcement was made by the FSB, declaring that any enemy of the regime of Uzbekistan was considered to be a threat to the security of the Russian Federation; several groups including the Islamic Movement of Uzbekistan were declared to be international terrorist movements subject to Russian security military action wherever they might be operating.

In the broader context it has to be noted that such Russian practices were not inconsistent with actions being taken by the United

States, announced publicly but conducted covertly by CIA paramilitary and JSOC teams around the globe. Black military operations, kidnapping, and rendition were carried out by Russian security forces following the terror attacks on Moscow and on Russian territory. The same types of activities were performed by American security teams following terror attacks on the United States and on American diplomatic missions across the Middle East and in Africa.

For more details on the evolution of the FSB and its move into a foreign intelligence / political action role, interested readers are encouraged to refer to the excellent independent research of two Russia journalists, Andrei Soldatov and Irina Borogan, who investigated and reported on developments within the Russian security services for over a decade. Their work, which became virtually impossible under new Russian security measures put into place circa 2008, provides us with some of the best early insights into the evolution of the FSB during the first Putin presidency.[9]

The evolution of the FSB, and its reach into both foreign intelligence and political action, is important to our understanding of Russian political warfare in the second decade of this century. Even more important is the extent to which that political warfare grew beyond simply the soft political action of establishing positive political and economic relations and ensuring that agents of influence were deeply embedded within key foreign nations. To some extent, up to 2004, Moscow's relations with its neighbors, and their governing regimes, was comparable to America's relations with many foreign nations following World War II—a matter of long-established social networks, economic ties, and mutual security alliances. There were close personal relationships, a good deal of history (some good, some not so good), and a great desire to maintain the status quo to the greatest extent possible.

In terms of American foreign relations, such ties enabled the support of pro-American regimes around the globe and generally opposed regime change. In those instances, where popular revolutions did threaten pro-American regimes, the United States moved first to active political measures (as in Italy and Iran) and if that failed to full-scale, deniable military action using surrogate forces (as in Guatemala, Indonesia, Cuba, Angola, Nicaragua, and elsewhere). While such responses were officially couched in terms of supporting democracy, supporting popular choice, and opposing communism, there seems no doubt that at the core it was a matter of sovereignty, of "spheres of influence"—both political and economic. It actually made no difference whether a particular regime had come into power in an open, popular election (as in Iran, Guatemala, or Chile) or through a revolutionary coup (as in Cuba or Nicaragua).

The great irony of the early twenty-first century was that, beginning in 2004, the Russian Federation would adopt the same pattern of response in its own foreign relations, pushing back against perceived political and economic threats to its own sphere of influence. The trigger would be a series of open popular elections, mass protests, and regime change in adjacent republics known as the color revolutions—the Rose Revolution in Georgia (2003), the Orange Revolution in Ukraine (2004), and the Tulip Revolution in Kyrgyzstan (2005). In response Russia turned to the same series of active measures and deniable surrogate warfare that the United States had used during the Cold War. The consequences would be…predictable.

The span of popular regime change in post-Soviet territories actually began in 2000 and extended through 2009, involving many more than just three countries. The causes and parties involved varied state by state, and regime by regime. They have been extensively debated by scholars, and propagandized for both Russian and American political factions according to their own worldviews and goals.[10] From the Russian perspective, the color revolutions in Georgia and the Ukraine were particularly shocking. Moscow perceived common elements in them: the American "democracy initiative" announced by President Bush in 2002—the open U.S. financing of NGOs promoting democratic elections around the globe (officially as a means to push back against terrorist takeovers such has happened in Afghanistan)—and pre-existing suspicion of incidents involving NGO personnel and political activity inside Russia itself.

The United States under presidents from Eisenhower to Reagan had consistently responded to pro-American regimes falling as being the result of efforts by local Communist Party factions supported by Soviet political warfare. The Russian Federation and in particular President Putin would see the fall of pro-Moscow regimes as the work of covert American and European political warfare, carried out locally (and deniably) though local efforts of NGOs. And there was always just enough evidence—in both instances—to feed such fears and justify an aggressive response.

In virtually all the Cold War-era American political warfare operations, there were active communist parties and populist movements involved in the politics of the nations in question. At times the communist parties were legally involved in national politics, in other instances they were considered illegal and not part of the electoral process. And those parties as well as other more covert media fronts were also consistently found to be involved in promoting a great deal of anti-American and anti-Western propaganda. In our review of the actual dialogues related to the American decisions to intervene, it was found that it was the ideological element—the fear of communism and Soviet influence—that took precedence over any factors.

A closer look at the Russian response to the color revolutions reveals a similar fear factor, one of Western ideological influence. There is no doubt NGOs were actively involved in virtually all the former Soviet republics, openly and actively promoting democracy and open elections. Several of those NGOs were an extension of an American democracy initiative that dated back to 1983 and Reagan-era legislation which had created the National Endowment for Democracy (NED). The stated goal of NED was to "strengthen democratic institutions around the world." In reality, that program was a relatively minor component of the Reagan Administration "push back" initiative, a peripheral form of political warfare effort intended to diminish Soviet influence, particularly in developing nations.

From a functional standpoint, NED served to route American government funding through organizations such as the Democratic Institute for International Affairs (NDI), the International Republican Institute (IRI), the International Foundation for Electoral Systems (IFES), the International Research and Exchanges Board (IREX), and Freedom House. It is important to note that the legislation which created the National Endowment for Democracy does not contain any language that would prohibit it from being used by the CIA in any fashion, nor does it forbid the employment or even participation of any active or retired CIA officer in its activities.

The initial language in the bill did contain such a ban, based in concerns over prior CIA involvement with international economic and humanitarian programs including USAID. A last-minute call on the night before the bill was going to the floor reportedly changed that. House Foreign Affairs Committee chief sponsor Representative Dante Fascell (D-NY) reportedly relayed a message from CIA Director William J. Casey requesting that the ban language be removed–and it was indeed removed prior to passage.[11]

We have no specific revelations on exactly how any of those organizations may have served as covers for CIA political action officers or as covert financial conduits to agents and groups of influence, however it seems quite understandable that KGB officers of that era would view NGO democracy efforts in the context of political action against Russia. While most likely not intended to be received in that vein, a remark by the National Endowment for Democracy's first president, Allen Weinstein, that "a lot of what we do today was done covertly twenty-five years ago by the CIA" would no doubt have confirmed the KGB view. Or, as an article in the *Washington Post* put it: "Working in broad daylight, the

United States and its allies were able to do things that would have been unthinkably dangerous had they been done in the shadows....And it includes political-support operations for pro-democracy activists, which may be best left to the new network of overt operators."[12]

Such Russian perceptions would be reinforced as the twentieth century ended and new administrations came to power in Washington, DC. President Clinton's first Secretary of State Warren Christopher talked of a new realism in efforts to promote democracy: "By enlisting international and regional institutions in the work, the U.S. can leverage our own limited resources and avoid the appearance of trying to dominate others."[13] Democracy-focused NGOs work to recruit and train locals in the techniques of political organization, of non-violent protest, and the use of modern communications both in coordinating protests and driving voters to the polls. The use of email, cell phones, and networking are all part of their programs. The only question is to what extent those groups and individuals within them may be knowingly or unknowingly used as covers for the placement of propaganda, disinformation, and media manipulation. In view of the history of political warfare, assuming that some level of active measures did not become involved would seem more than a little naïve.

The fact that NGOs were operating within the former Soviet republics and legally even within the Russian Federation itself, triggered the suspicions used to justify a dramatic increase in FSB domestic security activities. Ironically, the strengthening of FSB domestic operations mirrored the effect of Communist Party USA (CPUSA) on FBI domestic activities in the United States. The existence of the CPUSA, and its proven use as a front for the KGB, was a primary driver for the FBI for decades. And while it is obvious that certain NGOs funnel U.S. government funds into countries in pursuit of a democratic political agenda, the extent of any truly covert NGO activities are as yet undocumented. In contrast, we have solid, historical information on the extent that the KGB did attempt to use the Communist Party USA as a political warfare front.

That knowledge is based in FBI records in what was designated as the SOLO file, dealing with the activities and information provided by a high-level CPUSA member who became an informant, providing details on information obtained not only within the party but from visits to Moscow. That informant, Morris Childs, personally communicated with the highest levels of leadership in the Soviet Union and also served as the primary conduit for money carried directly from Moscow to the United States as financing for CPUSA activities.[14]

Childs was a loyal member of the CPUSA during the 1930s and 1940s, during the period when it had its greatest political impact within labor, academic, and progressive circles. He had even served as editor of its newspaper, the *Daily Worker*. However, Childs became unhappy over apparent political infighting and his forced removal from the editorial position. In 1947, his health and apparent disenchantment with the party leadership led him to discontinue his CPUSA activities. The following year he was secretly approached as part of an FBI initiative (TOPLEV) to recruit top-level party members as informants. With the FBI's encouragement, he again became active within the party and was able to rise within its ranks, being offered the position of courier between the CPUSA and Moscow in 1957.

The FBI then designated a new project dedicated solely to Childs—Operation SOLO.[15] During his first trip to Moscow, in addition to meeting with senior Russian and KGB leaders, Childs received a Russian commitment to CPUSA of almost $350,000, which was delivered over the following months by members of the Soviet diplomatic mission to the United Nations via drops at a restaurant in Queens, New York.[16] During the next two decades he traveled as a courier on over fifty overseas trips and assumed control over the CPUSA treasury. He ultimately helped move over $28 million in Soviet funding into the American activities of the CPUSA.[17]

Given the history of the KGB in channeling monies into America via the CPUSA and its use as a cover for a variety of political action activities including both propaganda and disinformation media efforts, there certainly was ample reason for experienced KGB officers to suspect that the CIA would be using NGOs in a similar fashion. And that leads us back to the eventual and very public Russian view that the 2004 political changes in Georgia, Ukraine, and Kyrgyzstan were primarily the result of American regime change efforts, carried out under the cover of NGO activities.

While our focus is on practices, it is also important to determine if the Russian conclusions as to the primary causes of the regime changes were as questionable as many of the U.S. assessments made during the Cold War. In other words, was Vladimir Putin making decisions of the same quality as those made by Eisenhower respecting Iran and Cuba, Nixon respecting Chile, and Reagan respecting Afghanistan and Nicaragua?

THE REPUBLIC OF GEORGIA: 2002-03

In the case of Georgia in 2003, there is no doubt that NGOs were involved with groups opposed to the government in power, to its leader, and to his overall regime. As previously discussed, in 2002 the Bush administration had continued the practice of support for democracy around the globe, initiating its own programs and putting the effort in the context of opposing the influence of terrorism though truly open elections and the support of democratically elected regimes. It had also continued government funding for the National Endowment for Democracy as well as similar organizations and encouraged private foundations and donors to do the same. That position would be continued by subsequent administrations and remains the same at the time of this writing in 2018.

The history of post-Soviet politics inside Georgia is far more complex than the change of government which occurred in 2003. However, in terms of the eventual Russian assessment, it is interesting to note that the Russian government had not been particularly pleased with the regime in Tbilisi. President Eduard Shevardnadze had formerly been Soviet foreign minister during the regime of Mikhail Gorbachev and many of those still in power in Moscow blamed him for being involved in agreements that allowed the ultimate fragmentation of the Soviet Union.[18]

During the 1990s his government had been seen as anti-Russian, particularly since it supported the development of a pipeline initially promoted by Turkey in 1992. The pipeline was intended to route oil collected in the energy-rich Caspian Sea region across Azerbaijan, Georgia, and Turkey to the Mediterranean Sea, totally bypassing Russia. Not surprisingly, the proposal was strongly supported by the United States. Upon its eventual completion in 2006, the United States Secretary of Energy Samuel Bodman joined the presidents of Turkey, Azerbaijan, and Georgia in inaugurating the first flow of oil. In May 2006 the tanker *British Hawthorne* docked at the Turkish Ceyhan oil terminal and loaded six hundred thousand barrels, which had originated at Baku in Azerbaijan and set sail across the Mediterranean.

Shevardnadze's Soviet history and Georgia's "collusion" in moving forward with a project bypassing Russia with the Baku-Tbilisi-Ceyhan (BTC) pipeline were not the only the issues that had made Russia unhappy with the Georgian government. Russia was incensed that Shevardnadze's government appeared to be allowing Chechen militants to collect and operate from its territory, in particular the Pankisi Gorge region of northern Georgia. The feeling in Russia was that the government of Georgia appeared to be under such stress that it had lost military control of key regions on the nation's borders. Russia carried out a number of air strikes on Georgian territory and Putin imposed travel sanctions on travel between the two nations.[19]

It also has to be noted that regional and ethnic identity issues had always existed among the non-Russian ethnic populations, even under the Soviet system. Georgia was proud to have been the native land of Joseph Stalin, yet it had been one of the first Soviet republics to see actual anti-Russian street riots and violence against Russian officials. That occurred in 1956, in response to the official Communist Party denigration of Stalin, the "Great Son of the Georgian People." Russian Premier Khrushchev had formally (and at length) denounced Stalin's crimes against the Soviet people. On March 7, with their pride seriously wounded, Georgians engaged in unapproved marches (spontaneous rallies and demonstrations were simply not permitted under the Soviet regime). Mobs formed in Tbilisi, further fueled by students who walked out of classes at Stalin University.

The next day the protests grew, eighteen thousand people filled the city's central square, with an increasing amount of anger aimed at "foreigners"—meaning Russians. Before long the protests took a nationalistic turn. Historic Georgian flags were flown, Soviet leaders were criticized publicly, and protests spread to other cities. Tbilisi was paralyzed, the huge Stalin Coach Works was shut down, and Soviet officials barricaded themselves in their offices, surrounded by armed guards. On March 9, with the main radio station under siege, Moscow authorized a military response. Soviet tank units went into action and in the end dozens of people were reported killed, and dozens arrested. The whole affair was officially blamed on "foreign spies and agents."[20]

In a new century and as of 2002-03, relations between Russia and Georgia were strained at best. It seems fair to state that there was little respect in Moscow for the economic performance of the Shevardnadze regime. Russia had recovered from its own economic crisis of the 1990s and was well into its recovery by 2003. In contrast Georgia was increasingly an economic disaster, its revenue collections fell far short of budget projections—largely due to extreme corruption—and it became nearly unable to pay its international loans, a very sensitive subject for Putin given his earlier experience with international lenders. Corruption was largely viewed as a legacy of the Soviet system, something that had become endemic, with up to 70 percent of financial deals being "off the books" and untaxed. The issue of corruption alone presented a major opportunity for anti-regime political groups.

The domestic consequences of the regime's economic failures were also quite public. In 2003 the Georgian debt on unpaid salaries and pensions reached $120 million and the lack of maintenance and spending on energy infrastructure (electrical service was repeatedly interrupted) was significantly hampering business and undermining revenues.[21] Economically, Georgia was almost a "failed state," with over half its population below the poverty level and no government revenues to sustain public support programs.

Under the stress of economic and social pressure, Shevardnadze's Citizens' Union of Georgia Party had begun to fragment as early as 2000, with deputies resigning from its parliament and new parties forming. Minister of Justice Mikheil Saakashvili left the Citizens' Union Party to launch the United National Movement (United Party) that same year. By the elections of 2002 the new party had gained a substantial number of seats (558) and independents held 2,724 seats in total, with the Citizens' Union only able to hold seventy seats. Established party control over the government had obviously shattered, and new elections were called for in November 2003.

The election of 2003 found Saakashvili leading an opposition coalition of the United National Movement along with the United Democrats, the Union of National Solidarity, and the youth movement Kamara—all in opposition to Shevardnadze's Citizens' Union party. There was a great deal of outside attention to and involvement with the 2003 election, not from the Russian Federation, but from NGOs pursuing a democracy initiative and also from the United States. Well before the elections, Secretary of State Colin Powell had talked with President

Shevardnadze, focusing on the need for and the mechanics of a fully open and representative election.[22] Later, Powell traveled to Georgia to attend the official swearing-in of Saakashvili as the new president.

The NGOs themselves (funded by both the American and European governments) provided funds and salaries that sustained a level of election involvement, which the local economy could not normally have supported. Training was provided on how to monitor the election process and on how to organize nonviolent government protests.[23] NGOs including the International Election Observation Mission (with representatives from the Council of Europe, the European Parliament, and the Organization for Security and Cooperation in Europe) monitored the vote and supported exit polling. Beyond that, private NGOs played their own role, with the Open Society Institute (OSI) funded by open society and democracy advocate George Soros. The OSI provided democracy training for student activists, including the techniques that had toppled certain of the former Soviet-era leaders, including Serbia's Slobodan Milosevic.[24]

During the election itself, a local group, the International Society for Fair Elections and Democracy, ran its own independent vote tabulation, providing tallies as a check against the government-released counts going to the media. While the government numbers showed Shevardnadze's candidates taking first place, voter exit polling definitely suggested an overwhelming loss for the Shevardnadze government. In addition, the independent vote tabulation quickly raised its own questions about irregularities in the official vote counts. Given the well-documented results of the previous 2002 election—with massive losses of seats for Shevardnadze's Citizens' Union Party—there was widespread public skepticism and disbelief in the numbers being officially reported.

Public mistrust was reinforced by the broadcasts of a major independent television station in Tbilisi, Rustavi 2. The station had allied itself with opposition to the Shevardnadze regime for a number of years, surviving attempts by the government to shut it down. One of the keys to its survival was that it received a level of financial support, training, and even legal aid from USAID and the Eurasia Foundation (itself at least partially funded by USAID) NGOs.[25]

Rustavi 2's ongoing broadcasts focused on the exit polling and the alternative vote tallies coming from the International Society for Fair Elections and Democracy. Media coverage touting apparent government election irregularities and promoting the United Opposition Party's messaging was most definitely a factor in fueling public protests over the election.[26] With no response from the government, matters escalated over a number of days, leading to continual demonstrations and the seizure of government buildings. The united opposition parties were able to collect sufficient funds to mobilize large crowds in the capital (including busing in people from surrounding regions) and sustain the street protests.

In contrast, the initial Russian response to the political situation in Georgia was quite moderate. At the time President Putin himself appears to have had little confidence in the regime—or its ability to stay in power.[27] With his hold on government in dire straits, Shevardnadze personally called President Putin, and in response Russian Foreign Minister Igor Ivanov (a native Georgian) flew to Tbilisi and met with old acquaintances from various parties, in the end advising Shevardnadze that he had best negotiate a political solution.

Shevardnadze had tried to remain in power by opening a new session of parliament but members of the opposing parties disrupted the session, forcing him to leave. His subsequent effort to declare a state of emergency and enforce power with the military failed when key commanders simply refused to obey his orders. In the midst of that political chaos, Ivanov inserted himself into the situation, helping organize a meeting between Shevardnadze and the three leading party heads. In the meeting Ivanov simply stated that President Putin had asked him to help facilitate a compromise. Then he departed.[28] Shevardnadze, left to his own devices and facing continually growing public protests, had little choice but to resign.

The foreign minister's visit and Russian influence are amply documented; Russia clearly exercised political action, but it was of a very soft form. After his election in 2003, new President Mikheil Saakashvili immediately traveled to Moscow, where he made statements of appreciation to President Putin, along with a commitment to government reforms. Soft Russian political action in response to the regime change had apparently been more than sufficient to deal with the situation, even though Putin certainly was aware of the role of the NGOs (and the Bush administration) and in particular the fact that democracy advocates and their media reach had seriously undermined the regime's control of the election results.

Foreign NGO involvement in the 2003 regime change in Georgia is more than obvious, its impact on opening the election process and exposing it via the media—as compared to previous years and especially the Soviet era of governance—was significant. Yet the political reversal was largely based in the nation's serious domestic problems; the fact that the regime was already in a minority position had been evident in the election results of 2002. The only question in 2003 was whether the regime could somehow maintain control, even if it meant the declaration of a state of national emergency and use of military force. In the end, the Russian leadership and moderate political action not only facilitated a peaceful solution but gave Putin the opportunity to improve the Russian relationship with Georgia through a positive relationship with the new Saakashvili government. In 2003 Putin chose not to make the election in Georgia a political confrontation, a contest of wills or a matter of spheres of influence. In doing so he seemed to have actually carried the day for Russian influence. The following year would bring an election in Ukraine, where matters would get much more personal, and much more emotional.

UKRAINE: 2004-05

The context for foreign political action in Ukraine in the mid-2000s was something far different than Georgian regime change. In 2003 Georgia had represented an actual security problem for Russia, with a central government that appeared to be unable to control regions on its own borders that were being used as bases for attacks against Russian territories. And there was no existing bond between Moscow leadership and the Tbilisi regime, which was still in the midst of an economic crisis and far different than Russia, where an energy-based economic revival was well underway.

In contrast Ukraine was and had long been a major resource for first the Soviet Union and then the Russian Federation. During the Cold War era, Ukraine had been referred to as the breadbasket of the USSR. The legal chaos and transition from centralized control significantly affected agricultural production (in both Ukraine and Russia) following the dissolution of the Soviet Union, taking large areas out of production. But that problem had largely been resolved by the end of the 1990s. Even when faced with issues of uncompetitive price supports and export subsidies, Ukraine remained a major global exporter of wheat and corn, with Russia and Europe as its primary customers.[29] Historically the eastern areas of Ukraine, in particular the Donbass region, had been a strategic resource for Soviet era industry in regard to coal production and metallurgy. Those industries had begun a serious decline in the last years of the Soviet Union, with coal mining heavily subsidized and largely untaxed.[30]

Much more important, Ukraine represented a vital strategic source for Russia in the area of military technology, particularly in military vehicles and shipbuilding, and in aerospace technology—specifically missile and rocket design and construction.[31] An estimated one-third of the Soviet defense industry was located in or supported by Ukraine's businesses and facilities. Ship construction involved heavy cruisers, missile cruisers, and antisubmarine warfare vessels. Certain factories in Ukraine were absolutely critical to the Russian military and would remain so even under increasingly stressed political relationships, including those supplying helicopter engines, transport planes, and rockets and missiles. Strategically Russia was also heavily dependent on Ukraine for the components used in its intercontinental ballistic missiles as well as for inspection and servicing of those strategic weapons. A great deal of the planned Russian military modernization would also require support from the Ukrainian defense industry.

The strategic technology relationship between Ukraine and Russia was a significant international bonding factor, as was the deep social network connecting Ukrainian politicians and Soviet leadership. Soviet Premier Nikita Khrushchev had been raised in Ukraine, as a youth he had been a metalworker in a coal mine there. During his ascent to power Khrushchev had personally represented Joseph Stalin in Ukraine, flying several times a week between Moscow and Kiev. During the Soviet era, Kiev would be one of the primary starting points on the road to political power in Moscow, with St. Petersburg being the other. Politically and socially the leadership of Ukraine and Russia had bonded throughout the Soviet era, and that continued into the twenty-first century.

However, there were elements of the relationship unique to certain regions of Ukraine that were most definitely not covered in Soviet history books. Those suggest the existence of deep strains of Ukrainian nationalism and regional dissatisfaction with Soviet rule. One illustration comes from World War II. Ukraine had played a major role in supporting the Red Army in ousting German occupation forces. Yet when Germany originally moved against Russia in World War II, there were areas within Ukraine actually receptive to the German presence—regions which had been taken over only in 1939 by the Red Army and other areas that had suffered millions of deaths in the early 1930s, with thousands executed or sent to labor camps. The Germans even managed to recruit a sufficient number of Ukrainians—up to four thousand—to support the first advances into Russia by creating disruption behind Soviet lines.[32] Although a horrendous German occupation ultimately quashed such support, in certain regions of western Ukraine, nationalism and hatred of Stalin's rule had been enough to even turn sympathies to invading German forces. Memories of Stalin-era atrocities in the west were not something that passed away in a single generation.

The political equation involving Ukraine and Moscow appears to have been one of ongoing Russian support for the established regime in Ukraine. For decades, successful Ukrainian politicians had gone to Moscow. Those that met approval returned to organize and control the governing regime in Kiev. If they were exceptionally apt, they succeeded to positions of power in Moscow. That was simply the way things worked, and that was exactly the scenario under which Russian political action towards Ukraine developed for what seemed to be simply another in a long line of elections.

Russia's political action involvement in the 2005 Ukrainian election was relatively restrained. President Putin personally took the initiative to convince the current term-limited president, Leonid Kuchma, not to attempt any political manipulations that would allow him to run again. Putin advised him to act strictly in accordance with the law and support a successor who would be acceptable to Moscow—Viktor Yanukovych.[33] What was made immediately clear was that Yanukovych had indeed been selected by Russia; he visited Putin monthly and the Russian president delivered a series of highly public endorsements. Official Russian involvement in the Ukrainian election would be very open. The relationship between Yanukovych and Putin was highly visible and obviously very close, enough so that Yanukovych attended Putin's birthday party.

Economic incentives were also part of the Russian endorsement. Energy prices and VAT-related taxes were reduced and restrictions were eased on Ukrainian migrant workers inside Russia. It was a new type of political action, a full-fledged "charm campaign" including a massive festival honoring Kiev's liberation from the Nazis by the Red Army, involving President Putin's personal participation. Putin even began a series of television appearances, endorsing Yanukovych on all the major Ukrainian broadcast channels. Russian news channels, widely watched in Ukraine, also gave a totally one-sided view of the election, emphasizing the virtually certain victory of Putin's candidate.[34]

There was a more covert side to the establishment public relations effort, but it was conducted not by FSB political action officers but rather by a large number of Russian political advisors, including the Effective Policy Foundation, a Moscow-based group which had worked for outgoing Ukrainian President Kuchma. These "election technologists," moving from Kuchma's administration to the Yanukovych campaign, took up residency in Kiev for the duration of the elections. Their propaganda campaign involved a variety of media efforts intended to position opposition candidate Viktor Yushchenko as anti-Russian, nationalistic, and even pro-fascist. And for reasons less clear at the time, a detachment of Russian Special Forces, along with a group of advisers to Putin's administration also appeared in Kiev.[35]

Certainly there was western NGO political activity in the Ukraine as well. Once again the National Endowment for Democracy (NED) trained local and international election monitors, organized exit polls, and worked with opposition parties to prepare them for the types of public protests that could be used to contest election results. It also appears that there were factions within Ukrainian ministries, security services, and even Ukrainian intelligence who were opposed to the overtly pro-Russian campaign being run by Yanukovych. Not only did they provide information to the opposition candidate's camp, but during the elections played a critical role in the government's security response.

The actual level of U.S. spending in the Ukraine during the 2004 election is difficult to determine, but later Russia would promote (via the RT television network) that some $5 billion had been dumped into Ukraine to steal the vote. That particular figure is certainly disinformation, lifted from the actual fact that a broad variety of aid efforts (initiated under the original Reagan-era programs and reinforced by the Bush democracy initiative) have indeed spent large sums of money in Ukraine. The specific $5 billion claim appears to be built around a total of all those monies from 1991 to 2014.[36] What can be said with certainty is that there was a democracy initiative in Ukraine, that USAID and NED were involved, and that the same activities described in the 2003 Georgian election were conducted in Ukraine.

In contrast, considerable detail is known about pro-Russian political action during the election, and that is largely thanks to the work of Taras Kuzio, whose in-depth research tells a great deal about the maneuvering that began even before President Kuchma was convinced by Putin not to try to set himself up as his own successor. It appears that Kuchma's pro-Russian oligarchic backers were quick to translate those efforts to the support of Putin's sanctioned candidate, who effectively became theirs. While Russia and Putin were carrying out what was a very open charm campaign, the Russian political technologists in Kiev carried out their own highly covert and classic, if far dirtier, political action efforts.[37]

Certain elements of those propaganda and media efforts should seem quite familiar. One initial action was an effort to spin the widely known Kuchma regime corruption to taint Yushchenko and his supporters. The Kuchma scandal (also known as the Cassette Scandal) of 2000, which led to massive Ukrainian public protests, had been based in secret tape recordings documenting Kuchma's involvement in a number of crimes, including the abduction of a Ukrainian investigative reporter. The tapes were given to the international media and broadcast worldwide, including via Radio Liberty. Given the pro-U.S.

history of Radio Free Europe/Radio Liberty, the fact that it had carried this news became the centerpiece of a propaganda campaign to portray the entire scandal as Western political intervention in Ukraine.

During the 2004 election the Kuchma affair was repositioned as an early U.S. effort to oust Kuchma and replace him with Yushchenko. Interestingly, rather than specifically calling out the CIA as an actor in the story, the allegations were that anti-Russian nationalists had acted as American surrogates, financed through NGOs such as Freedom House, the International Republican Institute, and the National Democratic Institute—all having been previously accused by Russia as responsible for the recent regime change in Georgia. In the twenty-first century, anti-Russian factions covertly in league with NGOs were now being pictured as the contemporary version of the ubiquitous Cold War threat from the CIA. In addition, the disinformation campaign appeared to gain particular traction as a conspiracy theory, and a variety of other conspiracy-related rumors were planted throughout the campaign.

Kuzio presents a strong case that the political entity driving the dirty tricks campaign against Yushchenko was the Ukrainian Social Democratic Party (SDPUo), assisted by the Centre for Political and Conflict Studies (a pro-Russian Ukrainian NGO) headed by Mikhail Pogrebinsky, a longtime supporter of Kuchma and his leading defender during the Cassette Scandal. The SDPUo was primarily funded by Ukrainian oligarchs and consistently represented established, traditional Ukrainian issues. With every reason to support the status quo in the upcoming election, it turned to the same Russian political "technologists" that had worked for the Kuchma regime.

Apart from conspiracy campaigns, the technologists' tactics introduced phony websites, placed telephone taps, and released political disinformation. They also created a new Russian Press Center in Kiev. Its media outreach was specifically targeted towards the demographics of the traditional Russian-speaking population of Ukraine. The overall goal of all those efforts was to position opposition candidate Viktor Yushchenko as anti-Russian and committed to a program of independent Ukrainian nationalism. It was most definitely an ethnically targeted campaign, focused on creating a solid block of votes for the Russian-supported candidate. In addition, fake leaflets and pamphlets were produced, supporting the anti-Russian campaign against Yushchenko. Extreme Ukrainian nationalists were even paid to claim they supported him.

In the final weeks of the campaign, huge amounts—over three hundred million items—of illegal campaign materials with anti-American and anti-Yushchenko themes were prepared, including posters featuring photographs of President Bush and illustrations of the American flag. There was little doubt that the campaign was being positioned by the Russian technologists as a pro-Russia versus pro-U.S. event. The posters, printed by Novyi Druk in Kiev as well as by printers in Slovakia and Hungary, were recovered from a privately leased warehouse. Another five million posters and leaflets were recovered from Novyi Druk itself. The origins of the posters became clear when Novyi Druk's owner was found to be the son of a former Kuchma regime foreign minister who was now acting as head of the People's Democratic Party and also serving as coordinator for all the anti-opposition parties. The anti-Yushchenko materials located in multiple locations were valued far in excess of the two million Ukrainian dollars required by campaign law. The actual estimated cost for them alone was in the millions, not to mention the quantities already distributed across the nation.

Perhaps the most interesting element of the Ukrainian election campaign is that while several of the Russian political technologists and their internet-savvy firms—such as the premier Russian government public-relations consultant Gleb Pavlovsky and the Foundation for Effective Politics[38]—were closely linked to Putin, it appears that they were being paid by and acting for Ukrainian political figures and parties. Evidence has emerged that Russian authorities were being advised of the actions, even though they were not the driving force involved with them. It also appears, and Kuzio concludes, that the leadership in Russia (including Putin) simply did not appreciate that anything had changed since the elections of 1994 and onward, which had installed successive pro-Russian regimes. In that same vein, traditional attitudes that the political leadership of Ukraine and Russia were intimately linked meant to Putin and Russia that the involvement of Russian political technologists was not truly outside interference, any more than Putin's highly public participation.

Perhaps the preliminary election should have been a warning. Even though there were other candidates, the campaign itself had been intentionally set up as a vote of confidence for the establishment, pro-Russian candidate Yanukovych. Yet the first round of voting came out with opposition candidate Yushchenko in the lead. The election technologists reportedly reassured both Moscow and Putin that there was no cause for concern—early second round results appeared to give Yanukovych the victory.

The official election committee declared Yanukovych the winner and, just as in Georgia, disbelieving crowds took to the streets claiming that the count had been rigged by the pro-Russian political establishment. The crowds grew, Kiev was in turmoil and as in Georgia there was no military response to force a new government into place. Once again Russia sent a political representative to talks, this time to lobby for Kuchma to stand firm and force a Yanukovych government into place, supporting it with whatever security measures were required. Still, given the results of the first vote, there was substantial popular opposition to Yanukovych.

Whether emotion and nationalism—or a flood of Western NGO dollars—kept the crowds in the streets will continue to be debated. Certainly Moscow viewed it all as yet another democracy movement conspiracy financed by the United States. Putin firmly took that position, publicly declaring on numerous occasions, including in animated statements given during a meeting at The Hague with European leaders, that the United States had orchestrated regime change in Ukraine. He protested that it had been a political warfare action from the very beginning.[39]

The one thing known for sure is that the dialogue in Kiev turned to nothing more than a demand for yet another election. Following a meeting between Kuchma and Putin, a statement was issued calling for the earlier results to be declared void and a new election to be held. New polling measures were introduced, in particular changes that made vote falsification more difficult. In the election that followed, opposition party candidate Viktor Yushchenko defeated Russia's choice Viktor Yanukovych by close to six percent. Moscow was stunned, and its political advisors took the stance that they could not possibly have misread the Ukrainian public so badly, that the ultimate shaping of the election as a pro-Russian contest could not possibly have been a mistake. It must have been a massive and cunning intervention by the NGOs, fronting for the Americans. And this time it was most definitely an affront to Russian sovereignty.

Strangely, despite the political angst in Moscow, for the next several years the new Ukrainian government took no dramatic moves to isolate itself from Russia or to abort the strategic technical and construction support that its industries provided to the Russian military. Yet by all accounts the Russian leadership truly began to consider Russian sovereignty to be at risk, with Moscow unable to maintain the longtime influence that had carried on even past the fragmentation of the Soviet Union. Perhaps it was simply too much change all at once. But at almost the same time as the final vote in the Ukraine, yet another former Soviet client state, small and not at all strategic, embarrassed President Putin with its voting.

ABKHAZIA: 2004

As with Ukraine during the Soviet era and even in following years, Abkhazia had a long habit of simply installing whatever local leader was sanctioned by Moscow. And in 2004, Putin and Moscow endorsed the head of the local state security service, Raul Khajimba. Putin even took time to visit while on a trip to his favorite resort at Sochi, the future Olympics venue. This was convenient since Abkhazia is just next door. In a further show of great efficiency, President Putin maximized his time by appearing on television with both Khajimba and Ukraine's sanctioned candidate Viktor Yanukovych, where he expressed support for both pro-Russian candidates.

Abkhazian statehood was a standing issue; it had proclaimed independence from Georgia, which had been unable to control it. In that context Russia was not unhappy about its independence, at least to the extent that it remained under Russian political influence. Political officers from the FSB cemented Putin's endorsement by traveling to Abkhazia in support of Khajimba, by going on television to endorse him, and by informing voters that "they should thank Russia for its support"—apparently by voting for the Russian candidate.[40] While consistent with the Russian political approach in Ukraine, the technique was a bit heavy-handed for the Abkhazians. They voted solidly against Khajimba, electing Sergei Bagapsh, a former Communist Party secretary and currently the head of a local energy company.

On his first state visit to Russia, President Bagapsh and his followers were reportedly severely chastised. Shortly afterward, Russia stopped purchasing Abkhazian oranges—its only export and sole source of any real income. While seemingly minor, that economic pressure appears to represent the first real pushback from Russia in regard to regime change in territories it considered within its natural sphere of influence. And it worked; Bagapsh was forced to call another election, with the agreement that if he again won he would have to appoint

Russia's pick, Raul Khajimba, as vice-president. That is exactly what happened. As will be seen, this tactic—combining economic leverage with political manipulation—was the first step in a new era of Russian political warfare.

KYRGYZSTAN: 2005

While there were no particular claims of NGO or Western involvement in Abkhazia, the same could not be said for yet another regime change, the expulsion of Askar Akayev in Kyrgyzstan following the 2005 election. Admittedly Kyrgyzstan is a small nation, a poor nation, and the Akayev regime had a reputation for large-scale corruption.[41] Of course that also could be said for several of the smaller, poorer Soviet-era republics. Russian concerns about Kyrgyzstan were fueled by the same fundamental scenario that had emerged out of the elections in Georgia in 2003.

Some individuals involved in that election, promoting election monitoring and training opposition leaders in nonviolent protest, were involved in the Kyrgyzstan campaign. In particular, representatives of the Liberty Institute of Georgia, who also worked with the opposition in the Ukraine.[42] Beyond that, funding from both the U.S. government and democracy initiative NGOs (National Democracy Institute, Freedom House, and the International Republican Institute) channeled to the government opposition parties allowed them to prepare flyers, leaflets, and other election materials they otherwise might not have been able to afford. American democracy initiative funding for activities in Kyrgyzstan during 2005 reportedly involved millions of dollars.[43]

As in Georgia, democracy initiative support also helped fund opposition newspapers such as *My Capital News*, allowed the creation and operation of "civil society centers" that served as meeting points for activists and government opposition groups, and even funded the purchase and operation of the country's first printing press (paid for by Liberty House) which was key in printing flyers and leaflets in large quantities for opposition party campaigns. Media reach included not only print but broadcasts by a new local Kyrgyz-language Radio Free Europe/Radio Liberty affiliate station, as well as political debates and talk shows (funded in part with U.S. democracy initiative grants), which were broadcast over the nation's independent television stations.[44]

The Organization for Security and Coordination in Europe also participated in monitoring the Kyrgyzstan voting, expressing criticism of the official totals which had pro-Akayev candidates well in the lead for virtually all parliamentary seats.[45] There were widespread reports of regime election suppression of the media. The country's single new printing press even had its electricity mysteriously cut just days before the initial election. The U.S. embassy provided two emergency generators to allow the press to keep running. Opposition candidates were also refused places on the ballot for highly questionable reasons. Matters did not improve before the final round of voting and only a handful of the opposition candidates were officially tallied to have gained seats.

In what was becoming an all too familiar pattern for Russian political sphere observers, street protests began in the capital of Bishkek and spread to other cities. A number of the opposition members in parliament supported a no-confidence vote. Within a week, cities were seeing protests ranging from three thousand to fifty thousand people. Many of the nation's southern cities were under opposition control—even while a great majority of parliament sided with Akayev, who in turn refused any sort of negotiation. President of Georgia Mikheil Saakashvili sent an official letter to President Akayev requesting that he exhibit "toleration" of the opposition parties and offered to personally mediate negotiations. Apparently viewing the offer as one more sign of attempted foreign intervention, Akayev made no response and stood firm on his position that his government supported the election results, was fully legal, and would remain in place.

In response, the leading opposition party members met and formed an opposition government. Adding to the confusion, the Kyrgyzstan Supreme Court ruled the pre-election parliament to still be officially in power but then officially recognized the opposition/ interim government. The interim government then announced new elections and ordered an investigation of election fraud. As in Georgia and Ukraine, the result was the creation of competing power centers and a confrontation between established and opposition regimes. The real question was whether or not Akayev would (or could) exercise the force required to remove the opposition.

He attempted to do so with riot police, and arrests were made. That was far from sufficient and Akayev fled with his family, first to neighboring Uzbekistan and then to Russia, where he was offered exile and submitted his official resignation. Akayev blamed all the controversy over the elections as well as the popular protest on Western agitators—essentially, it was all an American conspiracy. The sticking point with that claim was that, prior to the election, Akayev had been on very good terms with the United States, even allowing American access to an airbase outside the capital.[46]

In his absence there was mob violence, looting, and a number of deaths. At one point Akayev tried to reenter the country and inserted himself in the scheduled elections. In the end, an alliance of factions was established and stability returned, with certain of Akayev's former ministers still part of the interim government. Ultimately new elections were held, monitored by both the Western Balkan democracy initiative (OSCE) and the Russian Commonwealth of Independent States (CIS). The OSCE found improvement in the elections with some problems remaining; the CIS group endorsed them wholeheartedly. It had become clear that those supporting the established regimes and those supporting the new democracy initiatives were unlikely to agree on the subject of long-established election practices in the former Soviet states.

Perhaps the greatest irony related to the regime changes of 2003-05 is that popular elections and street protests came to be perceived as threats to Russian sovereignty. Decades earlier those events frequently opened a nation to Soviet political and economic influence. During the early years of the Cold War, the ousting of long-established regimes by democratic elections and street protests had become one of the key triggers for American political warfare. Even the possibility of popular election losses—as in Italy, Iran, Indonesia, and Chile—was enough to trigger pushback ranging from political action to hybrid warfare.

More than one American president, secretary of state, and national security advisor had taken the position that a popular election that put the wrong type of regime in place (whether communist, socialist, pro-Russian, or even neutral) represented a potential threat to America's national security. Beginning in 2005, the Russian leadership and President Putin moved to a similar view in the territories that were formerly part of the Soviet Union, especially those nations on their immediate borders. The new fears jelling in Moscow appeared to be confirmed by remarks from Washington, DC. In January 2005, President Bush said this in his second inaugural address: "It is the policy of the United States to seek and support the growth of democratic movements and institutions in every nation and culture, with the ultimate goal of ending tyranny in the world."[47] This initiative, known as the Bush Doctrine, may have been viewed in the White House as a strategy for dealing with global terror, choking it off at its source. However, in Moscow—which a former U.S. president had declared to be the heart of the "evil empire"—it was viewed quite differently.

The author recalls being on a street in London that year and encountering American tourists wearing "Got Democracy?" T-shirts. That seemed strange enough in England, but in Moscow it could understandably be seen as a challenge. Matters were made worse during

Bush's visit to Russia when the U.S. diplomatic party reportedly made it clear that Russia had no right to interfere in the political affairs of other nations, even those traditionally within their sphere of influence such as Georgia and Ukraine.

It was even more troubling that upon his departure, Bush and party visited Ukraine, where the president hailed the nation as a "beacon of liberty" throughout the former Soviet Union and around the world. Following the visit, a major thoroughfare in Kiev was renamed for President Bush.[48] It had been bad enough for those in Moscow who had come out of the USSR to see Russian statues tumble in its former republics; to see a street in the Ukraine named for an American president was a troubling omen indeed. And within a year, in 2006, U.S. Vice President Dick Cheney was in Vilnius to deliver a keynote address on freedom, democracy, and the rejection of (Russian) autocracy, before flying on to Kazakhstan for oil talks. Leading Russian political figures such as Vladislav Surkov would begin to speak openly about the perceived threat and the fundamental issue: "In 2008 we will either preserve our sovereignty or be ruled externally."[49]

It had taken the United States some six years to move into ongoing Cold War political warfare, from political action in Italy in 1948 to hybrid warfare using surrogates in Guatemala by 1954. Russia was going to follow the same path, adopting the same practices, and adding new tools. But Russia moved more slowly, at least from its perspective. After all, Putin did not consider Russian involvement in politics in the Ukraine to be intervention, it was simply the way things had been done.

Chapter Eleven:
Pushing Back

History demonstrates that the combination of democracy with truly open elections can be inherently destabilizing; it not only enables regime change but mandates that those in power accept the change without interfering with or opposing the process. The regime changes in the former Soviet republics were of particular concern to Moscow not simply because they appeared to be undermining traditional Russian sovereignty but because the elections themselves had become entangled with large, popular protests. And it appeared that both popular opposition to established regimes and a move towards large-scale protests of contested election results were increasingly enabled by something once considered anathema—open and essentially uncontrolled public communications.

One of the most fundamental aspects of life in the former Soviet Union had been the total control of communications by communist regimes. Speeches by leaders such as Lenin and Stalin had made it clear that in a communist society the media were to be used to "mobilize the masses, not inform them." Stalin had been quick to describe the press as simply a tool for the party—a "collective organizer."[1] Russian leaders were well schooled in the power of media as an organizing force for change.

Soviet-era domestic media control had been systematic and extremely thorough. When the United States began radio broadcasts into its territories, Russia responded by deploying 350 jamming stations in 1948. By 1955 there were 1,000 inside Russia and another 700 across Eastern Europe. The jamming effort also became a fundamental part of domestic media control. By 1986 the Soviet Union had 13 extremely powerful jamming stations operating across Russia with local jammers operating in eighty-one Russian cities, a total effort of over 1,300 radio jamming stations blocking Western broadcasts from no more than seventy transmitters.[2]

Radio sets produced in Russia had certain frequencies blocked and up until 1962 had to be individually registered. Possession of a radio capable of receiving the banned frequencies was a criminal offense. The number of international telephone lines into Russia was stringently limited and access-controlled. As late as 1972 the KGB had a law passed making it illegal to use international telephone lines in any fashion that might undermine public order. During 1973-74 more than a hundred international lines were simply shut down in enforcing that order.

Fully open, democratic elections with independent vote monitoring, uncontrolled media reporting, and real-time communications outside the governing regime's control were simply not part of the communist system political calculus, at least in nations previously under Communist Party control. The appearance of independent domestic media, radio, television, even the appearance of an opposition party printing press in Kyrgyzstan—appeared to have significantly changed the dynamic of politics in the new republics. Worse yet from the Russian perspective, in several instances the independent media outlets, even the printing press in Kyrgyzstan, had been funded and supported with personnel trained by the democracy initiative NGOs. The NGOs and even the American government were very open about their involvement, as early as the 1990s USAID listed democracy as one of its four main goals, significantly increasing aid for the open elections in response to congressional passage of the Support for East European Democracy Act and the Freedom Support Act (specifically dealing with the former Soviet Union).[3] It is easy enough to understand that the activities of NGOs formed and focused on totally open and democratic practices would almost certainly be regarded with suspicion by a Russian leadership whose world view had been formed within the Soviet Union, and in many instances by individuals trained and professionally developed within its security services.

Yet as of 2006 the Russian response to what it perceived as a very real Western challenge to its sovereignty was both measured and limited, with a primary focus on Europe rather than the United States. There were no new walls, no Iron Curtain, and Russia remained engaged both economically and politically with both Europe and the United States. President Putin and his chief economic advisor Igor Shuvalov asserted themselves within the G8 intergovernmental political forum (the Russian Federation had obtained a seat in 1997), the World Trade Organization, and the European Union—focusing on Russia's strategic position in providing natural gas to Europe and emphasizing the concept of energy security for Europe. At the same time, overall business contacts with the West expanded significantly. Russia's economy was well into its energy boom, producing money for a surge in consumer spending and foreign investment.

It seemed a rather untraditional approach to Russian foreign relations, more in the form of positive shaping, using a mix of personal and economic messages and with President Putin himself playing point. Of course, Putin's personal control over the major Russian energy companies—such as Gazprom, with majority ownership by the Russian government—provided considerable economic leverage in deal-making with European leaders, including Italian Prime Minister Silvio Berlusconi and German Chancellor Gerhard Schröder. But to a large extent it involved a Putin "charm initiative" similar to the Russian effort in the Ukrainian elections. Russian political action was largely being conducted by Putin himself, with aides and the Russian media following his lead.

Election activities in Ukraine had been a leading indicator of how foreign policy decision-making and official media messaging were going to be conducted in the new Russia. President Putin had personally expressed Russia's political desires, making himself extraordinarily visible in his public and very personal endorsements of preferred candidates. And in contrast to the need for covert planting of information in media outlets that was common practice for both American and Soviet political action during the Cold War, by 2004-05, the messaging of Russia's own domestic media outlets had been largely brought back under centralized regime control.

In 2001 the major Russian television channels, Channel One Russia (eighty-three percent viewership) and Russia-1 (seventy-five percent viewership), became state-owned and controlled. Russia-1 broadcasts in a number of languages with regional variations on programming and news. The director of the state channels as well as other state media outlets is appointed through presidential decree. Standard state broadcast media practices began to include weekly coordination meetings between the presidential administration and the editors and directors of the major media outlets. Those meetings served as briefs to ensure that the appropriate events and announcements of the coming week received prominent coverage. As of 2015, editorial content reportedly included the provision of lists for journalists of subjects to be avoided, such as domestic protests and coverage of Russian covert activities in the Donbass region of Ukraine. Regime-directed news influence is encouraged not only by state funding for the media but by the fact that the governing regimes oligarchic supporters comprise the major corporate advertising base for the media.[4] This appears to be a highly efficient media management strategy, integrating both state and corporate control over media messaging and creating a dual form of state/corporate media control via advertising revenues.

Putin, much as Joseph Stalin who was quoted earlier, had always been very open about his view of the media and the changes he instituted in order to direct its messages. For him the media is an asset of the state and it should serve the interests of the public though the regime in power: "There should be patriotically minded people at the head of state information resources," he told reporters at his 2013 annual news conference, "people who uphold the interests of the Russian Federation. These are state resources. That is the way it is going to be." Beyond the state-controlled media Putin fully expected that the owners of the "independent" outlets would be personally responsible for the content and editorial slant of their news. One of the major independent radio station figures, Alexei Venediktov, editor in chief of *Echo of Moscow*, described Putin's comments on that subject: "Here's an owner, they have their own politics, and for them it's an instrument. The government also is an owner and the media that belong to the government must carry out our instructions."[5]

The history of how the post-Soviet independent media evolved into a regime-controlled system is complex and evolutionary. Fortunately the story has been told by a number of Russian reporters and media specialists who experienced it firsthand, and their insights are available to interested readers. Investigative reporters Andrei Soldatov and Irina Borogan, working first inside the traditional Russian media and then with new internet news venues, provide key insights on the Putin-era transition and its extension into internet news and even social media in *The Red Web: The Kremlin's Wars on the Internet*.

Their research involved personal interviews with many chief media figures, editors, and news directors who personally experienced the transition. In one example, as early as 2001, two key figures from the Putin regime, Vladislav Surkov and Alexei Gromov, met with one of the nation's leading media groups, NTV, and delivered very specific regime demands in regard to the coverage of the Chechen conflict, a political scandal, and even a satirical news program, which focused on

Russian political figures. NTV's response was apparently not viewed as enthusiastic enough and within three months one of its newspapers was closed. Another news weekly's staff was simply "ejected from their offices" and NTV journalists working for its TV outlets were "thrown out" of their building.[6] Ultimately NTV was brought under control simply by arranging for one of Putin's affluent political supporters to acquire ownership. By 2004 both Russian state and independent print and television media were either under direct government control or owned by oligarchs supportive of Putin.

Media control and consistent messaging were very important to President Putin, especially as he began an effort in 2005 to convince Western European nations that Russia should be treated as a key strategic partner, vital to their own interests, and not as a target for their democracy initiatives and NGOs. Putin's new political influence program was based in a Russian energy strategy, the promise of "energy security" for natural gas to Europe. Given that Europe was forecast to be totally dependent on Russian gas supplies by 2010, the strategy offered Putin what appeared to be enormous leverage. As part of it he proposed new pipelines which would ensure distribution throughout Europe, thereby making state-owned Gazprom the owner of the largest gas distribution network in the world.

At the same time Putin was pursuing this new political outreach to Europe, the "carrot" for Europe was accompanied by a "stick" for Ukraine. It was all very public, communicated strictly in business terms. During the 1990s there had been occasions when Ukraine could not meet its full gas payments to Gazprom, and there had been brief delivery interruptions as a consequence. The new regime in Ukraine wanted to reset business agreements with Gazprom, seeking new financial arrangements and an agreement for future deliveries. As part of the new agreement Gazprom was to give a loan to the Ukrainian gas company that would settle past debts and establish a basis for deliveries through 2009. The agreement included a barter arrangement in which

Ukraine provided transit rights for deliveries to Europe. However, during the course of negotiations the government of Turkmenistan, a strong ally of the Putin regime, raised the price of its gas and also insisted that any sales to Ukraine be agreed upon by the Russian government.[7]

During 2005, a number of issues arose between Ukraine and Gazprom with the result that the negotiations and prior agreement entered a state of flux and clearly would have to be renegotiated. As 2005 was ending matters were further complicated by Gazprom's purchase of all the gas supplies from Turkmenistan, leaving none available for the existing contract between Ukraine and that country. In December 2005, Ukraine sent a negotiating team to Moscow and President Putin himself took the lead in the negotiations. Ostensibly it was all going to be just business, however it was clearly about more than that. To properly position the dialogue, Putin made a highly public speech in which he stated that he would no longer allow the "orange revolutionaries" to rob the Russian people.[8]

In the actual meeting the Ukrainians were told that gas prices would be substantially increased, at best they might receive a ninety-day support period, but long-term they would be paying European prices. Putin followed up the meeting with a state television broadcast, announcing the increase. Following this appearance Russian television reported that Gazprom might have to cease sales to Ukraine at the end of the year if the Ukrainians did not immediately accept the new terms.

The implication was that if Russia cut off Ukraine's total volume in mid-winter, Ukraine would face an energy crisis that would force it to violate transmittal agreements and take gas out of the pipeline which had been destined for Europe. It was a well-coordinated psychological warfare move. At the same time European customers were sent warning advisories that deliveries would very likely be affected if Ukraine failed to immediately accept the Gazprom terms. And at the end of the year that is exactly what happened, with European customers reporting shortfalls in deliveries ranging from twenty-five to forty percent during January 1-3. With no options at all, on January 4 Ukraine accepted the Gazprom terms. Deliveries resumed and by January 10 the Ukrainian government was dismissed in a no-confidence parliamentary vote. President Yushchenko's governance had been seriously undermined in the process. At the time, energy industry commentaries struggled to be objective about the Russian moves with Gazprom pricing, but it was impossible to avoid the fact that Ukraine had been shifted to a higher pricing schedule, at European levels, to a far greater extent than the pricing extended to openly pro-Russian regimes.

It was also noted that if the Russian-supported candidate had won in the 2004 election, it was difficult to believe that Putin would have acted so arbitrarily and with such dramatic deadlines. Global industry organizations such as the International Energy Agency went on record as stating that the Russian action had been damaging to its reputation as a reliable supplier of energy to Europe. [9]

Putin's energy initiative had captured Europe's attention, and if the Russian/Gazprom ultimatum had been intended to simply highlight the issue of energy security for Europe, it had done that. If it had been intended as economic warfare to destabilize the Yushchenko presidency, it had done that as well. But it had done much more, truly shocking Western Europe and most definitely undermining the personal confidence campaign President Putin had been conducting there.

During the following months of 2006, Russian political action would involve less charm and a great deal more of what we have come to understand as active measures. President Putin was moving into a far more confrontational mode, not yet actively pushing back in the political warfare sense, but making it clear that Russia was prepared to do just that. The first evidence of this became clear when U.S. Secretary of State Condoleezza Rice was kept waiting for hours for a scheduled meeting in 2006, followed by heated personal arguments about Russian actions in Georgia. Then there was Putin's heated attack on Bush administration foreign policies in a speech at the Munich Security Conference in 2007: "One state and of course, first and foremost, the United States, has overstepped its national borders in every way. This is visible in the economic, political, cultural and educational policies it imposed on other nations. Well who likes this? Who is happy about this?"[10]

Yet even in what was an increasingly confrontational context, other than maintaining SVR active measures programs inside the United States and increasing FSB monitoring of foreign business and NGO activities inside Russia, no covert political warfare would be conducted against America for a number of years. In fact, it would not be until first in 2012 and then in 2014 that Russia instituted laws that officially required NGOs financed from outside Russia and engaging in any activities related to politics to register as "foreign agents."[11] In comparison, the United States had a long history of "foreign agent" registration and as of 2007 some 1,700 individuals were officially registered as representing 100 foreign countries. In spite of the increasing discord between Moscow and Washington, Russia continued to encourage foreign business connections during the Bush and Obama administrations. Business sectors that were especially active included energy and investments.[12]

Yet while Russia showed a level of restraint towards any direct political warfare pushback that directly targeted the United States, its response to perceived domestic and regional sovereignty threats was something far different. Beginning in 2006, Moscow embarked on a campaign of regional political warfare that evolved into something that many of those in the West, including the United States, still cannot fathom. The new Russian initiatives would involve direct military engagement, deniable surrogate warfare, and a series of extensive destabilization and information warfare measures. It would be conducted in tandem with a huge military rearmament program and large-scale military intimidation operations—all of which seemed excessive and certainly beyond the scope of any direct threat to the Russian nation.

A variety of explanations have been offered as to why this twenty-first century Russian behavior would so closely mirror that of the United States in the earliest years of the Cold War. Much of that analysis has focused almost entirely on the personality and political career of Vladimir Putin. Yet while Putin himself bears direct responsibility for many of the specific political warfare decisions, it is also clear that he was able to channel a deep stream of Russian fears and concerns. As early as 2002, almost half of the Russians surveyed by the Pew Research Center expressed unfavorable views of the United States.[13] That level of concern remained constant though 2013, suggesting that there was a considerable base of support for government actions which would assert Russian national prerogatives, especially against Western and specifically American influence. The focus groups conducted in conjunction with polling also determined that the complaints were not so much about Americans as individuals. They were a backlash against what was perceived as United States government arrogance in "meddling" in the internal political affairs of other nations, by funding both foreign and domestic organizations involved in the elections of those nations.[14]

The focus groups also revealed that those negative comments were increasingly a direct repetition of President Putin's own public remarks, which were continually repeated in an extremely aggressive Russian media campaign beginning in 2006. The message was repeated by his successor Dimitry Medvedev and continued with Putin's return to the Russian presidency. It was a domestic propaganda drumbeat—containing sufficient examples to make it credible—which maintained and reinforced the perception of covert American political action for over a decade. In many ways it was as intense as, and possibly even more effective than, the anti-Communist, anti-Soviet media warfare that the CIA orchestrated during the first decades of the Cold War.

Niccolò Machiavelli would have fully appreciated both the need for and the probable success of such a campaign, having advised in his earliest writings that one of a ruler's primary concerns always involves ensuring that no foreigner should be allowed to gain a footing within a realm—especially as "it will always happen that such a one will be introduced by those who are discontented."[15]

A good deal of the success in messaging Russian government concerns over covert foreign intrusion inside both Russia and the new independent republics was due to the increased reach of the state-supported international television network RT (formerly Russian Today). RT operates cable and satellite channels and reaches a considerable audience outside Russia, broadcasting in a variety of languages. It receives funding from the Russian government and is evaluated through ratings and viewership as well as tasked with certain forms of government messaging. In 2008 an autonomous, non-profit RT business entity was established to help disassociate its American outlet, RT America, from Russian government sponsorship. That allowed RT America to avoid registering under the Foreign Agents Registration Act.[16]

While there are disagreements about RT America's actual television viewership in the United States, it is clear that—for a time at least—its YouTube viewership came to significantly exceed not only alternative news outlets such as the BBC but also CNN and CNN/International. RT also proved to be a major vehicle for extending the warnings about American political intervention globally. Its international media network was expanded to the point where it could reach 600 million viewers worldwide, in multiple languages. Satellite technology and the internet had given Russian messaging a reach that simply had never been available during the Cold War.

The broader Russian media story as it relates to political warfare practices is one we will defer until later, a decade later when full-scale information warfare came into play. As of 2005-06 it was simply one of the outlets used by President Putin in warning the world that Western pro-democracy aid efforts were subversive, and as far as his nation was concerned, actually anti-Russian. As a political device, Putin's highly vocal assertions of Western political meddling also helped minimize the rather dramatic failure of his own personal involvement in the Ukrainian elections of 2004. But warnings alone were not going to stabilize Russia's borders with Georgia, or assert Russian economic sovereignty among those newly independent republics, which only a few years previously had been part of the Soviet Union, with their economies, trade, and politics under direct influence from Moscow.

Russia had always been a major market for those regions and economic leverage was the first tool for reasserting Soviet influence. The first sign of that approach had been the Russian embargo of mandarin oranges from Abkhazia in 2004. While it escaped world attention, the oranges were that small state's only export and the almost immediate result was a compromise leading to new elections and a place in the nation's government for the preferred Russian candidate. The much more dramatic embargo of gas shipments to Ukraine had gotten the world's attention and clearly demonstrated to Ukraine that it ignored Russia at its own risk. The fact that President Putin was willing to essentially sacrifice his energy security initiative with Western Europe to make that point with Ukraine firmly established that Russian interests would be asserted—without over concern as to consequences or Western opinions. In that same vein, during 2006 Russia also employed economic sanctions against both Georgia and Moldavia, banning imports of wine and mineral water (wine being a particularly critical Georgian export). All Georgian migrant workers in Russia were expelled without warning and commercial air connections to the capital of Tbilisi were suspended.

There was little doubt that Russia was prepared to exercise its economic clout with the independent republics, however beginning in early 2007 a new element was introduced, combining propaganda with an outreach of a decidedly cultural element. Estonian nationalists triggered the incident with a relatively minor protest concerning a monument to the Red Army. Russian-speaking Estonians objected and were incited by Russian media accusations that the government of Estonia was "fascist." It was a line first introduced in the 2004 Ukrainian elections, an appeal to the cultural ties of Russian speakers and their debt of gratitude to the Russian Army.

Accusations of Estonia and Latvia violating the rights of its Russian-speaking minorities were also brought into play, with Putin beginning to speak of the leaders of those nations as "henchmen" of the Nazis.[17] In response, activist Russians laid siege to the Estonian embassy in Moscow, receiving public praise and expressions of pride from the Russian defense minister for their patriotism.[18] At the time it might have seemed a minor incident, in the longer term it indicated a new tactic—the use of volunteers to insulate the Russian government from illegal and potentially embarrassing actions. It was certainly not a new form of deniability, but it would prove to be exceptionally effective for the regimes in Moscow, especially later as it began to move off the streets and onto the internet.

Moscow's assertiveness and Putin's projection of a renewed Russian power focused significant international attention on both. It was becoming clearer that Putin was going to demand stability at virtually any cost. Stability over democracy, over free speech, and before freedom. Those points were so clear that they are quoted from *Time* magazine's designation of Putin as their Man of the Year for 2007. *Time* made it clear that Putin had not been selected for his finer qualities, not for principals or for ideals, but because he "brought Russia back to the table of world power."[19] *Time* was correct, and the following year Putin's interim successor as president, Dmitry Medvedev, would demonstrate that in a most direct fashion, adding overt military intimidation to the Russia's evolving projection of power.

As of 2007, Russia remained focused on the projection of power along its borders. The independent republics of Ukraine and Georgia were viewed as outstanding challenges for a number of reasons, beginning with the basic concern that candidates promoted by Russia were not leading either government. From the Russian perspective both nations also appeared to be flaunting their independence through increasing political dialogue with the West, each even exploring the possibility of joining NATO (the North Atlantic Treaty Alliance). Earlier, and for some years immediately following the collapse of the Soviet Union, Russia itself had seemed to be on a track towards increased mutual cooperation with NATO, with the possibility of actual membership.

In 1991 Russia had joined the North Atlantic Cooperation Council, and by 2002 consultations began to be carried out under a newly established NATO-Russian Council (NRC).[20] With both Russia and the NATO countries involved with increasing terrorist threats, there seemed to be a solid basis for cooperation. However, the political upsets of 2004, combined with increasing mistrust of Western democratic NGOs, soured the overall relationship with Western Europe and with NATO. Events of 2008 were going to demonstrate that Russia preferred to conduct its own military initiatives, and within a few more years Russia would begin actively demonstrating its military power in shows of force to NATO nations rather than discussing points of mutual defense.

The mistrust that ended in full-scale combat between the Russian and Georgian militaries had its roots in long-standing, unresolved territorial disputes relating to Russian-speaking enclaves in South Ossetia and Abkhazia. By 2008 those disputes led to open fighting. Reportedly the personal relations between Georgian President Mikhail Saakashvili and the new Russian President Dmitry Medvedev did nothing to moderate the relationship between the two nations.

Beyond that, the personal relationship between Saakashvili and new Russian Premier Vladimir Putin was "glacial." Yet when Saakashvili called Moscow over the two nations' foreign relations, he was connected to Putin.[21] It also appears that Saakashvili may have badly misjudged the possibility of NATO membership and the extent to which Western outreach would do more than irritate his Russian neighbor. In later years, he stated that he was assured by U.S. leaders that Russia would not respond to his threats of forcing a settlement. However, Secretary of State Condoleezza Rice has written that he was absolutely warned not to use force.[22] The entire dispute was exacerbated by actions of the Russian separatists, who began shelling villages in Georgia.

The upshot of the matter was that Saakashvili dropped out of the negotiations with Russia and sent peacekeeping forces to stop the separatist shelling. In turn Russia responded with its own "peacekeeping force" (there is evidence that Russian armored groups were already deployed inside the disputed region) and the end result was full-scale combat involving Russian air, land, and naval forces. There was no NATO or Western military support for Georgia. An estimated forty thousand Russian troops deployed and over little more than five days the Georgian military was soundly defeated. The full story of that conflict, who did what to whom—and the Western sanctions which it provoked—are not our focus here. Ultimately Russia did not annex the disputed territory, the regions were recognized as independent (although strongly pro-Russian), and within two years diplomatic and even trade relationships between Georgia and Russia had largely stabilized.

What is important about the 2008 confrontation, in terms of political warfare, is that Russia had once again leveraged cultural and language ties (as it had first in Ukraine in 2004, then in Latvia and Estonia in 2007) to encourage the separatists, and they had served as deniable surrogates, engaging in military provocations against Georgia, which led the Georgian leadership into military combat with far superior Russian forces. The end result was the creation of two pro-Russian independent regions and the demonstration of both Russian political and military sovereignty. President Medvedev personally took advantage of the confrontation in Georgia to emphasize the fact of Russian sovereignty to the rest of the world: "Russia, like other countries in the world, has regions where it has privileged interests. These are regions where countries with which we have friendly relations are located." When asked if such sovereignty applied only to Russian border regions, he stressed that Russian sovereignty was a broader matter than simply that of its "border regions."[23]

If that viewpoint sounds somewhat familiar, it should, we have indeed seen it before as an American practice. Supporting separatist enclaves was an American strategy in Indonesia, it was most definitely a consideration in landing the Cuban exile brigade at the Bay of Pigs in Cuba, and later there would be attempts to establish enclaves that would house an opposition government in Nicaragua. That effort involved two major Contra incursions into Nicaragua, but in neither case did popular support allow the enclaves to be held. Once again, now in the twenty-first century, Russia was beginning to mirror American Cold War practices. From a purely pragmatic standpoint it was doing so much more successfully.

The new push against foreign meddling was not something restricted to Russia's borders. The color revolutions had been at least partially enabled though relatively new and independent means of communications. While government control of the traditional media inside Russia had removed much of that risk, new technologies and new venues of communications had emerged. Cellular telephones, wireless networking, and the global internet had all come to Russia in a very big way. In fact, by 2008, print and broadcast media in Russia, as in the rest of the world, was beginning to suffer stiff competition from the internet. Investigative reporters were forced out of the establishment media and turning to blogs, to websites, to Facebook and YouTube—and their Russian social media equivalents (LiveJournal, VKontakte, and Odnoklassniki).[24]

Russian internal security services became concerned with domestic control of news and social media communications on the internet as early as 2002, when the FSB realized that the internet might be more than a threat: it might represent an untapped opportunity. Its potential as a tool for deniable political warfare was brought to the attention of the FSB by a group of pro-government students in the Siberian city of Tomsk. Apparently on their own patriotic initiative, the students launched a simple, brute-force "denial of service" (DNS) attack against a rebel website in Chechnya. The group continued its attacks over some three years, even contacting websites in the United States and Canada with protests about their hosting the rebel content. The students' action in support of the Russian intervention in Chechnya was well known to the FSB, which issued a public statement defending their activities as being within their rights as citizens and worthy of public respect.[25]

Later, in 2005, a Russian internet forum (Informacia.ru) began to acquire a considerable population of activist, anti-Western visitors, all upset with the Chechen protest messaging and even terrorist threats they were seeing on certain internet sites. The visitors were not themselves proficient in web techniques, certainly not what we think of as hackers. However they could and did organize, setting up their own website anti-center.org ("Civilian Anti-Terror") and offering a contract for a web tool that would let them shut down targeted websites.[26] That offer brought them a relatively simple, brute-force program capable of DNS attacks, a tool which could be used to literally overwhelm a targeted website with bursts of traffic, shutting it down for periods of time. During 2005, anti-center.org claimed some twenty-five successful DNS attacks, primarily against Chechen independence groups. The site even offered a downloadable file of the attack software. The new volunteer project did not go unnoticed by the FSB, which began to take a clear interest in "patriotic hackers." [27]

For the next two years the hackers organized themselves around websites such as meadiactivist.ru and, later, peace4peace.com, continuing to target Chechen insurgency sites and forcing those sites to be relocated to foreign servers, from a host in Sweden to one Georgia in 2006 and, following ongoing attacks, to a host in Estonia in 2008. Russian surrogate protests against Estonia were mentioned earlier, in 2008 those same physical protests were carried to the internet in simple but massive DNS attacks against Estonian banks, newspapers, broadcasters, and government websites.[28]

Some of the attacks were relatively sophisticated, others were simple and brute-force DNS assaults, carried out over some three weeks. They had an exceptionally serious impact due to the fact that as a nation Estonia had some of the most extensive internet access in all of Europe. Because of their severity, Estonia had to essentially turn off internet services for a period of time. Investigations revealed that the attacks had involved experienced hackers who had written malicious programs ("bot nets capable of automated operations") as well as relative novices who were simply following instructions posted on hacker websites.

The sheer variety of attackers had made the assault extremely difficult to cope with and track; suspicion of some type of Russian involvement was also suggested by the large numbers of computers that started and stopped attacks in a timed sequence, suggesting that rented machines were used to provide deniability.[29] In one instance an attacker was determined to be a Russian student living in Estonia and using his laptop for one series of target site attacks. His motivation was purely political, inspired by Russian media calls for protest action against Estonia.[30] The attacks were an early warning that proving the origins of internet political warfare was going to be exceptionally difficult, with the attack service requests and commands being sent via false requests for information, through multiple web servers, and hidden under many layers of redirected commands (addressing metadata). In short, it was virtually the ultimate in absolute deniability, at least in terms of legal proof.

A year later, Lithuania came under official Russian protest for actions denigrating Russian cultural values by banning public display of both Nazi and Soviet symbols. Almost immediately the websites of some three hundred Lithuanian government and businesses had their homepages overwritten with the flag of the Soviet Union as well as a variety of protest slogans. It was the type of attack well within the capabilities of moderately experienced hackers, again aided by the availability of instructions and programs posted on websites routinely visited by hacker novices (so called "script kiddies"). It was becoming clear that there was indeed a growing population of Russian patriotic hackers of various levels of sophistication, and a number of websites catering to them with training aids and actual attack code.

There is no doubt that the Russian government, both within the FSB and the military services (GRU/military intelligence), had access to extremely competent cyberwarfare specialists. Yet those specialists appear not to have joined in these sorts of attacks. What did happen was a Russian government initiative to persuade and assist "patriotic youth" in combating anti-Russian material being distributed on the Internet. By 2009 the Kremlin even began to host a school for bloggers headed by Alexei Chadayev, one of the senior political "technologists" and an associate of the individuals directly involved in developing messaging campaigns during the first Putin presidency.[31]

It was a brilliant move in deniability, one recognizing the potential of the anonymity inherent in internet messaging. During the Cold War the CIA had gone to immense expense establishing deniable, surrogate radio stations, trusted media outlets, and the deep cut-outs who would distribute information through print media. It had all been bureaucratic, operationally complex, and constantly open to public exposure. By 2010 the internet offered a viewing reach exponentially beyond any of those methods. And with the use of patriotic volunteers it offered the prospect of information warfare at minimal cost and with maximum deniability.

All of this takes us to the third presidency of Vladimir Putin in 2012. Initially there was some hope of a "restart" of the Russian/

American relationship, with President Barack Obama lifting trade restrictions put in place by President Gerald Ford in 1974. However, the law that lifted general trade restrictions contained specific sanctions related to the Russian persecution of journalists who had exposed excessive endemic corruption. The sanctions were imposed in recognition of basic Russian human rights violations. The related legislation is referred to as the Magnitsky Act, named for a Russian tax accountant turned citizen investigator who died in abysmal prison conditions.[32]

The Magnitsky Act was particularly irritating to President Putin and to a good number of his most affluent supporters, mostly because it involved a freeze on certain assets in Western banks and real estate. It also banned their entry into the United States. The individuals named were primarily oligarchs, investment and banking figures and others who had indeed made immense profits moving money outside Russia. For Putin himself, one particularly annoying aspect of the law was that it publicized the extent of corruption and theft of public assets that had been occurring in Russia, especially under his predecessor Dmitry Medvedev. Over time the Russian leadership and Russian lobbyists began to cloud the nature of the Magnitsky sanctions by associating them with agreements for the adoption of Russian children. In reality the Magnitsky Act sanctions have nothing to do with adoptions other than the fact that Russia had made them the subject of a retaliatory sanction against the United States.

While President Medvedev had spoken strongly about Russian sovereignty, President Putin made it clear that there was something even more fundamental at play. He described a fundamental cultural conflict between Russia and the West. It was not ideological—after all, Russia was now a capitalist nation—but something perhaps even deeper than political beliefs: "Do not harbor any illusions…we are not like you. We only look like you. But we are very different. Russians and Americans resemble each other physically but inside we have very different values."[33] One of Putin's advisors expounded on that difference, even relating it to Putin's Russian Orthodox religious beliefs and the essential Russian conservative agenda, which also involved defending the stability of other nations and peoples.

Sovereignty and stability were the new Russian watchwords. Putin's remarks certainly could have been interpreted as a warning, and in political warfare terms the response would quickly become clear. Anything that appeared to destabilize Russian sovereignty was going to bring about retaliation in a similar form. Destabilization would draw exactly the same response from Russia. In even simpler terms—and to match contemporary headlines—meddle with us and we will meddle with you. Given that Putin and the leadership in Moscow believed Russian Federation sovereignty was definitely at risk, and ultimately that it had been threatened with some degree of destabilization, the question was whether or not Russia would respond. The answer to that question would become quite clear during 2014.

Chapter Twelve:
Beachheads

Russia's leaders had clearly expressed themselves, claiming a sphere of economic, political, and even cultural influence that stretched beyond immediate territorial boundaries. President Dmitry Medvedev had openly claimed "privileged interests" extending to any nation with "friendly" interests and stressed that Russia's sphere of influence extended beyond its "border regions." His successor, Vladimir Putin, was equally adamant about that point and also the Russian cultural desire for stability. *Time* magazine had captured Putin's foreign relations agenda earlier, in remarks naming him their Man of the Year in 2007: "Putin has put his country back on the map. And he intends to redraw it himself."[1] As Putin entered his third term as president in 2012, that view seemed to be endorsed by a major part of the Russian public.

Advocating a sphere of influence is nothing new in foreign relations, it was a common practice during the age of empires. We began this study with the British and Russian struggles over spheres of influence across the Middle East and into Asia and Asia Minor. The United States had proclaimed its own sphere of influence in 1823 with a declaration by President James Monroe.[2] The Monroe Doctrine stated that any further efforts by European nations that represented an effort to take control of any independent state in either North or South America (several Central and South American nations had recently achieved independence from European nations) would be regarded as a sign of "unfriendly" intentions towards the United States and treated accordingly. It also included a pledge not to interfere in the internal concerns of those same European countries.

Attitudes and declarations on spheres of influence appear to be yet another constant in foreign relations, much the same as covert political action and political warfare. The same can be said for endorsements of "stability." Yet, under the czars, Russia actively worked to destabilize Afghanistan, Tibet, India, and other nations in order to expand its sphere of political influence. Russia, under the communist doctrine of the Soviet Union, endorsed political revolution and actively worked to destabilize states around the globe, challenging the Monroe Doctrine with major military installations (featuring ballistic missiles) in Cuba. The Soviet Union had also offered major military support to North Korea, North Vietnam, and Nicaragua during the Cold War and, even without the revolutionary demands of communist ideology, under Putin, the new post-Soviet Russia began renewing its global outreach in both Central and South America.

That outreach included a new security agreement with Nicaragua, supplying tanks, weapons, and military trainers as well as setting up what appear to be large-scale electronic intelligence collection facilities, staffed exclusively by Russian personnel. Russian arms sales to Venezuela are now estimated to total in the billions of dollars, with smaller sales going to Peru, Argentina, and Ecuador.[3] The new Russian outreach actually began in 2013, highlighted by the flight of two Russian strategic bombers through the Caribbean for landings in both Nicaragua and Venezuela. Russian military aircraft also resumed missions off Alaska and sent a pair of strategic bombers all the way down the West Coast of the United States, coming within fifty miles of California, something not seen even during the height of the Cold War.

In 2013, Putin staged summits in Cuba, Nicaragua, Brazil, and Argentina. The extensive nature of his presidential visits and the new Russian foreign relations initiative were striking, reinforced by a statement from General John F. Kelly that the Russian military presence was expanding to a level not seen for some three decades. There seemed little doubt that the new Russia indeed viewed its sphere of influence as extending considerably beyond its own borders.

At the same time Russia continued to feel that its influence on its immediate borders remained threatened, both economically and politically. The European nations and the United States basically ignored repeated Russian protests on that point. The democracy initiative remained in place and still funded by the United States, with NGOs active within the independent republics. The same NGOs remained at work within Russia, even under increasing FSB surveillance and harassment. In 2009 the European Union had announced a new Eastern Partnership initiative, focused on the former Soviet republics of Armenia, Azerbaijan, Belarus, Georgia, Moldavia, and Ukraine. The initiative opened dialogues on trade, travel, economic agreements, and related subjects. Russia immediately countered with an expanded focus on its own Eurasian Customs Union, which also addressed trade and travel agreements. But from the Russian perspective its protests simply were not registering, as illustrated by a story appearing in both the *Moscow Times* and *Izvestia* in 2015. It reported that $500,000 in funding was being offered out of the U.S. embassy in Lithuania, made available to regional media organizations to combat Russian propaganda. One of the grants available included money for a research project—the title of the study being "Investigative Journalism Training to Counter Russian Messaging in the Baltics."[4]

While military posturing and economic competition might be considered soft forms of political warfare, they certainly are not in the same category as active destabilization or hybrid warfare practices. In 2014, events in Ukraine triggered a Russian turn to exactly such practices, resulting in a type of political warfare not seen since the Cold War, using new tools to create a level of political chaos not achieved by even the most successful covert operations of the CIA or KGB. The events that ignited this new era are factually clear but will be debated for decades. Inside Ukraine, it began with essentially a repeat of the events of 2004, with the same participants and the same disagreements. In 2004 Viktor Yanukovych had been the pro-Russian Ukrainian candidate, personally and openly supported by Putin. In the end, to the embarrassment of Putin, Yanukovych had not become president. Yet there was considerable pro-Russian sympathy in Ukraine, especially in its eastern Russian-speaking regions, and over the next few years Yanukovych managed to reassert himself with those voters and was elected to the premiership within eighteen months. It was during this period that American political and communications consultants began to be employed in the Ukrainian political jousting. At the time, the turn to American consultants was seen as little different as the previous employment of Russian political "technologists." One of those new consultants—Paul Manafort—earned millions of dollars from his Ukrainian consulting while becoming increasingly visible in American domestic politics.

By 2010, Yanukovych had indeed become the elected president of Ukraine. He had done so by broadening his base and by an incremental advocacy for closer relations with Europe, even floating the prospects of an actual agreement with the European Union. It was practical, pragmatic politics—but not an approach appreciated in Moscow. In response, Russia and pro-Russian factions in Ukraine consistently and increasingly began to undermine Yanukovych. That effort focused on support for Putin's close personal friend Viktor Medvedchuk and his pro-Russian Ukrainian Choice movement.

Beginning in July 2013, Putin again made personal appearances in Ukraine. At one event he participated in a roundtable hosted by Medvedchuk on the subject of "Orthodox Slavic Values: The Basis of Civilized Choice in Ukraine." Putin's remarks focused on shared culture, including Russian Orthodox religious traditions.[5] However, unlike in 2004, neither man's message of cultural bonding and mutual interests appears to have made much impression on popular opinion, with polls showing strong support for an EU agreement. By October Putin was pursuing the matter directly with President Yanukovych. On three occasions that month, Yanukovych flew to Russia for meetings with Putin, who was adamant that Ukraine not conclude any agreement with the EU, offering a $15 billion loan as an incentive for Ukraine and as Russian support for Yanukovych in the upcoming election.

Objectively that would have to be considered political intervention on Russia's part, but as noted earlier, Putin did not view it that way. What he did view as intervention was the ongoing activity by Western NGOs in Ukraine. The NGOs were still there and still training, organizing, and advocating for popular elections and transparency, which in Putin's view was still simply more Western intervention. Historically there is a good deal of irony in the fact that by 2013-14 it would be Russia who viewed popular protest and political activism as dangerous to the established order of things, and public demonstrations as inherently dangerous and driven solely by foreign agitation.

A look at the National Endowment for Democracy spending in 2014 for Ukraine shows a total of approximately $4.5 million spent on NGO activities including seminars, media training and outreach, local civic initiatives, and online networking platforms. NED efforts openly developed youth activism and helped create a network of civic activists including business owners. Priorities included the monitoring of elections and responding to election-related coverage in regional media. Associations were formed to not only perform election monitoring but to ensure that candidates had equal access to mass media. NED partnerships produced and disseminated audio and video voter-mobilization materials as well as posters and billboard advertising placements.

As part of that effort, "public dialogue" on East-West topics and EU integration was promoted via broadcast television debates. Funds were also allocated to developing independent regional media, which would focus on elections and political transitions. This included operating popular news outlets on both television and the internet, as well as the production of content for news outlets. Correspondent salaries and basic operating costs were also funded.

Clearly this was political action, incorporating most of the practices the CIA might have used during the Cold War, and exactly the sort of action that tends to promote political change. Yet it was all done quite openly, reported and promoted by the NED itself.[6] The participants and trainees in these and other NGO programs were largely young, a high percentage being students. They also included individuals from community groups, charities, women's groups, and human rights groups. It must be noted that the democracy and open government-oriented NGOs were not engaging with the pro-Russian, traditional cultural segments of Ukraine's population, but rather with those groups more oriented to change and Western cultural values.

There is additional irony in the fact that these general demographic segments in the United States most often represented the opposition to U.S. foreign policies and military engagements during the Cold War. The profile of the Ukrainian population being reached by the NGOs matches the individuals and groups sought after by the KGB within the United States and targeted as agents of influence or unknowing assets in destabilizing and fragmenting American domestic politics. Those same types had also been repeatedly infiltrated by the FBI and targeted by the CIA in its domestic Operation MHCHAOS anti-war program.

The net of it all was that in 2013-14 Ukraine was indeed facing political intervention from outside, from competing camps. The democracy initiative inherently represented a challenge to long established alliances and links forged during the decades of Soviet political and economic dominion. That influence was essentially Western in culture, running counter to the traditional cultural links among the Russian-speaking population in segments of eastern Ukraine. While that political action was essentially playing to the "street" in Ukraine, Putin was exerting Russian influence with political action at the very top, directly with the president. And in a surprise to virtually everyone, Putin's influence prevailed. In November 2013 it was first announced that the agreement with the European Union would be delayed, and within days the President Yanukovych announced that it was being abandoned based on a decision of economics.

The events following that announcement, now known as the Euromaidan movement, received major media coverage and are well documented.[7] Massive street protests began almost immediately in the streets of Kiev, numbering as many as eight hundred thousand participants. A protest camp was formed, but special police immediately cleared it with the use of considerable violence. Yanukovych held to his decision, signed a $15 billion debt write-off agreement with Russia, and received promises of major reductions in the price of natural gas. However during January 2014 the central Ukrainian government in Kiev moved into increasing disarray, with major resignations and shifts in voting in opposition to Yanukovych's actions. On February 20, over eighty protesters were killed. Television footage showed them being fired on by snipers—further outraging the protest movement. Within a few weeks the United States and the European Union responded with sanctions against President Yanukovych and individual officers in his security forces.

In the interim Yanukovych moved on to promise corruption reforms, new elections, basically anything other than revisiting any form of EU agreement. On February 22, when the Ukrainian parliament voted to remove him from office, Yanukovych declared it to be a coup. In response, parliament issued an arrest warrant for him and ordered that the special police unit, identified as responsible for the recent violence and sniper fire incidents under his control, be disbanded. Ukrainian military and security forces refused to support Yanukovych, with the army issuing a statement that it would not become involved in political conflict and that it remained at the service of the people.[8] Without the backing of the army Yanukovych had no means by which to support any state of emergency declaration and in late February first fled Kiev and then went into exile in Russia, under Putin's protection.

RUSSIAN INTERVENTION

On March 4, 2014, Russia's UN ambassador presented a letter signed by Yanukovych, requesting Russian peacekeeping forces to restore order in Ukraine. The Russian parliament had already voted to approve a request by President Putin to deploy Russian troops. During March, the first signs of Russian surrogate military intervention (the "little green men") developed, with uniformed, very well-armed combat troops seizing government buildings in the Crimean region of the Ukraine. Later Putin himself would publicly admit to sending in Russian forces, expressing his satisfaction with the decision on Russian television and citing approval from the Russian parliament to intervene to "protect Russian interests."[9]

Those remarks were in total contrast to initial Russian statements; the military deployment had been conducted under full deniability, with a mix of Russian paratroopers (Pskov's Seventy-Sixth Guards Division with all identifying insignia and unit badges removed) flown into Sevastopol in ten aircraft and a smaller number of "volunteers." In an operation similar to the initial seizure of power in Afghanistan in 1979, the paratroopers quickly deployed and seized the Supreme Council building (Crimea's regional government) and the airfield. Russian forces also established airspace control over Crimea. The initial volunteers arrived within two days, some 170 veterans from Afghanistan and Chechnya as well as various political "clubs" known to be strongly supportive of Putin. Russian FSB and GRU officers were also covertly inserted and orchestrated the veterans in various public appearances, representing themselves as local, separatist partisans.

Using the "best practices" of such operations, Russia at first denied any involvement in the Crimean incident, with President Putin publicly stating that Russia had no intentions of annexing the region. However, a quick referendum was organized and by March 18 Putin signed a document granting membership of Crimea and the port of Sebastopol to the Russian Federation. Sebastopol housed a major Russian Navy base, with a large local contingent of Russian military personnel and local Russian Navy forces (including Marines). Those forces were sufficient to establish military control over the area. The economic and political integration of Crimea became a major priority for Russia—an accomplishment praised in the Russian press, citing the quicker-than-anticipated "adaptation" of the population.[10] In less than three years, Russia deployed significant numbers of missile systems into Crimea, including anti-aircraft, anti-ship, and wide area systems capable of broad air suppression over the Black Sea and Ukraine. By 2018, such deployments increasingly fueled air and naval confrontations in the ostensibly neutral Black Sea.[11]

The practices involved with turning Crimea into a political and military entity under Russian sovereignty were similar to those used in the breakaway Russian-speaking regions of Georgia. Both of those Russian successes took advantage of cultural fragmentation to politically destabilize targeted regions, using local agents of political influence and applying overt military force capable of blocking any action of the central governments involved. The effect of the actions in Georgia and Crimea was to create Russian beachheads that could be used for further destabilization of the independent republics, while offering territories for staging military forces for further action as necessary.

The Russian operations in the Georgian insurgent areas, as well as in Crimea, had been intense, surgical, and of very short duration.

What followed next in Ukraine was something quite different—"evo-lutionary" in nature—and in some respects similar to the early 1960s American involvement in Vietnam. In a political context Russia's next actions are best understood in terms of President Putin's own remarks on Ukraine, in which he referred to "Novorossiya"—a term from the era of the czars.[12] Putin's usage is telling, reflecting both his fundamental views of traditional Russian sovereignty and his deep belief that large sections of eastern Ukraine were not simply Russian-speaking, but possessed with elements of traditional Russian culture and deeply receptive to a political linkage to Moscow.

Originally Novorossiya was a territory of the Russian Empire, annexed in 1774. While it included most of southern Ukraine it had been settled by a broad mix of peoples, only to be more heavily popu-lated with native Russians during the Soviet era, with the region part of the Ukrainian People's Republic. There was a long history of inde-pendence movements. Circa 1990 a new Novorossiya movement had campaigned for either autonomy or for status as a "special state" within Ukraine. That movement did not gain wide popular support, some-thing that might have served as a warning as to the true political nature of the entire region, which was a good deal larger than certain of its heavily Russian enclaves. Later the same lack of broad popular support in the east undermined the Putin-backed political initiative of Viktor Medvedchuk in the summer of 2103. Ultimately it would become clear that, while much of the Ukrainian east had its own issues with the federal regimes in Kiev, it was even less excited about political control from Moscow.[13] Subsequent events would demonstrate that only in the Donbass region, specifically in the Donetsk and Luhansk administra-tive areas, was there any extensive support for union with Russia.

Yet in the spring of 2014 it appears that the belief in Moscow, and certainly the personal view of President Putin, was that a strong sepa-ratist movement would emerge throughout all of eastern Ukraine. At a minimum such a political movement would be amenable to strong linkages with Moscow, creating yet another beachhead, similar to but much larger than the addition of Crimea to the Russian Federation. In that context, it is far easier to understand the incremental nature of Russian action in Ukraine, beginning in 2014 and ongoing to the time of this writing in 2018. The first direct Russian involvement in eastern Ukraine was low-key, with the insertion of Russian intelligence officers and the appearance of a limited number of paramilitary surrogates, "volunteers," who were on the payroll of pro-Russian financial and political figures in the east.

The Russian approach to inserting paramilitary forces into eastern Ukraine through the use of private military firms set a pattern that was to appear in subsequent Russian foreign military involvement, similar to the methods the United States had earlier turned to in both Iraq and Afghanistan. As a practice, it appears politically efficient, providing a level of deniability but also minimizing official casualties and domestic political protests.[14] The "non-military military" appears here to stay: a return to American use of private military contractors was proposed as a new Trump Administration surge strategy for Afghanistan in 2017.[15]

While private military companies are illegal within Russia itself, in 2012 Prime Minister Putin endorsed the concept. The end result was that such firms began to be organized, legally chartered as business entities outside Russia itself. One of the known private military contractors, Wagner Group, provided civilian troops to the separatist oligarchs in the Donbass region of eastern Ukraine, and by 2018 would field similar paramilitary units to fight within Syria.[16]

Individuals involved with the Wagner Group appear to have connections to Putin—in 2016 one of its founders and senior military commanders, Dmitriy Utkin, was photographed with Putin at a national Russian awards ceremony, Day of Heroes of the Fatherland. Investigation of Russian activities in the Ukraine led the United States to impose personal sanctions against Utkin for his involvement, as well as against Putin's associate Yevegeny Prigozhin, reportedly a financial sponsor of Utkin's activities in the Ukraine.

Initially, the major protests against Kiev's moves towards EU accords had been centered around the Donetsk region of eastern Ukraine; that opposition was largely organized and funded by Rinat Akhmetov, a longtime Yanukovych supporter sufficiently wealthy to have been the sole contractor for the rebuilding of both the city of Donetsk and its airport. In the beginning, there were no actual declarations of independence and virtually no violence. However, there were discussions on separatism and the formation of an independent Novorossiya, to include Crimea. Activists from eastern Ukraine went back and forth to Crimea, and thereafter a number of the "volunteers" who had supported Russian intervention in Crimea moved on into east Ukraine.

Those volunteers were led by Colonel Igor Strelkov, who moved his small force into Slavyansk, a modest city in the Donetsk area in early May. He specifically chose a location where a small but aggressive group might make an impact.[17] Strelkov, who calls himself "Shooter," had an effect on the Donetsk region somewhat similar to that of the Contra military leaders the United States supported inside Nicaragua— bloody and brutal, but in the end not sustainable. His group initiated the first real violence in the east by seizing a police station and then taking control of Slavyansk's municipal government. The group was joined by a number of local pro-Russian volunteers and the violence escalated, with no particular response from Kiev, where the national government was trying to organize itself under newly elected President Petro Poroshenko.

During April and May, pro-Russian groups in both the Donetsk and Luhansk regions declared themselves fully independent people's republics. To some extent Strelkov, as the largely self-appointed defense minister for Donetsk, became the popular face of the independence movement in the east, publicly calling for Russia to intervene. There was no overt Russian response and no formal recognition of the insurgent Ukrainian republics. However, large Russian military formations were deployed on the Russian side of the Ukrainian border. Such overt intimidation is familiar to us from American political interventions, largely in the form of naval forces. Peak estimates put between thirty thousand and forty thousand Russian troops on Ukraine's border in the spring of 2014. In this instance, Kiev proved not to be intimidated, and the central government showed no signs of accepting the loss of its eastern territories. By early July, under increasing Ukrainian Army pressure, Strelkov was forced to shift his forces to the city of Donetsk, initially undefended by the Ukrainian Army. The resulting combat in a heavily urban area largely devastated Donetsk.

At that point, in early summer, Moscow apparently began to appreciate that a much broader Novorossiya was not emerging as an independent political entity. Given the case, the most pragmatic course of action was to turn to a destabilization agenda. Reportedly, Putin sent emissaries to pro-Russian political leaders encouraging they accept the integration of the insurgent regions of Donetsk and Luhansk back into Ukraine. Such a negotiated reentry would give the east (and the pro-Russian oligarchs) a much stronger influence in the central Ukrainian government.[18] From the Russian perspective such a course was quite acceptable, affecting all of Ukraine and helping to ensure that the EU accords did not happen. It would be a purely political action quite consistent with Russian hegemony goals, establishing a degree of influence without overt military intervention. Perhaps as part of the Russian encouragement, in late June Putin asked the Russian parliament to cancel its earlier resolution on the use of Russian forces in Ukraine, and the Federation Council did so, making it officially illegal to use the Russian military in eastern Ukraine.[19]

The problem with that approach was simply that both the Ukrainian Army and an increasing number of nationalist volunteers were putting serious military pressure on the insurgents, reducing any pressure on

Kiev to negotiate with groups it had declared to be terrorists. While there is ample evidence of Russian weapons shipments, Russian trainers, and a limited number of volunteers during the months of June and July, there was no large-scale deployment of Russian combat troops into eastern Ukraine. Although officially denied in the strongest terms at the time, eventually Putin was forced to acknowledge that Russian personnel, if not full-scale military units, had indeed been present in eastern Ukraine: "We never said there were not people there who carried out certain tasks including in the military sphere."[20]

In addition to supplying weapons, including artillery, there is also evidence that on occasion Russian forces engaged Ukrainian Army targets from within Russian territory. One the most devastating artillery attacks occurred in July 2014, when drones providing real-time targeting were used to vector in a three-minute artillery bombardment. Four Ukrainian Federal Army brigades had been assembled for an advance and the strike destroyed dozens of vehicles, killing two to three dozen personnel. Damage assessment determined that the attack had used advanced dual-purpose munitions including air-dropped mines and top-down anti-tank submunitions along with fuel air explosives.[21] It was a demonstration of some of the most advanced artillery available to the regular Russian forces and it led to a formal study by the United States Army's Capabilities Integration Center in an effort to determine new tactics for dealing with such sophisticated attacks.

The Ukrainian Federal Army was also deprived of much of its available air support by both the actual loss of aircraft and the extreme threat posed by shoulder-launched anti-aircraft missiles (manpads) provided to the insurgents, along with even more advanced anti-aircraft systems. Verified counts of Ukrainian Federal aircraft losses included nine combat aircraft, three cargo planes, and ten helicopters, all downed by shoulder-launched missiles and, in the case of the helicopters, rocket-propelled grenades.[22]

One of the cargo planes was determined to have been brought down by a Buk missile system, the same type of weapon which an official Dutch study determined to have brought down a commercial Boeing 777 airliner transiting at altitude above the combat zone.[23] A Dutch Safety Board report concluded that the weapon that destroyed the airliner was a very specific Buk surface to air missile rocket, noting that while both the Russian and Ukrainian armies fielded such systems, pro-Russian insurgents occupied the area from which the missile had launched. The report added that it had obtained photos showing a Buk system being driven into the Ukraine and around the suspected launch area before departing over the Russian border. Russia adamantly denied providing the system in question.

Yet despite the weapons and long-range artillery support, by August the Ukrainian Federal Army and a growing number of organized volunteer groups (from within the east) continued to advance. The insurgency had withdrawn from western Donetsk, which was increasingly surrounded, threatening its ground link to weapons and supplies via the Russian border. Calls for Russian military support increased, stressing that the Donetsk insurgency might well be overwhelmed within two weeks.[24] The city of Mariupol was no longer being contested and it appeared that many of the locals in the Donbass—much less all of "Novorossiya"—were far more nationalist and less pro-Moscow than Putin had originally believed. If the newly declared people's republics fully collapsed back to central government political control, even the minimal opportunity of creating a major Russian political beachhead on the border of eastern Ukraine would vanish. What followed serves as a strong demonstration of exactly how committed President Putin was to pushing back against any loss of Russian sovereignty.

At the end of July, heavy shelling of Ukrainian forces commenced from the Russian side of their joint border. Russian adamantly denied that it was occurring, though ultimately even Putin would be forced to acknowledge something of what followed—the arrival of a wave of Russian "vacationers." Officially the incursion involved only volunteers, admittedly Russian military but on vacation and acting strictly on their own accord. The vacationers were tasked with stopping the Ukrainian central government advance, diverting the Ukrainian Federal Army with a move against the second-largest city in the region where no serious fighting had yet occurred. Later Colonel Strelkov, Donetsk's former defense minister, would be quite specific about the deployment: "It was mostly the vacationers who attacked Mariupol... they could have taken it without a fight but they were ordered not to...the order was simply to halt the offensive...they were told not to occupy the city under any circumstances."[25]

Regardless of any such orders, the combat that followed the initial Russian military intervention was deadly. Indications are that this first intervention might have been intended as not just a blocking operation but as a message for Kiev, a demonstration of Russian will. This is suggested by the fact that even as Russian deaths began to mount, military death-benefit payments were kept secret and burials obscured with warnings to family members. In addition, Putin quietly issued a low-key but highly consequential order directing that military deaths occurring during peacetime "special operations" be classified. That order provided the authority for a formal declaration of secrecy in regard to any military deaths, especially those which occurred outside announced military activities—for example, while on vacation.[26]

By the end of August it was clear to virtually everyone, and especially to Kiev, that the Ukraine central government was involved in what amounted to full-scale war with a large, if deniable, Russian military force. Its Ministry of Foreign Affairs officially announced on August 27, 2014 that an invasion was in progress. The deniable Russian military offensive went far beyond special forces, trainers, volunteers, or intelligence personnel. In reality, the deployment of vacationers was more reminiscent of the force Soviet Russia had sent to Cuba in 1962.

The 2014 deployment into eastern Ukraine included full combat brigades, self-propelled artillery, and tank units. The Russian forces lacked the ballistic missiles of the Cuban crisis but employed surveillance drones and electronic warfare equipment.

One of the things that actually exposed the full extent of the Russian forces was the eventual press coverage of two destroyed Russian main line T-72 battle tanks, advanced fighting vehicles of a type not previously exported or made available outside Russia itself.[27] The tanks had been part of a major armored engagement with Ukrainian Federal Army forces; the Ukrainians had been routed, leaving dozens of their own tanks and armored vehicles behind. Similar engagements during August and into September demonstrated that even at their best, main line Ukrainian forces could not stand up to a mix of new Russian weapons and tactics, the same result as seen in the earlier Georgian/Russian combat.

Worse yet, a considerable number of central government volunteer units had been sent east, initially ordered to police and provide security in areas that had been retaken from the insurgents, territory where they appeared to have fallen back. The Ukrainian military command, with far less field intelligence than needed and looking to report the consolidation of rebel territory in the east, redirected the volunteer units into an advance with the intent of fragmenting the insurgent regions. The apparent collapse of the insurgents had moved the army into a broad move east. When the surprise Russian deployment struck, the main line Ukrainian units took losses, but the inexperienced volunteer units were totally unprepared to face the Russian armored advance. During August they were trapped and routed, suffering hundreds of deaths in the process.[28]

By September several things were evident. There were indeed solid blocs of pro-Russian separatists within the two self-declared independent republics in southeast Ukraine, and they wanted nothing to do with Kiev. They considered themselves under attack by the central government and viewed the Russians as defending them. Outside those enclaves, the Russian incursion had provoked equally virulent anti-Russian attitudes in areas of the east, producing the increasing involvement of nationalist volunteer military groups in the region. Regardless of that, it was clear that any new central government military initiative was going to be both bloody and fruitless. The result was a ceasefire accord, the Minsk Protocol, defining lines of control and buffer zones. The actual result was a cessation of any Kiev federal offensive (which had proved unsustainable), the continued existence of the separatist regions, and the withdrawal of some larger and more visible units of the Russian military.

Regardless of the Minsk agreement, the military reality was that certain locations still under federal government control—such as the Donetsk Airport—were not going to be acceptable to either the insurgents or Moscow. And that led to the second major Russian offensive, a tactically sophisticated engagement which further brutalized the regular Ukrainian Army.[29] Beginning in late September, Ukraine reinforced its forces at the airport, and in return the Russian forces deployed tactical units to surround the facility and slowly squeeze its perimeter. Insurgent groups were directed into the airport to contest individual hangars and the terminal. They were supported with tanks and armored vehicles as well as with artillery and rocket bombardment. In the end the Ukrainian infantry was ground down, the airport fell, and some two hundred troops were killed in action. Another five hundred were injured, and dozens of tanks, vehicles, and pieces of field artillery were destroyed.

The airport defeat essentially collapsed the central government's last remaining line of advance into Donetsk, which had been channeled through the city of Debaltseve. Combined Russian and insurgent forces immediately moved there, subjecting the city to massive rocket and artillery fire. With power and utilities cut and with the death of an estimated six thousand civilians, there was no choice for the federal government in Kiev other than to sign yet another ceasefire agreement in January 2015. The best available estimates suggest that from August 2014 to the time of that second ceasefire, a combined force of some ten thousand insurgents and Russian military personnel had shattered a combination of an estimated eight thousand regular Ukrainian Army and volunteer military units.

The Russian intervention had ensured the defeat of any attempts by Kiev to reclaim the secessionist enclaves on its far southeastern border. From that time to this writing, the Donetsk and Luhansk enclaves have remained in place. They are supported with some number of Russian military personnel being detached from their units and rotated for temporary tours of service, and with the appearance of pro-Russian volunteers from Azerbaijan, Belarus, and Tajikistan. However, increasing nationalist, anti-Moscow resistance in the broader areas of eastern Ukraine appears to have blocked any potential link between Crimea and those separatist regions, as well as any possibility of Putin's hope of a Novorossiya, dividing Ukraine and restoring its entire east to Russian hegemony.

Since then, tensions, sniping, firefights, probes, and limited shelling have continued. There were recurring incidents reflecting Russian troop buildups directly across the joint Ukraine/Russian border, fears of new interventions, and a general sense of instability. No major military initiative has been taken by Kiev nor has there been any new, large-scale deployment of forces from Russia. To that extent the ceasefire has held, but otherwise the shooting, explosions, and obvious destruction in the contested buffer zones show that there has been no fundamental change. A considerable number of the Ukrainian nationalist forces sparring along the demarcation lines are volunteers, many of the individuals from the east. They serve as paramilitary units organized under Ukraine's Interior Ministry.

As for the separatist republics, it appears that the hope in Moscow remains a limited version of what Putin had begun to express in the spring of 2014, that ultimately Kiev will tire of the drain on its resources, the tension that undermines its own internal politics, and accede to some sort of independence for the breakaway enclaves—officially acknowledging, along with Crimea, at least some level of Russian hegemony in its southeast. The standoff leaves an estimated eight hundred thousand civilians living near the contested demarcation lines and another one hundred thousand in the buffer zones.[30] In terms of combatants along the full extent of the contended lines, the total of actual military personnel and volunteers has been estimated in the tens of thousands—operating out of trenches, garrisons, and positions that change daily and weekly. Beyond that, an estimated three million or more people have simply moved out, going west into Ukraine or east into Russia.

While tragic for those involved, the ongoing violence initially forestalled Ukraine's agreement with the EU, an apparent victory for Russian political influence. However in September 2017 Ukraine entered into an initial association agreement with the EU, one involving the converging of regulations, workers' rights, movement of people, access to the European Investment Bank, and a free-trade zone.[31] With the signing—which followed by a week Ukraine's declaration of a unilateral ceasefire in the region of the breakaway insurgencies—Ukraine's President Poroshenko cited the "high price" that Ukraine had paid to be able to make such a move towards the EU. He also announced a program, which would allow Ukraine to apply for full membership by 2020.[32] September, 2017 also saw an expanded multi-nation training and interoperability exercise (Rapid Trident) between the Ukraine, the United States and some fourteen other nations including Bulgaria, Canada, the United Kingdom, and Georgia. The exercise involved both battalion and platoon level training as well as an integrated air and ground logistics operation.[33]

The Russian response to the agreement was best summarized in an RT news headline of September 1, 2017: "Ukraine's association deal bittersweet with no real hope for EU integration."[34] The RT story focused on the decline in trade with Russia (some twenty-five percent) and the lack of growth in exports to European Union nations (only three percent). It also pointed out that Turkey, which had signed a similar European agreement decades ago, never has become a full member of the EU. It also expressed the opinion that the agreement will favor foreign firms within the Ukraine and give primacy to European law over Ukraine's own statutes.

While the initial Ukraine/EU agreement clearly has left Moscow unhappy, it is likely that it will retain some political gains from its political warfare against Ukraine. The insurgent Donbass enclaves appear to have become permanent for the time being, albeit an economic drain on Russia. And although Ukraine has earnestly and repeatedly requested to join with NATO, the chances of that are virtually nonexistent.[35] The reason is simple, if allowed admission Ukraine could immediately invoke Article 5 of the NATO charter—demanding that NATO come to its aid in the low-intensity conflict in the Donbass. Given recent history that opens the risk of direct combat between NATO and Russian forces, a risk that NATO is not eager to incur.

Beyond that, Russia has made it quite clear that any agreements between the independent republics and the EU are something that it firmly opposes and will go to considerable extremes to prevent. This attitude obviously concerns certain of the former Soviet satellites. It seems particularly intimidating to Moldova, a small independent nation that faces its own pro-Russian regional insurgencies, the most significant being in its Trans-Dniester (also Transnistria) region that maintains its own constitution, parliament, and currency. Trans-Dniester broke away from Moldova in 1990 and has relied on Russia for military, economic, and political support. As with other insurgent enclaves, there are strong pro-Russian sentiments among the population, especially in the Dniester region which has a considerable Russian-language population. Russia actually maintains a military "peacekeeping" force in

Trans-Dniester, something continually opposed by the Moldova government.

Trans-Dniester contains most of Moldova's industrial resources, largely underutilized because the region's self-declared independence is not recognized within the international community. Reportedly Russia sustains the region economically and continues payments to those pensioned under the previous Soviet system. The elected regime has openly declared that its goal is ultimately a reunification with Russia. In contrast, Moldova had turned towards the EU, signing an economic assistance pact in 2014—and immediately facing the imposition of major import restrictions on its agricultural trade with Russia.

Moldova has also annoyed Moscow by demonstrating some cooperation with NATO and declining the Russian invitation into the Eurasian Economic Union. The political events of 2014 in Ukraine—and Russia's response—raised fears in Moldova that Russia might also move (covertly or overtly) to solidify full pro-Russian control over not only Trans-Dniester but Moldova as well. In response Moldova and Ukraine assumed joint control over their mutual border with the Trans-Dniester region. There is an active political competition between pro-Russian and pro-EU factions inside Moldova, and in 2016 the Russian faction made some gains in regard to the ceremonial position of the presidency, however the parliament remained EU-oriented.

In March 2017, Moldova arrested a member of its parliament for passing secrets to the military attaché in the Russian diplomatic delegation to that nation.[36] It also expelled five members of the delegation, accusing them of spying. Russia responded harshly, maintaining that it was an action orchestrated by the West, very likely the United States, to disrupt any improvement in relations between the nations. The Moldavan parliament also continues to call for Russia to withdraw its military from Trans-Dniester. In the spring of 2017 a protest from Moldova to Romania prevented the landing of a Russian military plane bound for Trans-Dniester carrying Russia's deputy prime minister. The flight took place at the same time the Trans-Dniester military conducted a river-crossing exercise, across the river that constitutes their self-declared border with Moldova.

Another self-declared autonomous region of Moldova, Gagauzia, is an almost perfect point of entry for Russian destabilization and for placing pressure on western Ukraine. Its population is Russian-speaking and Orthodox Christian, and the region was a longtime possession of the Russian empire. It is also poor and blames the Moldavian central government for many of its problems, in a fashion very similar to eastern Ukraine. It constitutes the strongest pro-Russian voting bloc in Moldova and has a pro-Russian governor. As with Trans-Dniester, Russia has moved to further isolate it from the central government by exempting it from the economic sanctions placed on Moldova.[37]

Moldova certainly is of strategic interest to Russia, flanking Ukraine on its western borders. Trans-Dniester is even more valuable, already housing a contingent of Russian troops, with a pro-Russian military force of its own of some six thousand soldiers, and access to the Don River, which carries oceangoing traffic into the Black Sea. The region serves as a serious check on Moldavan outreach to the west and at any point it could be used to stage "volunteer" forces or "little green men" to project pro-Russian intervention in Moldavan elections or parliamentary activities. The reality of Russian political warfare and NATO limitations certainly makes it clear to Moldova that it is walking a fine line—a line which it acknowledged in 2017 when it ejected Russian diplomats yet declined an invitation to participate in a NATO maritime security exercise, which would have involved its key port, Giurgiuleşti, on the Don.

The Russian political warfare in the Crimean and eastern Ukrainian conflict certainly served to demonstrate that Russia was willing to seize territory and redraw national borders, at least to the extent of supporting pro-Russian enclaves. It was also willing to deploy significant military formations to do so, both overtly and deniably. The Ukraine as a nation has been politically destabilized and weakened both economically and militarily. Russia has established protected bases of influence for further action, and those bases are culturally and economically aligned with Russia in a fashion that would make it virtually impossible to destabilize them in turn.

Up to the time of this writing Russia has demonstrated that it has the will and the military capability to impose a degree of both cultural and territorial sovereignty. What it has not been able to accomplish is to establish a broader hegemony throughout the former Soviet republics, which is what it clearly would have preferred. That may well be due to the fact that Moscow appears no more able to appreciate the divisive effects of nationalism, cultural and religious diversity, and resentment over former imperial control than the United States was at the beginning of the Cold War.

Chapter Thirteen:
Shaping

Beginning in 2008, Russian Federation leaders began to speak increasingly animatedly in regard to a threat to their nation's sovereignty, possibly even an existential threat to Russia's own domestic political security. While we lack the sorts of transcripts that give us a direct insight into their internal discussions—specifically the sort of documentation we reviewed in regard to American National Security Council meetings throughout the Cold War—the public statements issued in Moscow leave no doubt as to the nature of the threat and who was behind it.

The Russian response was direct, involving containment activities both internally and across its borders. Containment was followed by more active measures, opposing changes to the traditional political and economic hegemony that had existed across its self-declared sphere of influence for centuries, not just during the Soviet era but further back to the Russian empire under the czars. Ultimately that pushback extended to both overt and covert hybrid surrogate political warfare, destabilizing targeted regimes in Georgia and Ukraine and establishing territorial beachheads tied to Moscow.

That was largely the state of affairs that had come into being as of 2014. Other than economic pressure, primarily in the form of energy policy, there had been no direct action against either Western Europe or the United States. If anything, those foreign relationships were at a stalemate, with each side expressing its objection to the actions of the other.[1] While there had been an abortive "reset" during the Obama administration, objectively it appears that Russia and the West were simply talking past the other.

Although a dozen different examples of disagreement and discord could be cited, fundamentally the Russian view was that the West was driving change around the globe, particularly in Europe, but also in the Middle East and Africa. That change was degrading long-established Russian influence. In recent decades America and NATO had been both overtly and covertly engaged in military initiatives against Russian-affiliated nations with ties to the former Soviet Union, states that had long been Russian military clients and economic partners—Afghanistan, Bosnia, Iran, Libya, and most recently Syria. The United States had undermined Russian economic opportunities in Pakistan, in Iraq, and was looking to take away military sales to Russia's long-time client India. And American and European Union sanctions had undermined Russia's ability to leverage both its energy resources and its surplus of investment capital.

The West—America and the EU—were functioning as global change agents and Russia did not want change. It was almost that simple. As noted earlier, the disconnect ultimately became so great that President Putin brought it into the open in a flat statement about America and the West in general, "…we are not like you. We only look like you. But we are very different. Russians and Americans resemble each other physically but inside we have very different values."[2] Putin viewed Russia's culture as fundamentally tied to orthodoxy and stability.

Given that a virtual stalemate in foreign relations had developed, and that the West's democracy initiative was continuing, it appears that the Russian leadership determined to pursue two new initiatives, each of which offered the potential to either remove or at least alleviate the constant challenges coming from the West. Whether or not the two approaches were actually developed and coordinated as part of some master Russian strategy is impossible to say, especially since both appear to be continuing at the time of this writing. Still, it is possible to identify and illustrate both, elements of each first becoming visible during the period of 2014-16.

In general, both initiatives involved practices that are very familiar to us from earlier explorations of political action. As we found in reviewing America's history of active measures, it was not unknown to find such a bipolar approach, on one hand working to improve normal diplomatic relations with the targeted regime, while at the same time trying to destabilize and fragment it. Such a dual-track approach was explored in our examination of American political warfare in Indonesia during the Eisenhower administration.

It was also noted that a similar dual-track approach emerged between Cuba and the United States during 1963.[3] A number of very active CIA covert paramilitary and political action projects remained operational against Cuba during that year. However, President Kennedy was personally involved in a second track exploring the possibility of moving Cuba out of the Soviet bloc and into a more neutral foreign policy position. That dialogue was just beginning at the time of his assassination. Following JFK's death, President Johnson rejected further backchannel overtures of a similar nature, some of which included significant concessions on Castro's part.

Over the decades information on those American activities has been documented to the point that they can now be detailed with considerable historical accuracy. In the following exploration of an apparent dual-track Russian political action approach to the West and in particular America, the best we can do is offer as many concrete indications as possible, acknowledging the risk of sketching out historical events at virtually the same time they are emerging.

The first track/tactic to be explored is the relatively benign practice of shaping. In this instance positive shaping, an attempt to establish a new foreign relations context between the Putin regime and what might be a brand new American presidential administration, is one without the same seemingly confrontational policy positions as its most recent predecessors. As previously detailed, the practices of such soft positive shaping are exceptionally innocent in appearance. The approach involves the expression of mutual interests, the establishment of common goals, essentially a bonding to support the development of complimentary foreign policies.

Given the Russian perception of the threat it was facing, American foreign policy would need to be modified to pull the United States back from its deep involvement with the international community, from its established role as change agent to the world, focusing America on its own affairs and ceasing its tendency to insert itself into the business of other nations. Establishing the context for such a change necessarily involves contacts both within and beyond the formal, official arena of diplomatic relations. To be truly effective, as we saw with American influence in Mexico City during the 1960s, positive influence needs to be as personal as possible. And in looking at events during 2015-16 we do indeed find a number of indications that Russian actors were interested in exerting a positive shaping influence on United States foreign policy, beginning efforts to do so in conjunction with the election of 2016.

Specifically, certain Russian actors made contact with the presidential campaign of Donald Trump. In some instances those contacts came from Russian diplomatic personnel. We now know that Russian Ambassador to the United States Sergey Kislyak discussed possible communications backchannels that might be used to deal with issues relating to Syria with Donald Trump's son-in-low Jared Kushner. Kislyak also discussed a United Nations resolution condemning Israel's West Bank settlements with Trump's designated National Security Advisor Michael Flynn—while the Obama administration was still legally in place and conducting U.S. foreign policy.[4]

The possibility that there will be attempts to shape national policies of course works both ways in foreign relations. That reality was illustrated in the passage of the Logan Act by Congress in 1799. It criminalizes any effort by an American citizen, without official authority, to communicate with foreign government representatives in any fashion that might reflect an effort to "influence the measures or conduct of any foreign government."[5] Under that law "official authority" is held only by the president and officials designated within the current administration. Private citizens are not allowed to interfere with an administration's foreign policies and possible negotiations through their own contacts with foreign officials. In the instances of the Kislyak contacts, both Kushner and Flynn appear to have made their contacts and begun the exploration of topics of foreign policy prior to Donald Trump's taking office as president.[6]

Other Russian contacts with the Trump campaign staff (and future administration figures) were unofficial or ostensibly quite personal in nature. One such approach involved Sergei Millian, a Belarussian-American businessman who had previous business dealings with candidate Trump.[7] Millian was president of the U.S.-based American-Russian Chamber of Commerce. Reportedly, Millian floated the idea of a meeting with Trump during the candidate's campaign speech to the National Rifle Association, a meeting that could eventually set the stage for personal dialogue with President Putin.[8] That particular outreach was ultimately rejected by one of Trump's senior advisors, but only because the individuals involved did not appear to actually have high-level Russian connections. Eventually individuals with seemingly higher-level connections would approach and meet with a senior Trump advisor and other campaign members.

It is those other meetings that are most interesting in terms of the active measures practices we have explored. One of the most successful examples of American political action during the Cold War was the extent to which the CIA leveraged intelligence it was collecting in regard to both Cuban activities (Castro regime plans) and the activities of Mexican domestic opposition parties of all stripes. The majority of that intelligence came from communications intercepts and telephone wiretaps placed by CIA operations officers. That information was offered, incrementally and over a period of time, to senior regime figures in the Mexican government. Ultimately it became a matter of vital interest to the president of Mexico, and his desire for ongoing data resulted in extensive cooperation with the CIA station chief in Mexico City as well as a general receptivity to a number of American foreign policy positions.

The simple fact is that among the hooks available to gain access to figures of influence, information is as attractive and sometimes far more tempting than the classic tools of money and sex. The CIA success in Mexico demonstrated the extreme value of covertly collected political information. Access to such political dirt can be shown to be at the heart of a good number of both American and Russian efforts to gain influence and leverage policy within targeted regimes. At the time of this writing in 2018, there are indications suggesting that the practices of offering covert intelligence as a tool to gain influence are still very much in contemporary use, brought into play by Russian political operatives as recently as the American elections of 2016.

During the 2016 campaign, on at least two known occasions, offers were extended to provide dirt on the presidential campaign of Hillary Clinton. Both offers received a positive response from Trump campaign members. One offer was extended to George Papadopoulos, named early in the Trump campaign as a foreign policy advisor, with expertise in the area of energy policy. Within days of joining Trump's campaign, Papadopoulos became involved in contacts between the Trump campaign team and purported representatives of the Russian leadership. A number of his own internal campaign emails dealt with establishing direct Russian contacts and improving relations, ultimately seeking a high-level meeting between Trump and Putin. In his communications he touted his own Russian connections and relayed Russian interest in engaging with the Trump campaign. Between March and September, Papadopoulos proposed such meetings on seven different occasions.[9]

To what extent Russian contacts were directly encouraged by Papadopoulos is currently unclear, but he has admitted that in one instance a Russian professor he knew "to have substantial connections to Russian government officials" contacted him within days of his joining the campaign. The implications of the timing of that contact are important, as is the fact that when questioned on that point by the FBI, Papadopoulos now admits that he lied—stating that the discussion had occurred prior to his being appointed as a foreign policy advisor. Specifically, the professor offered "thousands of emails" containing "dirt" on Hillary Clinton and the offer of that dirt was used as one of the reasons in which Russian contacts should be established.[10]

The professor also introduced Papadopoulos to a third party, representing himself as associated with members of the Russian Ministry of Foreign Affairs, which was interested in organizing a meeting on the subject of relations between the two governments under a Trump presidency. The contacts were reported within the campaign organization and in emails Papadopoulos was told the he was doing "great work" and that he should "go for it."[11] Exactly how far such dialogues extended remains unknown at the time of this writing. However, with the advent of the Justice Department's Special Council investigation of Russian involvement in the 2016 election, Papadopoulos was questioned and investigated.

On October 30, 2017, Papadopoulos pleaded guilty to charges of making false statements to the FBI. Among the materials introduced with the charges were emails he had sent to one of his Russian contacts in regard to a meeting with Trump's then national campaign chairman, Paul Manafort. An email states that the meeting had been "approved from our side." A follow-up email of July 14, 2016 proposed an August meeting in London, which would have included the "national chairman," possibly one or more other Trump foreign policy advisors and members of President Putin's office.

In the affidavit connected to the George Papadopoulos case, there is reference to what appears to be a corroborating email Papadopoulos sent to a foreign contact regarding setting up a meeting with a person (referred to as his "national chairman") who appears to be Paul Manafort. Papadopoulos writes that the meeting has been "approved from our side." A separate email, forwarded along with the meeting message by unnamed Trump staff, emphasized that the initial Russian contacts needed to be at a level that would not "send any signal" regarding the opening of dialogue between the campaign and the Russian leadership.[12] Such language appears to reflect an effort to ensure that at least the initial dialogue remained secret and did not become exposed to press scrutiny.

The larger story of Russian attempts to gain policy-level influence within a future Trump presidency will very possibly emerge over time. However, other incidents from the campaign suggest that there was an orchestrated effort to extend the offer of Clinton dirt in an effort to engage with individuals within the campaign, indeed individuals personally close to the presidential candidate. In June well after the initial outreach to Papadopoulos, Donald Trump Jr. received an email from a former business associate of his father—someone known to Trump from a period when he was actively involved in an entertainment project (the Miss Universe pageant) and potential business investments in Russia.

The message related that the former business contact had been approached by a "senior Russian government official" who was interested in providing the Trump campaign with "dirt" on Hillary Clinton. The email specifically mentioned documents that "would incriminate Hillary and her dealings with Russia and which would be very useful to your father." The information was positioned as being very sensitive and coming from a high level within the Russian government. Donald

Trump Jr.'s reply to the outreach, expressed within minutes via email, was quite positive and encouraging (from a Russian perspective): "If it's what you say I love it especially later in the summer." Within days, the former business partner proposed a meeting in New York which would include a "Russian government attorney."[13] Trump Jr. also responded that he would likely invite "Paul Manafort, campaign boss" and Jared Kushner, one of the closest personal advisors to Donald Trump. The reference to Manafort would certainly seem to suggest a deep interest in the political value of the information being offered.

While the offer of such "sensitive" political information—presented as coming from a "high level" within the Russian government and reflecting "incriminating" behavior on the part of a former senator and secretary of state in regard to dealings with Russia—would be very much in line with standard active measures practices, the response by Trump Jr. is somewhat shocking. First of all, the information was presented as coming from within the Russian government and as being sensitive, obviously raising questions not only as to what it was but how the Russians might have obtained it. If it was what it appeared to be, issues of national security were immediately obvious, including to what extent State Department or other government communications channels might have been compromised. That possibility, along with whatever was implied by the reference to "incriminating" information, called for immediately reporting such an offer to one or more United States intelligence agencies. In prior decades, any such outreach from an adversary nation would have been considered suspect and very likely reported to the FBI as well. In 2016 Russia and individuals within its political, financial, and business leadership had been and were still under a variety of U.S. legal sanctions, including the new sanctions resulting from events in the Crimea and Ukraine in 2014. It was noted earlier that the long-established cautions concerning Russian contacts during the Cold War had faded away following the collapse of the Soviet Union. Incidents such as this, during the election campaign of

2016, seem to confirm that the old cautions and sensitivities had not just faded—they had totally disappeared.

The result of the Russian outreach to Donald Trump Jr. was that on June 9, a Russian lawyer, Natalia Veselnitskaya, did appear for a meeting at Trump Tower in New York City (a meeting held only one floor below the personal offices of Donald Trump). Veselnitskaya was known to represent individuals still under investigation by U.S. federal prosecutors and had been an active lobbyist, supporting Russian opposition to a series of 2012 sanctions, which the United States had imposed on individuals as a response to human rights violations in Russia (the Magnitsky Act).[14]

The Russian meeting also included Emin Agalarov, a popular singer and the son of a Russian real estate multimillionaire closely tied to Vladimir Putin, who awarded the senior Agalarov with the Order of Honor of the Russian Federation. Agalarov worked with Trump on the Miss Universe pageant and the Agalarov families were well known to him. Agalarov's initial communication to Trump Jr. mentioned that his father had been in touch with the Russian prosecutor general, who had volunteered the possibility of providing incriminating information about Clinton.

Given the emails eventually released by Trump Jr. himself, there is no doubt of the political nature of the meeting, and the offer of sensitive Russian information on Clinton. Initially Trump Jr. obfuscated that entire aspect of the contact, stating in a public response that the meeting was strictly about the adoption of Russian children and that Manafort and Kushner had simply dropped by for introductions. Later he did acknowledge that information about Clinton had been mentioned but that Veselnitskaya had not made any reference to the type of highly sensitive and incriminatory details that had been the subject of the pre-meeting communications. Veselnitskaya stated that it might have been true that there was a desire for dirt on Clinton, but she herself had mentioned nothing of that nature during the meeting, thereby putting her story in direct conflict with the statements by Trump Jr. that she had indeed offered such information.

While Trump Jr. later expressed, during Judiciary Committee testimony, that he had anticipated consulting lawyers about any information that the Russians might have provided, he did not report the Russian offer of confidential information concerning a former secretary of state to the FBI or any other agency of the American intelligence community. In a similar vein, he failed to report the contact with Veselnitskaya to the FBI even though he claimed she had indeed offered information, albeit of a questionable nature. Indeed Trump Jr. stated he did not even know the lawyer's name, implying he certainly did not order any sort of background or security check on her, which would have confirmed that she was indeed known to the FBI and Justice Department.

Beyond exactly what the intent of this particular Russian outreach may have been, it clearly did involve the bait of serious dirt on Clinton and exposed those in the meeting to accusations that they were soliciting valuable political intelligence from a foreign national, especially a known Russian lobbyist. In that regard, the simple act of Donald Trump Jr., Paul Manafort, and Jared Kushner meeting with the Russians exposed them all to compromise.[15] In addition, a test of receptivity—along with the earlier approach to Papadopoulos—and the acceptance of the meeting would certainly have confirmed that the American election campaign was fertile ground for active measures focused on political destabilization and disinformation. Anything that might open the American political dynamic to Russian influence, particularly in regard to reducing or eliminating sanctions, was a high priority for the Russian leadership. To some extent that was a purely personal issue for the Putin regime and its supporters, but it was something that had been very publicly expressed by President Putin and was endemic among leading Russian political and economic figures. There was a deep and overriding desire to reduce (or otherwise mitigate) the growing number of economic sanctions that the United States had in place against Russian business and finance figures.

As of this writing, one other incident—involving a senior figure not only in the 2016 campaign but in the initial Trump presidency—deserves exploration as it appears to provide further insight into a much deeper aspect of active measures, the recruitment of active agents of influence. We have previously noted that such recruitments can be a very long-term investment, occurring over years until (and if) the target (normally with the potential for either current or future influence on political decision-making) actually ends up in a position to be of some value. To appreciate the context in which modern-day agents of influence may be developed, we need to begin with a review of the extent to which Russian practices and tools have evolved during the period 2005-2010. We previously covered the point that the most fundamental Russian active measures programs continued unchanged as the SVR took over operations from the KGB within the United States. Covert intelligence collection continued and efforts to identify and recruit agents of influence continued, increasingly within the business sectors including trade, investment, and banking. The new, open, capitalist business environment in Russia made it far easier for intelligence officers and especially their cut-outs, installed in perfectly legal business and trade jobs, to make ostensibly routine contact with Americans.

Such practices were initially targeted on foreign businesspersons and consultants and involved both unwitting agents of influence and individuals who could be suborned with money or blackmail. *Kompromat* is the Russian term for the practice of compromising individuals with money or with the collection of information on illegal or immoral activities. Compromising foreigners with sexually active translators (covert intelligence officers) or even with prostitutes seems to have been a favorite ploy, used by both American and Russian intelligence. Individuals who had been or could be compromised in any fashion were referred to as "trusted assets."[16]

The opportunities for FSB kompromat activities significantly increased during the first decade of this century, not only in regard to the number and quality of potential assets but in terms of FSB ability to target individuals, monitor their activities, and collect virtually any of their private communications. The FSB's twelfth department, responsible for technical collections, had dramatically increased its ability to tap into and record virtually any communications going on within Russia.[17] The advanced tapping system used by the FSB inside Russia (the SORM system) was also implemented in Ukraine. In 2014 a conversation between two American diplomats, one being the U.S. Ukrainian ambassador, using a non-encrypted voice line was intercepted and recorded. The conversation involved a discussion of Ukrainian political problems, and mentioned the names of preferred individuals for a new regime. The call was uploaded to a pro-Russian YouTube channel and reposted. It seriously embarrassed the United States, providing information used in Russian propaganda claims about American conspiracy in Ukraine. The Ukrainian security service simply declined to investigate the incident.[18]

These advanced Russian communications surveillance capabilities and the new SVR and FSB practices related to targeting foreigners doing business with Russians were most definitely known to the American security services, in particular the CIA, FBI, and NSA. In contrast, American businessmen and investors appear to have become much less concerned about foreign intelligence exposure in the post-Soviet, post-Cold War years, and American diplomats were somewhat less security cautious than they should have been.

Still, the laws pertaining to foreign agents, to Americans lobbying for or representing foreign parties of any sort, remained in force and the NSA had its own set of highly advanced snooping tools, including not only name and keyword searches but computer algorithms for much more sophisticated scanning and sorting of all types of communications. And, as in years past, the CIA generated its own intelligence collections target lists, not just for military and diplomatic monitoring but also for individuals and topics related to foreign commercial and business activities.

Neither the Russian or American services had abandoned their Cold War practices or suspicions of each other. And that is why certain individuals known to have had extensive business contacts inside both Russia and Ukraine came under scrutiny when they assumed roles of political influence in American politics. Standard counterintelligence practice demands that individuals who might be (or might become) agents of influence or trusted assets of an adversary power undergo investigation. If it is determined that those individuals have not reported the full details of their associations under the Foreign Agents Registration Act, the investigations become much more detailed.

As early as 2005, Paul Manafort began working as a paid consultant to an extremely wealthy Russian metals billionaire, Oleg Deripaska. By profession Paul Manafort is a lawyer, his extensive career has also involved positions as a lobbyist and political consultant. In fact, Manafort was a political consultant and advisor to the presidential campaigns of Gerald Ford, Ronald Reagan, George H. W., Bush and Bob Dole, and clearly he has broad personal connections at the top of the American political spectrum.

Oleg Deripaska owned several mills and factories in Russia and was an early supporter of Vladimir Putin. By 2005 his own public image inside Russia was not all that positive and Manafort was hired as a political/image consultant. In the mid-2000s Russian/U.S. business dealings like these had become quite common. Manafort made introductions for Deripaska, who traveled internationally and met with numbers of influential Americans and Europeans, including politicians such as Senator John McCain. Eventually Manafort and his business partner Rick Gates became involved in a joint effort to purchase New York City's Drake Hotel, which ended with Deripaska in court with a legal action against the partnership.[19] Deripaska's close ties to the

Russian leadership and the importance of his connections were further confirmed in April, 2018 when he and his metals company (Rusal) were signaled out for special American financial sanctions.

Manafort's most intensive political consulting was in Ukraine. Press reports there indicate that Manafort was first hired by Rinat Akhmetov, whose iron ore and steel business gave him an estimated worth of some $2.8 billion. Manafort was ostensibly hired as an advisor on corporate communications for one of Akhmetov's companies, System Capital Management. In reality, Akhmetov was a major supporter of Yanukovych and the pro-Russian Party of Regions. Through Akhmetov, Manafort offered political advice to Yanukovych. Apparently disillusioned with Russian political technologists efforts in the 2004 election, Yanukovych felt that an American political advisor might be of more assistance. Manafort's consulting in the Ukraine began in 2006 and would continue into 2012. As reported in his own financial statements, he earned over $17 million in professional fees during that period.[20]

In 2014, Manafort became a subject of interest to the FBI, partly as an outgrowth of a U.S. investigation of Yanukovych, whose pro-Russian regime had been ousted amid street protests. Yanukovych's Party of Regions was accused of corruption, and Ukrainian authorities claimed he had hidden millions of dollars in foreign accounts outside the country. Investigators conducted extensive probes of the possible roles played by Manafort's firm and other Ukraine-associated U.S. lobbyist and consulting groups (including the Podesta Group and Mercury Public Affairs LLC) in illegal foreign transactions and money-laundering. One of the things that began to emerge from those inquiries was that the firms had not registered under the Foreign Agents Registration Act. That failure alone could have potentially exposed the two men to compromise and recruitment.

The FBI investigation confirmed Manafort's foreign business relationship and payments, and in June 2016 Manafort acknowledged his employment by the pro-Russian Party of Regions. He also admitted to his lobbying activities for them, involving more contemporary efforts to improve Yanukovych's image during the period 2012-14. One example of his American outreach was an email to then U.S. Ambassador to Ukraine John F. Tefft, concerning a State Department charge that the 2012 elections in Ukraine had been a "step backward" in terms of democratic process. It was only in June 2016 that Manafort "retroactively" filed as an agent of a foreign government.[21]

In and of itself, Manafort's work for pro-Russian politicians in Ukraine is interesting and consistent with the practice of soft political action—the use of politically connected individuals in an effort for imaging and shaping positive perceptions. However, his outreach to the American ambassador in an effort to temper the State Department's view of Ukraine was something else. More important, his position as a senior political advisor in both a national American political campaign and his potential direct policy advisory reach to an American president is potential shaping of an entirely different magnitude.

This potential for serious pro-Russian policy influence came into play when Manafort volunteered his consulting services—at no charge—to the 2016 presidential campaign of Donald Trump. Reportedly Manafort's offer was extended via Trump's son-in-law Jared Kushner. The offer was accepted and in March 2016 Manafort joined the campaign's effort to obtain delegates to the Republican Party National Convention, an effort in which Manafort reportedly played a key role. Following Trump's successful effort to obtain the Republican presidential nomination, Manafort was promoted in June 2016 to the position of campaign manager. Manafort's business partner Rick Gates also assumed a role as an official in the campaign.

The FBI's initial 2014 interest in Manafort had involved his services as a business consultant and lobbyist for the pro-Russian Ukrainian party of Viktor Yanukovych. By 2016 Yanukovych was in exile in Russia, obtained though his personal friendship with Putin.

And reportedly, at some point during 2016, the FBI was advised by the NSA that Manafort was involved in a number of ongoing conversations with Russian political operatives. Beyond that, internal communications between Russian figures (exactly who they are is obviously heavily classified) were also monitored by the NSA.[22]

With our understanding of political action practices, it is virtually impossible to think that Russian intelligence would not have recognized the potential of having a pro-Russian political consultant in direct contact with an American president (or even within an influential role within U.S. party politics). Given his position in the campaign and his potential future access to Trump as president, the FBI reopened its investigation. When rumors of his former Ukrainian relationship appeared in the press, Manafort almost immediately resigned from his campaign work. However, news reports described his partner Rick Gates's visits to the White House following Trump's election.[23]

With the appointment of Justice Department Special Prosecutor Robert Mueller, tasked with investigating Russian involvement in the 2016 campaign, Manafort and Gates became objects of interest in the inquiry. On October 10, 2017 they were formally charged with a number of violations including "conspiracy against the United States, conspiracy to launder money, unregistered agent of a foreign principal, false and misleading FARA statements, false statements, and seven counts of failure to file reports of foreign bank and financial accounts."[24] In February 2018, Gates entered a guilty plea to charges of conspiracy for money laundering and lying to investigators. Manafort was indicted on additional charges of illegal lobbying activities.

In regard to our exploration of political warfare, the primary point of interest in those charges is that FARA was created to ensure that, according to the State Department, "the U.S. government and the people of the United States are informed of the source of information and the identity of persons attempting to influence U.S. public opinion, policy, and laws." Obviously, such influencing activities are a basic part of political warfare. Manafort and Gates's unreported involvement in foreign lobbying illustrates yet one more type of entanglement, and could well have provided new political action opportunities for intelligence agencies or private pro-Russian actors supporting Putin's policy goals.

There is little doubt that Russian political action was in play during the U.S. election of 2016, yet efforts to gain access through personal contacts, the offering of political dirt, and the potential use of agents of influence were only part of the picture. The American election campaign-related activities of 2016 can now be seen to have been only one element of a much larger destabilization effort targeting the United States as well as key NATO nations—an active measures effort employing sophisticated information warfare that began well before the American campaigns, continued though the election itself, and continues as of this writing in 2018. That effort involves old practices with very new tools and runs far deeper than a single election. It appears far broader and harshly divisive, intended to politically fragment Western nations viewed as still targeting Russian sovereignty and hegemony with long-term open election/democracy initiatives.

Chapter Fourteen:
Fragmentation

By early 2015 Russia had completed a series of actions that demonstrated that it would not hesitate to intervene either politically or militarily within its sphere of influence, including states on its borders and the newly independent former Soviet republics. Those interventions brought rounds of American and European sanctions in March of 2014. Its economy damaged, Russia pushed back with sanctions of its own, just as it had in response to the Magnitsky human rights sanctions. But those sanctions proved to be only a small part of what now appears to be a much broader set of Russian active measures begun that year.

To fully appreciate the nature of the Russian response it is important to understand that, to President Putin and the broader Russian public, the 2014 sanctions were just one more example proving the West, in particular the United States, is fundamentally unwilling to respect Russian sovereignty or to acknowledge Russia as a truly independent global power deserving respect. Putin projected that basic Russian concern, quite sincerely, years earlier in a 2007 *Time* interview: "Sometimes one gets the impression that America does not need friends. Sometimes we get the impression that you need some kind of auxiliary subjects to take command of…that is the reason why everybody is made to feel that it's OK to pinch the Russians somewhat…

they are a little bit savage still…and probably need to have their hair brushed and their beards trimmed somewhat."[1]

The Russian public increasingly expressed the same feelings. Unfavorable opinions of the United States doubled from forty to almost eighty percent within a single year.[2] Beyond that, polling showed that during the course of 2014 Putin's personal popularity increased by over twenty percent. Polls also showed that confidence in the overall direction of the Russian nation had improved by the same twenty percent.[3] Following Russia's annexation of Crimea, Putin and the Russian political figures who had endorsed intervention in Ukraine were treated as heroes. In announcing the acquisition of Crimea during a speech outside the Kremlin, Putin left no doubt about the solidified Russian position on foreign affairs and Moscow's worldview: "Russia strived to engage in a dialogue with our colleagues in the West. We are constantly proposing cooperation on all key issues; we want to strengthen our level of trust and for our relations to be equal, open and fair. But we saw no reciprocal steps. On the contrary they have lied to us many times, made decisions behind our backs, and placed before us an accomplished fact. They kept telling us the same thing, 'Well this does not concern you.' That's easy to say."[4]

A much more personal insight into Putin's view of the West as of 2014 is found in his response to a question during a press session following an economic forum in May. The forum was to have been held in conjunction with the G8 economic forum, but Russia had been expelled as part of the sanctions. In a follow-up press session, the president was asked about freedom of speech in Russia. Putin, clearly sensitive to the issue, was outraged: "You Americans have no right to lecture us! Your TV stations blatantly lied about the events in Kiev. You have no moral authority to breathe a word about freedom of speech."[5]

The events of the next few years would certainly prove that neither the United States nor the West was going to be able to ignore Russia. On the other hand, they would do little to develop any level of increased trust. What would increase substantially was the degree of political chaos among the Western nations that were clearly the targets of President Putin's remarks.

INTIMIDATION AND DIVERSION

Russia's first step towards gaining the West's attention, and forcing its respect, was to emphasize its strength as a global, nuclear superpower. For the first time since the height of the Cold War, Russian bombers routinely entered American and NATO airspace. In one particular surge Russian aircraft were detected sixteen times in ten days. And for the first time ever the flights were not simply obvious reconnaissance missions by individual Russian bombers. In a number of instances they were full-fledged "strike packages" consisting of bombers, tankers, and long-range fighter escorts. In November 2014 the Russian military advised that it would routinely send flights not only along both the east and west American coasts, but into the Gulf of Mexico as well, another practice not seen during the Cold War.

Russia was obviously sending a strategic military message to the United States; it proceeded to send a very tactical message to NATO and Western Europe. Beginning in October 2014 a series of large-scale Russian military penetration missions were flown over NATO nation borders. On four occasions formations of six strategic bombers, four long-range fighters, and a larger number of short-range fighters, all accompanied by aerial tankers, moved along Western borders, forcing the launch of interceptors from the United Kingdom, Denmark, Finland, Sweden, Turkey, and even Portugal.

Again, nothing of that nature had previously been seen in Europe, even at the height of the Cold War. Equally alarming was that all the Russian flights were unannounced. All flew with their transponders turned off, leaving air-traffic control radar blind to them, and creating the risk of collision with commercial aircraft. By the end of 2014

NATO announced that its aircraft had responded repeatedly to large groups of Russian aircraft flying over the Baltic Sea, off the Norwegian coast, and in one instance from the North Sea all the way down the west coast of Europe to Portugal.

The second part of the Russian military message, part intimidation but in another key aspect highly political, represented a major destabilization of ongoing efforts towards reducing nuclear weapons deployments. It began with a series of new and extremely assertive statements on the importance and commitment to advancing Russian nuclear weaponry. The *Moscow Times* increasingly carried articles on the development of the brand new Borei-class nuclear-powered ballistic missile submarines (in September 2014 sea trials launched the first of Russia's next generation Bulava ICBMs) as well as a new system of road mobile TOPOL-M strategic nuclear missiles. In touting the new weapons, the newspaper proclaimed that they demonstrated "that Russia remains a nuclear power to be reckoned with even as Moscow's relations sour over Ukraine."[6]

The Russian focus on nuclear weaponry continued, asserted by the most senior Russian leaders. In December 2016 Putin claimed that Russia had already modernized almost sixty percent of its nuclear force. In January 2017 Russia's Defense Minister Sergey Shoygu described a massive program of nuclear rearmament, including land, sea, and air (with a new strategic nuclear bomber to be developed), and in March Putin confirmed that Russia's strategic forces were the highest priority in its ongoing push for military modernization.[7]

Russia continued to do more than talk about its nuclear focus. In October 2017 it conducted what was possibly the largest coordinated nuclear strike drill on record, comparable to only one similar exercise in the early 1980s. The exercise involved three submarine-launched ballistic missiles fired from units of both the Russian Northern and Pacific fleets, as well as three separate cruise missile launches from long-range bombers flying out of widely separated airfields, and a ground-based

ICBM launch.[8] It was something far more intense than an individual weapons drill. Given the extent of the worldwide command and control required, it simulated what can only be described as a first strike nuclear exercise.

Russian leadership remarks also generated an active discussion about Russian policy on use of nuclear weapons. There was a suggestion that Russia had now returned to the possibility for "first use" in tactical (kiloton class) versus strategic (megaton class) weapons. Early in 2018, Putin fueled concerns over Russian use of nuclear weapons with a high-profile presentation on five next-generation nuclear strike weapons, including stealthy air- and sea-launched devices, as well as hypersonic and even atomic-powered unlimited range cruise missiles. In introducing the advanced weapons system, Putin once again hit on the point that Russia would not allow itself to be contained or ignored: "No has listened to us," he said, according to the Associated Press. "You listen to us now."[9]

Putin's assertion that the world was not giving sufficient attention to Russia was not totally accurate. In response to the ongoing Russian focus on nuclear weapons and warfare, the United States and NATO have resurrected practices for the use (and defense against) low yield "tactical" nuclear weapons in combat, something that had almost disappeared from military planning since late in the Cold War. NATO ground exercises, especially in the East, surged following the Russian incursions in Crimea and Ukraine. With the new Russian emphasis on nuclear weaponry, a deterrence exercise named Steadfast Noon has begun to involve the control and use of B61 tactical nuclear bombs.[10] A planned phase-out of those weapons in Europe was put on indefinite hold, with a new program for upgrading the weapons.

Russian focus on nuclear warfare has quite literally reversed what had been an ongoing American push towards nuclear force reduction into a sprint towards investing in a modernized force of upgraded weapons and delivery systems. By November 2014 U.S. Secretary of

Defense Chuck Hagel was proposing a Defense Innovation Initiative which called for an annual increase of ten percent in the nuclear force budget for five years—an investment comparable to the huge defense programs of the 1950s and 1970s.[11] That move was followed during the next two years with the announcement of ICBM missile moderni-zation programs and the development of a next-generation long-range strategic bomber, the Northrop Grumman B-21 Raider. The modern-ization and new weapons programs for all three military services are estimated by the Congressional Budget Office, as of 2017, to cost $1.3 trillion.[12]

Lots of exercises, lots of fantastically expensive weapons, and a huge drain on the American budget—so how is this political warfare? What makes it an element of political/hybrid warfare is that Russian nuclear intimidation diverts the United States, and NATO, from spending money and resources on ground forces, tactical air units, and air defense systems—the real weapons of necessity which NATO would need, even in the form of military aid, should Russia decide to reassert itself in eastern Ukraine or engage in another round of deni-able hybrid warfare in Eastern Europe. Limiting NATO's ability to respond helps maintain feelings of both stress and tension among the former Soviet satellite republics in the East, even for NATO member states. And stress and tension—insecurity—provide political leverage for Russia. Actual military incursion is not absolutely necessary, simply maintaining the possibility is in itself politically destabilizing.

DISINFORMATION

Intimidation, diversion, and the creation of beachheads for potential political or military initiatives are very real and contemporary Russian political warfare practices in Eastern Europe, especially in the regions of the former Soviet territories. When compared to American contain-ment and push-back operations conducted by Truman and Eisenhower following World War II, they appear to be more sophisticated and more successful, at least in the short term. The longer-term legacies of mistrust produced by such efforts are a different story, as America learned from what it perceived as its own initial successes in Iran and Guatemala.

The longer-term consequences of the destabilization campaign, which appears to have been launched against Western democracies beginning in 2014, are even greater, despite what appears to be the initial success of the effort. As we have seen, President Putin was furious with the second failure of Russian political influence in Ukraine and, in addition to blaming it on Western agents, felt that it was an illegal coup against an elected government. In his view, Western media totally misrepresented what had happened, and only the Russian media had accurately reported the events. He made it clear that Western media was totally untrustworthy, whether with regard to Russia, Ukraine, or even the Olympics. Whatever the story was, it would be recast for "anti-Russian" propaganda purposes: "Whatever we say we cannot convince anyone, because they have their own agenda."[13]

Putin was able to project his own view of a coup inside Ukraine internally through the Russian media because by 2014 he had very effectively arranged for almost total Kremlin control. He was unabashed about controlling state-operated outlets, declaring them national resources that would be operated by "people who uphold the interest of the Russian Federation…the government is an owner and the media that belong to the government must carry out our instructions"[14] As for the independent media, by 2014 it was largely owned by oligarchs supporting the regime in the Kremlin, with the ability to increasingly exert the same degree of editorial control. In a previous chapter, we noted Kremlin efforts to ensure that "patriotic" sources made use of the internet to aggressively project its messaging.

The establishment of a "patriotic hacker" community had evolved over time, moving beyond internal messaging, and by 2006 aggressively targeting anti-Russian websites in support of Chechnya as well as against Estonian banks, newspapers, broadcasters, and government websites.[15] In 2007 hundreds of Lithuanian government and business sites came under pro-Russian attack, demonstrating that there was an expanding population of patriotic hackers operating at varied levels of technical capability. That capability was enhanced in 2009 with the opening of a Kremlin school for bloggers, headed by Russian political "technologists" and oriented towards increasing the political sophistication of internet "messaging." By 2014 there was a well-developed capability to project any pro-Russian message globally, against any target on the internet. The only question would be the extent to which Russian hacking and political messaging was "self-directed" or organized and controlled.

The evidence of a new wave of Russian internet political messaging specifically directed towards Western targets became increasingly evident in early 2014. The events in Ukraine appear to have dramatically accelerated the messaging, making it highly visible and increasingly noted in regular news coverage. Some of the earliest Western reporting came from *The Guardian*. Founded in 1821, it has long been one of Britain's leading newspapers, with a history of investigative reporting and independent criticism, and it is especially well known for its foreign correspondents. During 2014, *The Guardian* carried some of the most detailed field reporting on events in Ukraine. Its articles were particularly assertive in countering official Russian statements. In March 2014, it went head-to-head with Putin, immediately and directly repudiating five specific claims made in a highly public press interview.[16]

On the same day the article—"Five fibs from Vladimir: how Putin distorted the facts about Ukraine"—appeared, *The Guardian*'s website comments sections were overwhelmed by a series of pro-Putin rebuttals at such volume that monitors could not respond to them. The posts were exceptionally rude, abusive, and harshly critical of any news stories related to either Putin or Russia.[17] Comments on pro-Russian posts were highly repetitive, seemingly written from a common template, and immediately supplemented with an extensive set of "recommends." Predictably, it was impossible to absolutely prove it was a troll attack, but the experienced moderators, who deal with over forty thousand comments a day, certainly felt it to be an organized effort. Such orchestrated political messaging—focused on events in Ukraine—also appeared on Russian social networking sites such as VKontakte, particularly important since it has twenty million Ukrainian users.

The campaign then moved onto the global social media networks Facebook, YouTube, and even Twitter. And as with *The Guardian*, messaging exhibited a great deal of comment similarity and a rate of commenting and recommending that suggested something far beyond the work of random, patriotic posters. It was not similar to the DNS attacks or web-page smearing discussed earlier, nor was it hacking in even the simplest sense; it was trolling: simply using individuals (or in some instances automated scripts referred to as robots or "bots") to post scripted comments, photos, or video clips. Given its extensive focus on politics and its mode of specifically repeating official Russian government talking points on Ukraine, the overall information effort was relatively obvious when viewed in total—but potentially quite effective when seen by a social network user looking at an individual comment thread, a tweet, a photo (which was often doctored or from a totally different incident than the purported context), or a streaming video clip.

Its weakness was that as an overall effort it was so obvious that some of the remaining investigative reporters inside Russia itself—working largely for independent internet news sites—focused in on the campaign's probable sources, including certain of the paid "troll farms" that had been established to project the Kremlin's views.[18] It must be noted that such basic information campaigns need not be planned or even directed from within the Russian government, and are not likely to be an FSB or GRU (military intelligence) matter. Given their technical simplicity and that the primary need is for them to be deniable and focused on political messaging, the simple solution is privatization, allowing supportive and financially well-endowed regime associates carry out such initiatives at their own discretion.

Certainly privatization of political warfare is not a new practice. On some occasions during the Cold War, a U.S. president simply had to remark that something needed to be done about a certain issue for CIA officers to take the initiative and make it happen, without direct orders or anything in writing. Such activities occurred at the senior levels of the CIA and to a lesser degree much further down the organizational chain of command.[19] We also explored the privatization of such operations, with the second phase of the Contra effort against Nicaragua involving a number of individuals and groups (including some very wealthy donors) acting independently from the United States government. Perhaps the highlight of such deniability occurred when, during the Iran-Contra scandal, President Reagan was able to claim that he had no knowledge at all of events taking place in an ongoing secret war against Nicaragua.[20]

Such stated lack of knowledge is certainly not unique to American presidents, we have seen that even their own aides and agencies act to preserve deniability on their behalf. By his third presidential term, Vladimir Putin—trained and developed to be a politically sensitive senior KGB officer in an earlier life—apparently has become a master of the opaque. He reportedly routinely deals with even direct questions from senior aides in an intentionally deniable fashion. In one instance in 2011, First Deputy Chief of Staff Vyacheslav Volodin queried Putin on a specific problem they had discussed: "Shall we do as agreed?" asked Volodin, trying to elicit an answer. "Do as you think is best," replied Putin."[21]

Future years—or perhaps decades—may reveal exactly who initiated the Russian psychological warfare campaign that began to emerge during 2014. For now the information available only allows it to be described and characterized in terms of its targets and its levels of sophistication. Beyond that it can be evaluated in terms of the overall political warfare practices put into play. Certain of the actors involved have already been identified and a number of individuals have been formally charged; both the true extent of the information warfare and the practices involved have emerged relatively quickly. In February 2018, thirteen Russians, one American, and three companies were indicted for a variety of illegal activities, part of a sophisticated campaign to subvert the American election of 2016.[22]

Perhaps the most sensational aspect of the Russian political action was not simply the massive quantity of messaging but the fact that Russian operatives, using stolen identities, had illegally traveled across the United States, collecting information to fine-tune and target the campaign. The operatives had focused their attention on election battleground states, and even gone so far as to organize political rallies, even competing rallies—all with the objective of creating maximum political, cultural, and racial fragmentation. Even the earliest findings show it to have been an information warfare effort in the classic tradition of the Cold War, comparable to the best practices of the CIA or KGB.

It is now a matter of record, as reflected in the United States Justice Department charges—and supporting details in the indictments—that the origin of much of the Russian troll warfare appears to have come out of a business establishment in St. Petersburg.[23] That company, The Internet Research Agency, has no official connection to the Russian government. However, at least some of its financing has been traced by Russian media investigators to shell companies such as Concord Management and Consulting, linked to Russian oligarchs such as Yevgeniy Viktorovich Prigozhin with personal ties to President Putin. Prigozhin, known familiarly as "Putin's chef" for his apparent willingness to do whatever Putin asks of him as well as for his career origins as a hot dog vendor, was among those indicted in the 2018

Justice Department filing.[24] He had previously been under American sanctions related to his involvement with covert Russian paramilitary activities in eastern Ukraine.

Internet Research Agency staff, some of whom had been previously interviewed about their work, were simply paid employees, assigned to put posts on blogs or place comments on the threads of news sites and forums. A number had formerly done such work voluntarily, as members of the patriotic hacker effort discussed earlier. They had simply moved to being paid for work in which they fully believed. Beginning in 2014, troll farm campaigns began to be managed in a much more structured fashion, with attention given to what types of content worked and which did not. Initial efforts were evaluated and those in charge determined that it was far too easy for Western internet users to spot the types of messaging that had become common. Techniques and messages that were working effectively in Russia and even in Ukraine did not make an impression on Western viewers, in fact they were so easily spotted they were evaluated as counterproductive.[25]

In addition to increasingly organized trolling efforts, during 2014 and 2015 a highly targeted form of hacking appeared that was well beyond the DNS and website "graffiti attacks" of earlier years. The first known targets to be claimed were the email servers of NGOs operating in Ukraine. The website CyberBerkut published a series of supposedly hacked emails, which purportedly demonstrated that the Ukrainian NGOs were in communication with the U.S. Embassy and receiving funds from American foundations. Both practices were fairly common NGO activities, but the emails proved extremely inflammatory in terms of the political crisis of 2014.[26] In early 2015 the same hacking group claimed to have penetrated web servers of the German government, and by April had successfully hacked a French television network, taking control of eleven channels for some three hours. French cybersecurity ultimately tracked the hack to a group of Russia-based hackers who would become known as "Fancy Bear."[27]

FRAGMENTATION

While much of the contemporary news dialogue revolves around the extent to which Russia conducted an influence campaign (i.e., "meddled with American politics") targeting the U.S. presidential election of 2016, our broader view reveals something of far greater scope, with deep and by now more familiar goals. Those goals center on the fragmentation of a targeted adversary: politically, racially, religiously, and ethnically. In addition they seek the disruption of the adversary's political framework, including calling into question the legitimacy and trustworthiness of its electoral process. One of the most destabilizing aspects of the NGO democracy initiative has been its challenge to the stability of "legacy governments," regimes in which parties, political power centers, and even individuals tend to repeatedly recycle themselves with little real change in governance. To the extent that the tools of political warfare can create a challenge to the confidence in the electoral process itself, they represent a major opportunity for destabilizing any government, including that of the United States.

In short, what we are describing is not just meddling in a single election nor positioning one candidate over another, it is a destabilization effort with the overall goal of fragmenting the American public and inserting chaos into its political system. In one sense it is the same sort of campaign that Russia had consistently accused Western democracies of conducting against the independent republics and Russia itself. As to the question of whether or not the Putin regime would see such practices as improper or unethical, we can only turn to President Putin's 2016 remark when challenged with "meddling" by President Obama. It was simple and direct—had not the United States itself funded media groups and civil society groups that meddled in Russian affairs?[28]

Given the destabilization operations covered here, it appears to be an axiom that fragmentation of an adversary's population is a fundamental starting point in increasing political and social chaos—the first stage in political warfare. Intuitively it might seem that fragmentation would be more difficult to bring about in the internet age of maximum openness, connectivity, and communications. As it turns out, an immense new opportunity for destabilization lies in turning that connectivity against itself, and the tool that makes that possible is social media. The keys to weaponizing social media for political warfare lie in its potential for hiding true identities and the amazing degree of demographic targeting that has become available on major social media platforms.

The current destabilization campaigns targeting the West and most intensely the United States are distinguished by the sophistication of their targeting, their reach in terms of numbers of reads/viewers, and their potential for not simply fragmenting segments of the population but in encouraging personal confrontation and potential violence. They span the entire spectrum of social media, from obvious forums such as Facebook, Twitter, Google, and YouTube to unexpected outlets such as Reddit, Instagram, 4Chan, Imgur, and even Pokémon Go.

One of the key indications that a true psychological warfare campaign has been in progress, rather than simply an effort by independent patriotic posters or hackers, is the extent of the social media reach which began in 2015 and continues as of this writing. Initial efforts to quantify the scope of Russian activity were quite challenging for the social media companies involved. The total reach may well grow in time but even the initial numbers are staggering, in terms of number of accounts involved, quantity of messaging, and respectable funding.

In congressional testimony Facebook executives stated that from 2015 through 2016 some 126 million American viewers were potentially exposed to advertisements and content circulated via Facebook that originated from the Internet Research Agency (a.k.a. Glavset), a Russian troll farm.[29] Some 470 pages and profiles directly linked to the Internet Research Agency were identified by Facebook, some masquerading as gun rights ("Defend the 2nd"), gay rights, militant black rights, and even animal rights activists—all placed in a form of counter-messaging to provoke negative responses.[30] These Russia-linked trolls not only performed direct messaging using a variety of fake Facebook accounts but also paid for "boosted posts," Facebook's name for one of its paid advertising options that intersperses material in a user's news feed.[31] Posts were also used to urge individual users to share the post or to actually join fake pages and groups. Such advanced tactics can and do spread messages quickly throughout targeted social communities.

The Internet Research Agency appears to have been formed in 2013, joined by Internet Research Limited in 2014. That association provided what had largely been a brute-force troll factory with the sophisticated techniques and tools necessary to maximize targeting and placement of messages as well as automating certain messaging to select demographics. Documents obtained by news organizations indicate that the group's activities were allocated $1 million per month, divided between its work in the Russian language and operations strictly targeted to English-language social media outlets.[32]

Facebook's research and data has also confirmed that the overall Russian messaging campaign was much more than election related, with more than half its advertisements (fifty-six percent) placed following the 2016 election. In fact the majority of the Russian placements "appear to focus on divisive social and political messages" across the ideological spectrum, with an emphasis on topics relating to race, gun rights, religion, and gay rights and transgender issues.[33] Facebook's general counsel Colin Stretch specifically described them as "an insidious attempt to drive people apart."

Initially Twitter representatives told the same congressional committee that at least 2,752 accounts from the same source (the Internet Research Agency) had been used for Russian messaging. Beyond that it identified another 36,746 accounts apparently associated with Russia that had generated automated content of a political nature—with a large percentage of the messaging devoted to race issues and immigration policies.[34] One major Twitter source for Russia-driven content was RT (formerly Russia Today) which spent $274,100 on three different accounts—@RT.com, @RT.America, and @ActualidadRT—and generated some 1,823 tweets to the U.S. market.[35] As with Facebook, the Twitter accounts were used to send messages highlighting divisive topics such as race and immigration. Within weeks intensive investigation determined that the Twitter effort had actually been at least four times larger, with over 130,000 messages tweeted.[36]

Twitter also reported on a detailed analysis of some 600 accounts clearly connected to Russian messaging. Those accounts involved obviously pro-Russian users, a network of trolls who tweeted as part of a campaign linked openly to Russian media sources and a third network of robot tweets (bots), which were associated with other accounts involved in the messaging. The analysis of the messages suggested that there were both knowing participants and other users who were simply retweeting messages amplifying preferred themes. Beyond that, analysis of the retweets suggested that the smallest activity was associated with the attributed content (from RT and Sputnik), while the vast majority was from third parties including "hyper partisan" and "fake news" sites.

Facebook advertisements and Twitter tweets were only part of the overall social fragmentation effort. Google reported to Congress that it had found eighteen channels associated with "Russian agents" which had been used to post politically-charged videos to YouTube. Beginning in 2015 those accounts had been loaded with at least 1,100 videos containing forty-three hours of content. Videos and images continued to be uploaded through at least the summer of 2017. Viewership had not been extraordinarily high in relative YouTube terms but in the first year they yielded 309,000 views.[37]

Although widely discussed even by Congress and the president simply in terms of election meddling, it is clear that the Russian-sponsored efforts were truly information warfare, focused and targeted as a fragmentation campaign intended not just to impact a single election but to broadly stimulate emotional reactions on issues that would separate the American public on the most divisive issues possible, creating discord and both social and political chaos. In order to illustrate that point it is necessary to turn to a more detailed illustration of the demographic targeting available in placing Facebook advertisements. The following examples will also demonstrate that the anonymity of personal accounts on social media are of great value to "false flag" activities, including those specifically intended to provoke confrontations and violence.

As a commercial entity, Facebook collects huge amounts of information on its users, profiling them explicitly in terms of location, background, and interests. Its own marketing pages tout its ability for "intelligent" advertising, through the selection of exactly the audience that would be most receptive to a particular message. Location can be defined by country, state, city, or zip code; demographics by age range, sex, and relationship status; and beyond that "likes and interests" can be matched to the home pages of individuals based on their profiles. Advanced targeting includes education, workplace, job title, language, and more, such as hobbies and interests, and even purchasing behaviors and device preferences.[38] It's a level of targeting and reach that would no doubt make any Cold War covert action officer, who was involved in efforts to simply get a newspaper article placed or a leaflet posted on a wall, positively weep with joy.

The availability of such discrete user-targeting amplifies the ability to use false accounts and identities (both online and supplemented with surrogate telephone calls and contacts) to promote discord and confrontation. Jonathan Albright, research director at Columbia University's Tow Center for Digital Journalism, has built a database of Russian propaganda efforts. He found that while the main themes were the radicalization of viewers into more hardline political positions, there were actually a set of groups and posts that actively promoted violence.[39]

Provoking violent measures against both illegals and refugees was a real theme for the fake pages of certain groups. One group calling itself "Secured Borders" focused on the threat of dangerous illegal aliens and continued to call for violence months after the 2016 election. It advocated killing illegals as the only solution, advising anyone who came back after being deported that they would be fair game and should be shot. Its position on refugees was equally aggressive, calling for the U.S. State Department to be destroyed in retaliation for dealing with them. In terms of impressions, one particular message from Secure Borders—claiming that there would be extensive nationwide riots if Hillary Clinton should win the election—was viewed over one hundred thousand times. One of the Russian-associated Facebook groups, "Being Patriotic," took the position that Black Lives Matter activists should immediately be shot for disrespecting the American flag. Other themes on the page were more political and clearly targeted. Before being shut down the account had gained two hundred thousand followers.

Another class of Facebook groups was equally aggressive, but much more sophisticated—supported by unidentified local surrogates who followed up with personal contacts. A Russia-linked group, "Blacktivist," carried on after the election, focusing on police brutality and demanding that "Black people have to do something. An eye for an eye. The law enforcement officers keep harassing and killing us without consequences." Blacktivist was also supported by a Twitter feed allowing responses to messaging. In one instance Blacktivist called for a rally and street march in Baltimore, an obvious provocation since it came after the death of a local activist, Freddie Gray, while in police custody. When local Baltimore pastor Reverend Heber M. Brown III replied, asking if the organizers were from Baltimore, the response was vague but an obvious attempt to cultivate his participation with the group.

Not satisfied and unhappy with their message, he asked for an apology—which never came. Eventually he was amazed to learn that the purported black activist group had actually been a Russian messaging front.[40] In terms of context, the Russian racial fragmentation campaign was a much broader effort than the more focused, highly covert FBI dirty tricks effort against black activist groups in the late 1960s. That Cointelpro campaign was designed to fragment black activist groups, to obstruct possible group mergers and prevent joint organizing and protest efforts. There was a FBI concern that groups such as the Black Panther Party would join with the Young Lords, Young Patriots, and the Mau Maus. Popular leaders such as Fred Hampton promoted the idea of reaching out to radical student groups such as the SDS in a "Rainbow Coalition."[41]

In response the FBI created fake letters from individuals prominent within the groups, letters containing personal slurs or provocative statements against other groups. Other letters promoted violent acts and confrontations in contrast to peaceful protest or demonstrations. While similar in the intent to divide and encourage violence, as well in basic propaganda practices, the reach of the FBI campaign was minimal compared to the goals of the Russian effort.

Facebook ad buys with provocative racial themes were tightly targeted. At this point it's impossible to know exactly how widespread the effort truly was, but in addition to the fake Baltimore rally ad at least one Russian ad buy was specifically focused on Ferguson, Missouri.[42] Targeting both Baltimore and Ferguson—and specifically focusing on the activist group Black Lives Matter—reveals not only that the information warfare campaign was sophisticated but that it was synchronized with current American events. Both Baltimore and Ferguson had experienced street violence and tempers were most definitely on edge. The Ferguson ad was constructed as a supported piece for Black Lives Matter but its content clearly suggested the threat of more confrontation and violence.

One of the strangest and most sinister gambits in the racially targeted segment of the fragmentation campaign was the use of one of the world's most popular internet-enabled games, Pokémon Go.[43] Players are encouraged to take their smartphones to various physical locations where Pokémon characters are electronically inserted into the game. Once they locate the Pokémon, they can either train them or battle them. In this instance an account presenting itself as part of Black Lives Matter started a campaign called "Don't Shoot Us," which directed players to give their characters the names of young black people who had recently been killed in police shootings—incidents which had produced not just protests but some form of violence. The Pokémon Go page contained some two hundred videos but it was also linked to a Tumblr account. It's virtually impossible to confirm how many players actually participated, and to what extent. For those that did the messaging was quite subtle. It was also carefully designed to be hidden from those not being targeted, and only exposed by one message delivered to a reporter.

One additional example illustrates both sophistication in targeting and in constructing the messaging campaign, as well as the extent of its attempted political destabilization. In the spring of 2016 a Facebook page calling itself the "Heart of Texas" promoted what can only be described as Islamophobia, actively organizing protest rallies at locations in Texas called "Stop Islamization of Texas." Its calls for action managed to mobilize demonstrators who not only carried signs warning of Sharia law being legalized but proclaiming White Lives Matter. One post on the page had even called for blowing up the Islamic Center in Houston.[44] Going beyond Islamophobia and warnings about refugees, Heart of Texas also devoted itself to a campaign for Texas to secede from the United States. By November 2016 it was calling for rallies across Texas in Dallas, Fort Worth, and even Lubbock.

It is unclear to what extent those calls were answered. The rally in Lubbock was apparently canceled, possibly for lack of interest. In the earlier Houston Islamic Center protest, participants expressed their irritation that nobody claiming to actually be a member of Heart of Texas had showed up. Ultimately, Heart of Texas grew to have 225,000 followers, with no individuals ever identified with the movement and no contact information given. That seemed strange because other Texas secession groups already existed and their members were both vocal and quite public. Yet Heart of Texas had quickly garnered more viewership than any of their information efforts.[45] The page also introduced and focused on one idea that had been integrated into other Russian messaging during 2016—that the upcoming American election was rigged. The concept—very much a part of the Russian destabilization campaign—was ironically consistent with the Putin and Kremlin leadership objections to the earlier claims of the democracy initiative NGOs.

Perhaps the most obvious example of the political outreach of the Russian messaging can be seen in a Russia-affiliated Twitter account designated as @tpartynews, which claimed a well-defined position in the American political spectrum. With a profile photo consisting of a teapot, the words "Tea Party," and an American flag,[46] the account routinely posted conservative and anti-immigrant messages as well as endorsements of Donald Trump. It also routinely retweeted messages from conservative news sites and commentators such as Ann Coulter. @tpartynews was followed by twenty-two thousand viewers including one individual, Sebastian Gorka, who became a White House advisor to President Trump. In reality the account was yet another Internet Research Agency outlet, one of fifty such Twitter accounts which in total had six hundred thousand followers and produced an estimated seventeen million tweets and retweets. Many of the accounts were driven by automated bots and many were created to give the impression of being Trump supporters. In total the entire effort was intended to enhance the impression of widespread support for a particular candidate. Studies revealed that in terms of quantity, the messaging was definitely tilted towards support for presidential candidate Donald Trump.

The theme and targeting of @tpartynews was quite clear, but the overall scope and reach of the full political messaging campaign may never be known. However, even early studies show that messaging focused on the most highly contested states in the election, including Michigan and Wisconsin, where the final vote totals would be extremely close (within one percent). Russian-sponsored ads in those states appear to have particularly focused on not just divisive themes but on anti-Muslim messages. States geographically targeted in the Russian ad campaign included Alabama, California, Florida, Georgia, Maryland, Michigan, Mississippi, Missouri, New York, Ohio, Texas, and Wisconsin.[47]

What makes such advertising tactics especially hard to trace and estimate is that fact that Facebook also allowed an option for unpublished page posts ("dark posts") where a post does not actually appear on the user's page but is only seen by those to which it is targeted. That makes it almost impossible to check sourcing and with sufficient demographic skill can also be sent to users least likely to do fact-checking.

As of mid-2018, there is some indication that the true threat of information warfare conducted via "free" social media has yet to register with certain levels of American political leadership. In April 2018, Facebook CEO Mark Zuckerberg was called to testify before a Congressional committee. The committee's questioning focused almost exclusively on the theft of personal data, rather than on issues of media responsibility in terms of Facebook's role as a commercial entity.

DESTABILIZATION

In order to appreciate the full nature of the Russian information warfare campaign, it has to be viewed in a much broader scope than simply "meddling" in the election of 2016. As previously noted, other than the purely political ads and posts, the racial and social fragmentation aspect of the campaign continues, minimized only to the extent that the social media companies have modified certain of their practices and are on alert for the more obvious sources of such content. Given the apparent skill and sophistication of the media targeting described above, as well as its source in actors not directly connected to the Russian government, it seems likely that other entities are already in play and will be used to carry the same fundamental themes forward.

Pro-Russian activists have become increasingly vocal in Europe and to some extent in the United States, encouraging extreme nationalism and nativism. The Russian political party United Russia (the ruling party associated with Vladimir Putin) actually signed a cooperation agreement with the most extreme right-wing party in Austria, looking towards collaboration on economic, political, and business projects.[48] The head of the far-right National Front Party in France made a very visible bid for the French presidency, putting forward a very nationalist theme and touting President Putin's support and their "common values." Similar outreach to ultra-nationalist parties can be found in Germany, Greece, and Hungary.

In terms of Russian geopolitical strategy, the extent to which any of the Western nations do turn inwards, either due to increased social fragmentation or political instability, will undermine the common initiatives of the European Union and reduce its perceived economic influence in Eastern Europe—certainly a plus for maintaining Russian sovereignty. Perhaps the most dramatic example of weakening the EU can be seen in the activity of the United Kingdom's nationalist Independence Party, a leader in the effort to move Britain out of the Europe Union. Well after the fact of the British EU exit referendums, indications are emerging that suggest that Russian actors were taking advantage of the EU membership controversy in yet another destabilization effort.

Wired magazine conducted a study of cached Twitter posts during the EU exit campaign of 2016 and even its first assessment revealed twenty-nine accounts using Brexit-related hashtags in posts that originated in Russian accounts—the same sources identified in the American information messaging. The Brexit-related tweets focused on anti-Muslim and anti-immigration themes, not only for Britain but generally for Europe.[49] The Russian tweets posed themselves as coming from Americans. One series of widely retweeted posts came from @SouthLoneStar (self-described as a proud Texan and American patriot) who had almost 17,000 followers. After the Brexit vote, the posts congratulated the British for leaving the EU and encouraged them to clean up the United Kingdom and fight the Muslim invasion that was turning it into a Caliphate. The purported Texan also tweeted about France and its Muslim problems. Social media metadata tags used on Twitter other similar services illustrate the divisive themes being promoted in this messaging: "@PriceForPierce, #IslamKills, and #StopIslam".

While the true scope of such Russian messaging against Britain is still being investigated, the initial findings have been sufficient for U.K. Prime Minister Theresa May to openly warn Russia regarding the planting of fake news stories and divisive messaging. In a major address in November 2017, May discussed the Russian messaging in conjunction with other issues such as Russian military airspace violations, cyber espionage, and the hacking of both the Danish Ministry of Defense and the German Bundestag.[50]

The exposure of the various Russian-sponsored and -associated social networking activities sensitized a number of governments, as well as the major vendors such as Facebook and Twitter, to the information warfare issue. By the end of 2017 both Spain and France had become concerned about targeting by Russian internet actors. Spain's foreign and defense ministers publicly announced that they had obtained evidence of an effort to promote separatism within Spain and support the succession of Catalonia.[51] The Spanish Defense minister cited accounts that had been traced to Russian territory, and in language similar to that of Prime Minister May, accused Russian actors both public and private of "trying to influence the situation [the secession vote] and create instability in Europe." A heavy separatist vote in what was later declared to be an illegal election was certainly highly destabilizing, forcing Spain's most significant political crisis in decades—in what is the EU's fourth-largest economy. Even after the voting, other sensational posts such as "EU officials supported violence in Catalonia" and "Global powers prepare for ground war in Europe" obviously targeted the broader EU community.

Spain's Foreign Minister Alfonso Dastis elaborated on the proof of interference by stating that investigations had detected fake accounts on social media, tracing half of them to Russia and some thirty percent to pro-Russian sources in Venezuela. All the accounts were involved in actively posting and reposting messages on the benefits of secession and an independent Catalonia. The postings from Venezuela would not be anything unexpected since we have already examined instances of pro-Russian web-page and DNS attacks coming from surrogates outside Russia itself. However, a campaign supported by accounts originating in Latin America certainly indicates how rapidly internet-based information warfare can be adapted to foil monitoring.

To a large extent, the major internet media companies had essentially avoided the issue that their services were increasingly being used as news outlets, with none of the content or editorial control—much less the regulations—historically demanded of the public media. When current events made it clear that they were indeed seeing their services hijacked for not just political purposes but true information warfare, they began to respond, at least to the extent possible without major system and policy changes. As an example, Facebook, duly concerned about fake news and postings in the United States, conducted a search of French accounts ahead of that nation's election. As a result some thirty thousand questionable Russian-affiliated accounts were deleted.[52]

Yet despite that move by Facebook, the French campaign saw extensive retweeting of both factually questionable news items and obvious endorsements of pro-Russian candidates—stories and content which were foreign in origin, originally appearing in Russian state-controlled media such as RT and Sputnik. French readers and viewers might not even know those media exist, but once their news becomes tweeted, retweeted, or blogged it acquires an internet life of its own. Charges that RT and Sputnik were serving a Russian political agenda were immediately rebutted by those organizations, with the response that they are simply serving all points of view. One RT spokesperson even responded with a statement that seemingly paraphrased rebuttals to similar types of stories which appeared during the American campaign of 2016: "There are many different truths…there has to be a pluralism of truth."[53]

It remains to be seen whether it is even possible to isolate political warfare messaging on the internet. One of the more recent illustrations of that challenge occurred towards the end of 2017, when a Russian troll account resurfaced on Twitter. Presenting itself as being that of a conservative American woman with the pseudonym "Jenna Abrams," the account posted real photographs—of an actual Russian woman.[54] The rather obvious problem was that this was not a new persona, it had been active during the 2016 elections, posting more than twenty thousand tweets to some seventy thousand followers, including several members of the Trump campaign and advisors to Donald Trump. Posts from the account appeared in a number of American and international news organizations, including CNN.

The account itself was determined to have been on Twitter for years, opened by the Internet Research Agency as only one of some three thousand Twitter accounts and used as part of its earliest troll posting programs. Even more significant was that it was only publicly exposed through the work of Russian investigative reporters. As it turned out, Jenna Abrams had also appeared in major blogging/publishing platforms including WordPress and Medium. Medium removed the account after its nature became public, but WordPress did not. In

November the WordPress blog had new posts, denying it was run by Russians and advising Americans that they were responsible for Trump being president, not Vladimir Putin. The posts also announced a new Twitter account: @realJennaAbrams.

The new account was blatant in using the name and photo of a known troll; indeed "Jenna" began promoting herself/itself as Russia's best troll. Whether or not the account was really Russian or not remains an open question. The real Jenna, a St. Petersburg resident, claimed no knowledge of it. What cannot be argued is that within only a matter of weeks one of the more notorious troll accounts identified in the American investigation of Russian "meddling" had resurfaced on both Twitter and other commercial internet venues—without generating any challenge from the social media companies carrying it.

INFORMATION WARFARE

It is hard to deny that the ongoing information warfare campaigns have produced some degree of both social fragmentation and political destabilization within the United States, Great Britain, Spain, and within the EU nations as a whole. As with all effective psychological warfare, the messaging did not create the divisions involved, they worked diligently and deeply to amplify them. To some extent it hardly matters whether the information warfare itself originated from within the Russian state, whether it was covertly encouraged by state sources, or whether it was carried out by commercial entities.

As we traced its evolution from domestic use inside Russia, through an expanded role in the former Soviet republics, and on to the targeting of EU nations and the United States, the Russian information warfare became more organized, more directed, and more sophisticated. In the period of 2014-17 the volume of fake, themed posting increased dramatically. There is also no doubt that it became institutionalized. Given the large numbers of accounts tied to Russia's

International Research Agency, there obviously were funds and management resources devoted to it. Of course, in that regard, it certainly is not the first privatization of political warfare we have explored.

In the context of our overall historical study, the Russian containment and pushback efforts described in the last few chapters almost exactly mirror the equivalent activities of the United States during the Cold War. During that era, as a champion of stability over change, the United States turned first to containment, then to pushback, not just along its own borders and in its own hemisphere but globally. In a new century, in a new Russia, Vladimir Putin and the Russian political leadership came to view the democratic initiative sponsored by the United States and the EU as being a fundamental threat. Viewing the West as a source of political change, it would be Russia that would assume the mantle of defending stability, through containment, pushback, and political warfare utilizing a variety of active measures.

Russia and its spokespersons have made their position completely clear—they will act in opposition to change and in defense of stability. Most recently, when British Prime Minister May challenged Russian meddling, tweets by Russian Senator Aleksey Pushkov were brutally dismissive: "The international system of rules must be saved not from Russia but from the advocates of intervention, coups and regime change. Russia will not accept those 'rules.' […] The world order that suits May, with the seizure of Iraq, war in Libya, the rise of IS and terrorism in Europe, has had its day. You can't save it by attacking Russia."

Political warfare. You shove me, I shove you. Déjà vu. Mirroring. The Territorial Imperative. Regardless of what it is called, the same fears come into play, and the responses are virtually identical. The political warfare practices remain the same as well, only the tools change. And there are always consequences.

Chapter Fifteen:
Consequences

Kings, queens, and presidents, rulers of all stripes, have never hesitated to turn to the darker side of foreign relations. At its most simple, that involves efforts to shape positive views and influence political policies—both with allies and adversaries. Still, there is often a shadowy element to be found in virtually all foreign relations, exemplified in the active measures conducted under diplomatic cover, or by surrogates associated with embassies, consulates, legations, trade missions, or even business and professional associations. During the Cold War, patriotic American businessperson and corporate leaders were more than willing to collect information and even to provide operational support for the CIA. In the new Russia, regime-associated oligarchs and pro-Russian surrogates can be found assuming the same roles. The privatization of American political warfare is surely mirrored in contemporary Russian political shaping, as well as both hybrid and information warfare.

The even darker practices of active measures, agent-of-influence recruiting, surrogate operations, hybrid warfare, and information warfare have been extensively examined—as have the associated measures of deniability, political and operational covers and cutouts, including layered and shell company financing for covert activities. Hopefully, at this point, the reader is better prepared to recognize and follow discussions of such activities, regardless of their source.

But what of the consequences? Simply because all major powers appear to routinely engage in at least some level of political warfare—sometimes in pursuit of opportunities but more often based in their fears of others acting against them—there is the outstanding question of whether or not doing so is a sound decision. While an attempt to fully answer that question here would be overreach, some observations can be made based in the history explored in this work.

First, political warfare may be covert, it may be officially denied, but in reality it is never truly deniable in terms of public perceptions. In all of the American and Russian operations we have covered, the actual sponsors of active measures, surrogate warfare, regime change, and even information warfare were exposed, discussed openly in public forums in real time, with many operations investigated and documented in considerable detail. The consequence of that visibility is almost always a growing mistrust and suspicion of any further overtures from those engaging in the practices, whether diplomatic, economic, or military.

Even American deniable political warfare operations initially deemed successful—placing or maintaining pro-American regimes in power—produced a legacy of anti-American prejudice and guilt by association, fueled by the repression and brutality of the regimes themselves as well as ongoing regional political instability.[1] Regime change in Iran and Guatemala poisoned long-term American foreign relations with those countries long after the pro-American regimes were ultimately ousted. A host of 1970s political action activities across South America (in Argentina, Chile, Peru, Bolivia, Uruguay, and Paraguay) established and maintained dictatorial military regimes friendly to the U.S.—but only for a time, producing an immense number of civilian deaths and suffering as collateral damage.[2] Surrogate warfare forced the Russians out of Afghanistan, at the same time enabling decades of global jihad and terror. And in the twenty-first century, democracy initiatives have become a factor in leading to regime change across North Africa and into the Middle East (the Arab Spring) and among former Soviet republics (the color revolutions). Yet several of the nations in the Arab Spring have spiraled into civil warfare while mistrust of American and Western intentions has dramatically increased even within the independent, formerly Soviet republics, not to mention in Russian public perceptions of the West.

As far as Russia is concerned, beyond the immediate post-World War II years when it used communist parties and the Red Army to establish dominion in Eastern Europe, its own political warfare was more limited, simply because it was most often following along behind regime change driven by nationalism, anti-imperialism, and cultural conflicts. When it did turn to regime destabilization and change, as in Indonesia, the long-term results were much the same as those experienced by America—with extensive civilian casualties and a highly repressive, military-backed regime coming to power. Of course, the Soviet Union did conduct extensive global propaganda and active measures campaigns, with the goal of shaping anti-American popular opinion. Such campaigns certainly did work to some extent—in Iran, Turkey, India, and elsewhere. However, creating concerns over foreign influence by America often translated to creating concerns over foreign influence of any type, even Soviet. That can be seen in the extensive number of incidents in which Soviet diplomats, foreign mission personnel, and even Russian citizens were charged and expelled for subversion, propaganda, destabilization activities, and other similar actions. We offered a limited listing of such incidents, including not only obvious Western targets such as the United States, Canada, Great Britain, and France but global incidents involving expulsions from Spain, Mexico, the Republic of the Congo, Costa Rica, Liberia, Pakistan, Malaysia, and Egypt.

For some four decades Russian political action within the nations of the Soviet bloc proved generally effective at regime maintenance, establishing what can only be described as puppet governments under direct and obvious control from Moscow. However, on numerous occasions those governments were only maintained through the use of the Red Army. The extent to which those Soviet practices failed over the longer term can be seen in the virtual implosion of the Soviet Union once centralized communist political control failed in the face of domestic Russian political change—change that removed the threat of Russian military intervention across the former Soviet bloc nations.

Soviet bloc regime change came about internally, first within Poland and Czechoslovakia at the end of the 1980s. Other satellite states began to split along cultural and ethnic lines and separatist movements grew within Ukraine, Belarus, and across the Baltic states. With domestic instability in Moscow and no orchestrated Soviet military response, by 1991 the former Union of Soviet Socialist Republics was no more. Neither Marxist economic theories nor Russian political dominion had eliminated the most fundamental fragmentation factors of nationalism, racial/ethnic/religious diversity, and rejection of foreign economic manipulation. The same factors that had brought about the wave of global government changes following World War II. Political and military dominance simply suppressed them for a time. The consequences of current Russian efforts to restore the historical dominion and sovereignty of the Russian Empire and Soviet Union are still emerging, but at best they have created enclaves of pro-Russian influence within the larger territories of Georgia and Ukraine, while creating anti-Russian fears and further fueling independent nationalism within many of the former Soviet republics.

In a truly historical view, the political warfare practices of active measures, hybrid/surrogate warfare, and even regime change appear to have had little truly long-term positive effects—and severe negative consequences including extensive loss of life. In many instances what were perceived as successes actually failed over a period of a few years, on occasion within a few months. The practices of psychological warfare, disinformation, propaganda, and information warfare have often been more efficient but only in terms of creating fragmentation and political chaos for less investment of money and personnel. However, even when conducted covertly, their true sponsors were quickly identified, and even more quickly suspected.

Given the level of fragmentation that exists within most states, the recruitment of agents of influence and the conduct of destabilization practices are perhaps the most tempting of all political warfare alternatives, at least in terms of weakening potential adversaries. Certainly there is nothing unique about that particular observation, Machiavelli himself described that avenue of opportunity early in his work *The Prince*: "…one always finds malcontents and such as desire change. Such men, for the reasons given, can open the way into the state."[3] Of course, in his entirely pragmatic view, it would matter little whether the malcontents were essentially good or evil, moral or immoral—it was simply a matter of their usefulness. And as to his advice on the ongoing use of agents of influence in destabilizing or taking over an adversary state after success is achieved, it was equally pragmatic, a warning that it would be necessary to deal forcefully with "both those who have assisted you and those who you have crushed."

What Machiavelli could not have envisioned was the possibility that the recruiting and destabilizing practices he described would become available to not just princes and kings but to virtually anyone. The consequences of sophisticated and individual customized propaganda, psychological warfare, disinformation, "fake news," and "malcontent recruitment" might well have been beyond his grasp. Yet as we have seen, social media and the availability of advanced demographic profiling and message targeting via the global internet have brought us to exactly that.

PANDORA'S CLOUD

The same advanced population analysis and demographic targeting seen in the Russian information warfare campaigns against the United States is available to virtually any major private, political, or commercial user. Firms such as Cambridge Analytica tout their capabilities of "data driven" campaign messaging, citing its effectiveness in both congressional and presidential elections.[4] The company even claims to have constructed extended personality profiles on every single American, allowing it to conduct "psychographic targeting" by personality type. Of particular note is the fact that Cambridge Analytica developed out of a British consulting company's defense contract work—specifically psychological warfare operations—in Afghanistan.

During the 2016 U.S. campaign, Cambridge Analytica worked with both the Republican National Committee and the Trump campaign. Reportedly some $85 million in digital advertising was spent on Facebook by the Trump campaign. In one dramatic illustration of targeted internet messaging, on a single day in October 2017 the Trump campaign ran 175,000 variations of the same advertisement on Facebook.[5] Such sophisticated internet messaging is now available to any political or commercial entity willing to pay for it, and to fund and organize the follow-up internet media campaigns. Given the opportunities for hiding the sources of such messaging, it can be delivered in a number of anonymous, fake, or even personally disguised forms. The extent to which efforts can truly be personalized is rather amazing, with very deep personal data being collected by seemingly innocuous means such as Facebook trivia quizzes or personality self-tests. Tests developed and used on Facebook are by none other than Cambridge Analytica.[6]

Cambridge Analytica has seeded Facebook with a variety of personality quizzes, allowing viewers to evaluate their own top five psychological traits. The traits include openness and agreeableness as well as tendencies towards being extroverted or even neurotic. Through their paid Facebook quizzes, Cambridge has collected such data on hundreds of thousands of individuals, as well as individual personal profiles and real names. It is exactly that data that supports the claim that it can indeed build not only voting histories but profile individuals with a level of detail never before available in mainstream marketing—age, income, debt, hobbies, criminal histories, purchase histories, religious leanings, health concerns, gun ownership, car ownership, and home-ownership. While Facebook ultimately moved to separate itself from Cambridge Analytica, the overriding issue of targeted user messaging remains. Any "free use" social media company which operates as a commercial entity must differentiate itself by delivering customized content to users— and customized content can only come though the collection and application of individualized user interests and preferences. This is the sort of resource that has become available to private firms and nations and which can be used so anonymously that the viewer has no true idea of its source.

The same can be increasingly said for alternative news, distributed via the internet. Some alternative news comes via known websites, but a great deal of it simply consists of blog and Facebook posts, tweets, and retweets, with the true source of the "news" totally unknown. This unsourced news (defined here as "virtual" news) is offered with no fact-checking nor any objective review by professional news organizations. It is "virtual" to the extent that it may or may not be true, even partially true, but it is presented as true and unbiased fact.

In reality, virtual news is often little more than opinion, at best it can be the packaging of real information to match a particular opinion or world view—more editorial than true news. An equally misleading variant is "satire" news, often well-crafted but intended as humor. Because this form of news item is created as satire on real news, when reposted, retweeted or otherwise circulated without attribution (or the warnings and advisories found on the original sites) it is often taken as real news, especially if it matches the reader's attitudes. The following warnings and disclaimers posted on the actual sites clearly indicate how damaging virtual news can become, especially when reposted with no qualification:[7]

Daily Feed News: This website has a disclaimer that reads:
DailyFeed.news is a satirical publication that may sometimes appear to be telling the truth. We assure you that's not the case. We present fiction as fact and our sources don't actually exist. Names that represent actual people and places are purely coincidental and all images should be considered altered and do not in any way depict reality. All people, places, names, and images should be considered fictitious or fictitious representations.

The site is registered through WhoisGuard, Inc., a company that hides the identity and location of the owner of the website.

Morning Herald: This website has a disclaimer that says in part:
We make no representations or warranties of any kind, express or implied, about the completeness, accuracy, reliability, suitability or availability with respect to the website or the information, products, services, or related graphics contained on the website for any purpose. Any reliance you place on such information is therefore strictly at your own risk.

The site is registered to an owner in Macedonia.

365 US News: A disclaimer on 365usnews.com says:
This information is provided by 365 US News and while we endeavor to keep the information up to date and correct, we make no representations or warranties of any kind, express or implied, about the completeness, accuracy, reliability, suitability or availability with respect to the website or the

information, products, services, or related graphics contained on the website for any purpose. Any reliance you place on such information is therefore strictly at your own risk.

The site is also registered to an owner in Macedonia.

The majority of such sites, whether either uncorroborated news sites, sensation-oriented sites, or simply satire sites—contain no advisories or warnings at all. The problem with false and at best unverified virtual news sites has become so serious that a new genre of fact-checking websites have emerged in an effort to allow those internet users who take the time for it to attempt to claim some sort of grip on reality. At the time of this writing there is no widely used computer program or smart device application which allows automated filtering or warning in regard to "virtual" news or its sources.

Virtual news should not be confused with contemporary references to "fake news" although that term has become a staple of political dialogue in the twenty-first century. Russian President Vladimir Putin began using the term "fake news" during his first term, as a means to push back against Russian media coverage of a variety of embarrassing events—true news ranging from reports of oligarch corruption and the brutality of Russian military activity in Chechnya to the failure to recover the sunken Kursk atomic-powered ICBM submarine and the bungling of official responses to a variety of domestic terror attacks.

In its most current incarnation, President Trump and various American political candidates routinely use the term "fake news" either to attack media reports they view as biased or to defend their own performance. Trump himself has given considerable traction to the term, at one point maintaining that he either created it or is the first major figure to use it.[8] However, Trump's use of the term appears quite similar to the way Putin began to use it years earlier—and not at all like the intentionally planted and truly fake news used in the information warfare we have been exploring. That fake news is constructed for a specific purpose, matched to a particular viewer profile, and targeted for maximum effect.

Perhaps the most dangerous form of false internet news is found in uncorroborated stories which have the potential for creating panic. In one 2017 incident, the Coast Guard and local law enforcement responded to the threat of a "dirty bomb" on a container ship coming into Charleston harbor in South Carolina.[9] A unified security command was established and the ship as well as sections of the huge port facility were blocked off and evacuated. A one nautical-mile safety zone was established around the vessel, and boaters were warned away. The adjacent section of the Port of Charleston was closed for some seven hours while fourteen agents with radiation detectors and hazmat gear searched the boat.

Investigation eventually determined that warning telephone calls to the Coast Guard had been prompted by an individual active on both Twitter ("TruthLeaks") and YouTube—active in posting on government corruption and conspiracy theories and with some seventeen thousand followers on Twitter and forty thousand on YouTube. (Posters covering similar material reach more than two million followers). The dirty bomb incident had begun with a warning from anonymous sources described as "American patriots," individuals self-dedicated to protecting the nation from terror attacks. Although the warning was totally baseless, it was circulated and retweeted on at least four additional accounts.

Fake news is also being created to feed off tragic, real world news. In October 2017, a number of politically-radical domestic posters attempted to leverage the mass shooting in Las Vegas to place blame on their own preferred villains.[10] Viewers turning to Facebook, Google, or anonymous forums such as 4Chan found not real news but misinformation. In the rush for news, intentionally false shooter identifications and manufactured motives were picked up by politically-oriented websites, repeated, and then picked up on Google so that searches on the fake information would show up as top link results, as well as in its Top Stories section, feeding viewers to the intentionally planted fake news.

In a similar vein, Facebook unknowingly promoted several of the fake shooting stories on its "Crisis Response" page, a key social media site which allows users to check on the safety of friends and relatives. In other instances of mass shootings, the same sets of trolls have continued to be among the first to promote the incorrect names of shooters, apparently in an effort to undermine the credibility of more mainstream outlets and even of politicians who fall for their ploy in the earliest minutes of a news story, only to embarrass themselves.[11]

Another American domestic tragedy, the Parkland Florida school shooting of February 2018, generated a wide range of politically opportunistic fake news items, as well as confirmation of the ongoing Russian information warfare campaign. First, almost in real time, a spate of social media outlets began simultaneously relaying the identification of the shooter as a radical Islamic terrorist, an illegal immigrant, or a nativist radical affiliated with right wing militia units; they offered details and even photos to back up their identifications. Within a few hours, a variety of conspiracy oriented blogs and Twitter feeds were offering up stories that actual survivors of the attack were actors paid to push gun control advocacy.

That theme proved to be the precursor to a much more extensive series of pro-gun conspiracy messaging on Twitter, found on hashtags such as #falseflag, #fbi, #gunreformnow, #fbigate, and the more innocuous #parklandschoolshooting. In turn, numerous gun control and gun law reform tweets and posts began to appear, feeding and exacerbating the argument in the immediate wake of the shooting. Over twenty-four hours some 1,500 political propaganda "bots" were found to be actively tweeting and retweeting on the shooting. Early research tied a great number of those bots to Russian associated sources.[12]

Political warfare always has consequences, whether it is covert, deniable, anonymous, or simply privatized. The history we have explored suggests that state-sponsored political warfare is literally a constant, regardless of those consequences. What has changed over the decades is the extent to which the failure of state-sponsored deniability has migrated its practices to the private sector. There seems to be less and less of the tight, bureaucratic operational control that we saw with both the CIA and the KGB during the Cold War. Heads nod and funds are channeled through multiple financial shells. Cut-outs and on occasion dedicated regime supporters patriotically proceed with their own funds knowing the respect and influence it brings them. Corporations provided covers for the CIA during the Cold War; today, NGOs are likely do the same thing. In turn Russian oligarchs, investors, and professionals carry out the various practices required to support the views and ambitions of those in power in Moscow.

It is the global reach of the internet, the ubiquitous influence of social media, and the anonymity of the "cloud" that has added new elements to the calculus of political warfare. With the tools now available, its practices are no longer limited to empires, kingdoms, or nation states. Political parties, activists, and radical groups have access to almost the entire toolkit of practices, short only those of hybrid warfare (hopefully). Beyond that, even individuals are now free to independently pursue social, racial, ethnic, and religious fragmentation; destabilizing their own nations or others through psychological warfare, disinformation and weaponized virtual news. The potential consequences of that capability are still emerging.

The only defense—as with political warfare of all stripes—is recognizing it before it succeeds.

Endnotes

Introduction

1   Niccolò Machiavelli, *The Prince* (Simon & Brown, 2011), 21 and 67.
2   Ibid., 70-71.
3   Ibid., 44-46.
4   Larry Hancock, *Shadow Warfare: The History of America's Undeclared Wars* (Berkeley, California: Counterpoint, 2014), 498.
5   John Barron, *KGB Today: The Hidden Hand* (New York: Berkley Publishing Group, 1987), 34.
6   Neil MacFarquhar, "Yevgeny Prigozhin, Russian Oligarch Indicted by U.S., Is Known as 'Putin's Cook'", *The New York Times Europe*, February 16, 2018
7   Ibid., 150-51.
8   "George Kennan and Containment," A Short History of the Department of State, Office of the Historian, United States, Department of State. https://history.state.gov/departmenthistory/short-history/kennan
9   Richard Rhodes, *Dark Sun*: *The Making of the Hydrogen Bomb* (New York: Simon and Schuster, 1995), 234-35.
10 George F. Kennan, *Russia and the West: Under Lenin and Stalin* (New York: Little, Brown and Company, 1961), 392-93.

Chapter One

1   Peter Hopkirk, *The Great Game: The Struggle for Empire in Central Asia* (Tokyo, New York, London: Kodansha International, 1992), 21-22.
2   Ibid., 77-78.
3   Ibid., 163.

4   3rd Viscount Lord Palmerston, British Prime Minister in diplomatic correspondence as cited in *The Great Game: The Struggle for Empire in Central Asia*, 190.

5   Peter Hopkirk, *The Great Game; The Struggle for Empire in Central Asia*, 288.

6   Ibid., 503-04.

7   Peter Hopkirk, *Setting the East Ablaze* (Tokyo, London, New York: Kodansha America, 1995), 15.

8   Ibid., 121-22.

9   Ibid., 142.

10   George Cuzon, British Foreign Minister, diplomatic note, 1921, as cited in *Setting the East Ablaze*, 142.

11   Peter Hopkirk, *Setting the East Ablaze*, 171-72.

12   Ibid., 163-64.

13   Ibid., 192.

14   Alan Armstrong, *Preemptive Strike: The Secret Plan That Would Have Prevented the Attack on Pearl Harbor* (Guilford, Connecticut: The Lyons Press, 2006), 36, 56, 59, 96, 103.

15   Ibid., 150–54.

16   Ibid., 25–27.

17   Ibid., 6, 87–89.

18   Ibid., 92.

19   Ibid., 93.

20   Ibid., 97.

21   Ibid., 169–171.

22   Lt. Gen. James H. Doolittle, *Report on the Covert Activities of the Central Intelligence Agency*, Washington DC, July 26, 1954. https://docs.google.com/viewer?a=v&q=cache:TFz1prqQ6NsJ:www.foia.cia.gov/helms/pdf/doolittle_report.pdf+&hl=en&gl=us&pid=bl&srcid=ADGEESgGUVEdReoO2XsyRPZ_i0qYexDzo2SacjgOvnTYN4vFx_WdNEBxYSAXtAq4C7uB2ii9oGy6mnJkivsCKOzjgualrL81TkWeYpeXDOaPgVyTWPUWn4tT9oxfF2YMmJb2XwFXAqkJ&sig=AHIEtbSXI69AsoUYL3q028QNiSxg8KJ32w

23   *CIA Memorandum for the Record*, Conversation with Mr. Thomas Corcoran, signed by Stuart Hedden, April 16, 1952 http://www.foia.cia.gov/sites/default/files/document_conversions/89801/DOC_0000924155.pdf

24   *Memorandum of Conversation with Mr. Joe Montgomery and Mr. Thomas Corcoran*, created July 22, 1954 http://www.faqs.org/cia/

docs/106/0000920234/MEMORANDUM-OF-CONVERSATION-
WITH-MR.-JOE-MONTGOMERY-AND-MR.-THOMAS-
CORCORAN-OF-T.html

25   *CIA Memorandum to Deputy Director of Plans*, July 22, 1954, *Foreign Relations of the United States, 1952–1954, Retrospective Volume, Guatemala, Document 279,* Meeting between Mr. Joe Montgomery and Mr. Corcoran and Col. J. C. King, Chief CIA Western Hemisphere. http://history.state.gov/historicaldocuments/frus1952-54Guat/d279

Chapter Two

1   Joseph Persico, *Roosevelt's Centurions; FDR and the Commanders He Led to Victory in WWII* (New York: Random House, 2013), 462.

2   William Burrows, *By Any Means Necessary: America's Secret Air War in the Cold War*, 66.

3   Joseph Persico, *Roosevelt's Centurions; FDR and the Commanders He Led to Victory in WWII*, 496-98.

4   Richard Rhodes, *Dark Sun: The Making of the Hydrogen Bomb,* (New York: Simon and Schuster, 1995), 225. Rhodes notes that neither the U.S. government nor any of its presidents ever formally endorsed the preventive war concept, but that the extreme convictions of military, and in particular Air Force leaders led to decades of military planning and preparation for surprise attacks of either interdiction or preemption against the Soviet Union.

5   Jerry Miller, *Stockpile; The Story Behind 10,000 Strategic Nuclear Weapons*, (Annapolis, Maryland: Naval Institute Press, 2010), 5.

6   Richard Rhodes, *Dark Sun: The Making of the Hydrogen Bomb*, 181.

7   Rumania, Summary Document S-12, October 5, 1949, Central Intelligence Agency Report Sent to the President. http://nsarchive2.gwu.edu//dc.html?doc=3220860-01-CIA-Intelligence-Report-Rumania-sent-to-the

8   Ibid., 32.

9   Geoffrey Stone, *Perilous Times: Free Speech in Wartime: From the Sedition Act of 1798 to the War on Terrorism*, (New York: W. W. Norton, 2005), 12, 44-45.

10   Stephen Kinzer, *The Brothers: John Foster Dulles, Allen Dulles and Their Secret World War*, 33.

11   Ibid., 56.

12   Ibid., 24.

13 Norman A. Graebner, *National Security; Its Theory and Practice, 1945-1960*, (Oxford, New York: Oxford University Press, 1986), 17.

14 Stephen Kinzer, *The Brothers; John Foster Dulles, Allen Dulles and Their Secret World War,* 60-61.

15 Ibid., 79-80.

16 Richard Rhodes, *Dark Sun: The Making of the Hydrogen Bomb,*186-198.

17 The National Security Act, Office of the Historian, United States State Department, https://history.state.gov/milestones/1945-1952/national-security-act also The National Security Act of 1947, July 26, 1947, Public Law, 253, 80th Congress; Chapter 343, 1st Session; S. 758 https://www.cia.gov/library/readingroom/docs/1947-07-26.pdf

18 Stephen Kinzer, *The Brothers; John Foster Dulles, Allen Dulles and Their Secret World War*, 89.

19 "Position of the United States with respect to Italy", National Security Council Report, February 10, 1948, Office of the Historian, United States State Department. https://history.state.gov/historicaldocuments/frus1948v03/d469

20 Note On U.S. Covert Operations, Foreign Relations of the United States, 1964–1968, Volume XII, Western Europe Office of the Historian, United States Department of State. https://history.state.gov/historicaldocuments/frus1964-68v12/actionsstatement

21 Secretary of State to United States Embassy in Italy, February 4, 1948, Foreign Relations of the United States, 1948, Volume III, Office of the State Historian, United States Department of State. https://history.state.gov/historicaldocuments/frus1948v03/d510

22 Director of the Policy Planning Staff (Kennan) to the Secretary of State, March 15, 1948, Foreign Relations of the United States, 1948, Volume III, Office of the State Historian, United States Department of State. https://history.state.gov/historicaldocuments/frus1948v03/d523

23 The Acting Secretary of State to the Embassy in Italy, April 16, 1948, Foreign Relations of the United States, 1948, Volume III, Office of the State Historian, United States Department of State. https://history.state.gov/historicaldocuments/frus1948v03/d539

24 CIA memorandum to the Forty Committee (National Security Council), presented to the House Select Committee on Intelligence (the Pike Committee) during closed hearings held in 1975. Cited in CIA—The Pike Report, Nottingham, England, 1977, 204-05.

25 Allesandro Brogi, *Confronting America: The Cold War between the United States and the Communists in France and Italy* (Chapel Hill: The University of North Carolina Press, 2011), 109.

26 Silvio Pons, "Stalin, Togliatte and the Origins of the Cold War in Europe," *Journal of Cold War Studies*, Volume 3, Number 2, Spring 2001, 3-27.

27 "Shots from a Luce Cannon; Combating Communism in Italy," 1953-1956, CIA HISTORICAL document, National Security Archives. http://nsarchive2.gwu.edu//dc.html?doc=3456983-01-Shots-from-a-Luce-Cannon-Combating-Communism

28 Ibid.

29 Stephen Kinzer, *The Brothers: John Foster Dulles, Allen Dulles and Their Secret World War*, (New York: St. Martins Griffin, 2013), 157.

30 Stephen Kinzer, *The Brothers: John Foster Dulles, Allen Dulles and Their Secret World War*, 21.

31 "Report by the National Security Council on the Position of the United States with Respect to Soviet-Directed World Communism," NSC 7, March 30, 1948. https://history.state.gov/historicaldocuments/frus1948v01p2/d12

32 "Policy Planning Staff Memorandum," Policy Planning Committee, Department of State, May 4, 1948. http://academic.brooklyn.cuny.edu/history/johnson/65ciafounding3.htm

33 Hugh Wilford, *The Mighty Wurlitzer: How the CIA Played America*, (Cambridge, Maryland: Harvard University Press, 2008), 25.

34 Ibid.

35 Ibid., 25-26.

1   "Coordination and Approval of Covert Operations," A Historical Evaluation, Central Intelligence Agency, released February 22, 1967. https://www.cia.gov/library/readingroom/docs/DOC_0000790232.pdf

Chapter Three

1   *The National Security Act of 1947*, July 26, 1947, Public Law 253, 80th Congress; Chapter 343, 1st Session; S. 758. https://global.oup.com/us/companion.websites/9780195385168/resources/chapter10/nsa/nsa.pdf

2   Hugh Wilford, *The Mighty Wurlitzer: How the CIA Played America*, (Cambridge, Massachusetts: Harvard University Press, 2008), 28.

3   "Office of Policy Coordination 1948-1953," CIA History Document, Released March 1997, 12. https://cryptome.org/2012/05/cia-opc.pdf

4   Hugh Wilford, *The Mighty Wurlitzer: How the CIA Played America*, 31.

5   Walter Hixon, *Parting the Curtain: Propaganda, Culture and the Cold War* (Palgrave McMillian, 1998), 66. Also The Report on the President's Committee on International Information Activities, also known as the

"Jackson Committee." https://www.cia.gov/library/readingroom/docs/DOC_0000476939.pdf

6   Hugh Wilford, *The Mighty Wurlitzer: How the CIA Played America, 37*.

7   "The National Committee for a Free Europe," A Look Back, Central Intelligence Agency, 2007. https://www.cia.gov/news-information/featured-story-archive/2007-featured-story-archive/a-look-back.html

8   Michael Nelson, *War of the Black Heaven: The Battles of Western Broadcasting in the Cold War* (Syracuse University Press, 1997), 49.

9   "Office of Policy Coordination 1948-1953," 10.

10   Walter Hixon, *Parting the Curtain: Propaganda, Culture and the Cold War*, 63.

11   Hugh Wilford, *The Mighty Wurlitzer: How the CIA Played America*, 35.

12   Richard H. Schultz Jr., *The Secret War against Hanoi; The Untold Story of Spies, Saboteurs and Covert Warriors in North Vietnam*. (New York: Harper Perennial, 2001), 11.

13   Larry Hancock, *Shadow Warfare: The History of America's Undeclared Wars*, (Berkeley, California: Counterpoint Press, 2015), Chapter Oakland, 145-54.

14   Charles Gati, "No Inside Information" and "Little Outside Information," National Security Archive, November 3, 2006. https://nsarchive2.gwu.edu/NSAEBB/NSAEBB206/index.htm

15   Ibid.

16   Charles Gati, *Failed Illusions: Moscow, Washington, Budapest and the 1956 Hungarian Revolt* (Stanford University Press and Woodrow Wilson Center Press, 2006).

17   Thomas Blanton and Malcolm Byrne, National Security Archive Electronic Briefing Book No. 206, Posted October 31, 2006. http://nsarchive2.gwu.edu/NSAEBB/NSAEBB206/

18   Clandestine Service History, The Hungarian Revolution and Planning for the Future, Volume 1 of 2, CS Historical Paper No 6. http://nsarchive2.gwu.edu/NSAEBB/NSAEBB206/CSH_Hungarian_Revolution_Vol1.pdf

19   Dr. Roland D. Landa, "Almost Successful Recipe: The United States and East European Unrest prior to the 1956 Hungarian Revolution," Draft historical study by Dr. Ronald D. Landa of U.S. policy toward Eastern Europe in the 1950s, Historical Office, Office of the Secretary of Defense. http://nsarchive2.gwu.edu/dc.html?doc=3473778-Document-01-Almost-Successful-Recipe-The-United

20   Ibid., 25.

21 Memorandum of Conversation held in the CIA conference Room, Subject: Psychological Strategy Board, May 22, 1951. https://www.cia.gov/library/readingroom/docs/CIA-RDP80R01731 R003400010025-1.pdf

Chapter Four

1 Greg Behrman, *The Most Noble Adventure: The Marshall Plan and How America Helped Rebuild Europe* (Free Press, 2008), 29.
2 Ibid., 30-31.
3 Ibid., 29.
4 Ibid., 33.
5 Ibid., 92.
6 The Secretary of State to the Embassy in Italy, Washington, February 4, 1948, Foreign Relations of the United States, 1948, Western Europe, Volume III, Office of the Historian, State Department of the United States. https://history.state.gov/historicaldocuments/frus1948v03/d510
7 Mario Del Pero, "The United States and Psychological Warfare in Italy; 1948-1955," *The Journal of American History*, March 2001, 1307-08. http://www.academicroom.com/article/united-states-and-psychological-warfare-italy-1948-1955
8 The Secretary of State to the Embassy in Italy, Gala showing "Thanks America," Washington, March 24, 1948, Foreign Relations of the United States, 1948, Volume III, Office of the State Historian, United States Department of State. https://history.state.gov/historicaldocuments/frus1948v03/d532
9 The Ambassador in Italy (Dunn) to the Secretary of State, Rome, April 15, 1948, Foreign Relations of the United States, 1948, Volume III, Office of the State Historian, United States Department of State. https://history.state.gov/historicaldocuments/frus1948v03/d538
10 Memorandum of Conversation, by the Assistant Secretary for Economic Affairs (Thorp), Washington, April 7, 1948, Foreign Relations of the United States, 1948, Volume III, Office of the State Historian, United States Department of State. https://history.state.gov/historicaldocuments/frus1948v03/d536
11 The Acting Secretary of State to the Embassy in Italy, Dept fully appreciates desirability June allocation 50,000 tons to aid Ital Govt in program abolish political prices and subsidies, Washington, May 27, 1948, Foreign Relations of the United States, 1948, Volume III, Office of the State

Historian, United States Department of State. https://history.state.gov/historicaldocuments/frus1948v03/d542

12   The Ambassador in Italy (Dunn) to the Secretary of State, Rome, April 7, 1948, Foreign Relations of the United States, 1948, Volume III, Office of the State Historian, United States Department of State. https://history.state.gov/historicaldocuments/frus1948v03/d535

13   Richard and Gladys Harkness, "The Mysterious Doings of the CIA," *The Saturday Evening Post*, November 6, 1954, 66-68. https://www.cia.gov/library/readingroom/docs/CIA-RDP60-00321R000100090002-0.pdf

14   Richard Cottam, *Nationalism in Iran*, (Pittsburgh: University of Pittsburgh Press, 1979), 229.

15   Readers who desire a much deeper background than that which appears in the released State Department and CIA documents are encouraged to refer to Richard W. Cottam's *Nationalism in Iran* and James A. Bill's *The Eagle and the Lion: The Tragedy of American-Iranian Relations*.

16   Foreign Relations of the United States, 1952-1954, Iran, 1951–1954, Editor: James C. Van Hook, General Editor: Adam M. Howard, United States Government Publishing Office, Washington, 2017. https://history.state.gov/historicaldocuments/frus1951-54Iran

17   "Paper Prepared in the Directorate of Plans," Central Intelligence Agency, Washington, undated. Summary appraisal of the current situation in iran, Foreign Relations of the United States, 1952-1954, Iran, 1951–1954, Office of the Historian, Department of State, United States of America. https://history.state.gov/historicaldocuments/frus1951-54Iran/d4

18   Foreign Relations of the United States, 1952-1954, Iran, 1951–1954, Office of the Historian, Department of State, United States of America. https://history.state.gov/historicaldocuments/frus1951-54Iran/d5

19   Draft Statement of Policy Proposed by the National Security Council, NSC 107 Washington, March 14, 1951, Iran, Foreign Relations of the United States, 1952-1954, Iran, 1951–1954, Office of the Historian, Department of State, United States of America. https://history.state.gov/historicaldocuments/frus1951-54Iran/d6

20   Memorandum Prepared in the Office of National Estimates, Central Intelligence Agency, Washington, March 9, 1951, Memorandum of Information Number for the National Estimates Board, Subject: The Situation in Iran. Foreign Relations of the United States, 1952-1954, Iran, 1951–1954, Office of the Historian, Department of State, United States of America. https://history.state.gov/historicaldocuments/frus1951-54Iran/d3

21 Memorandum for the Record, CIA, Operations in Iran, Washington, October 9, 1951, Foreign Relations of the United States, 1952-1954, Iran, 1951–1954, Office of the Historian, Department of State, United States of America. https://history.state.gov/historicaldocuments/frus1951-54Iran/d48

22 Memorandum of Discussion at the 136th Meeting of the National Security Council, Washington, March 11, 1953, SUBJECT: Discussion at the 136th Meeting of the National Security Council on Wednesday, March 11, 1953, Foreign Relations of the United States, 1952-1954, Iran, 1951–1954, Office of the Historian, Department of State, United States of America. https://history.state.gov/historicaldocuments/frus1951-54Iran/d176

23 Memorandum From the Chief of the Near East and Africa Division, Directorate of Plans, Central Intelligence Agency (Roosevelt) to Mitchell, Washington, July 14, 1953, Foreign Relations of the United States, 1952-1954, Iran, 1951–1954, Office of the Historian, Department of State, United States of America. https://history.state.gov/historicaldocuments/frus1951-54Iran/d238

24 Richard Cottam, *Nationalism in Iran,* 224.

25 Memorandum of Conversation, Washington, June 26, 1953, Memorandum of Conversation Between Brigadier General H. Norman Schwarzkopf, Administrative Director, Department of Law and Public Safety for the State of New Jersey, and Mr. John H. Waller, CNEA/4, Foreign Relations of the United States, 1952-1954, Iran, 1951–1954, Office of the Historian, Department of State, United States of America. https://history.state.gov/historicaldocuments/frus1951-54Iran/d227

26 Memorandum From the Chief of the Near East and Africa Division, Directorate of Plans, Central Intelligence Agency (Roosevelt) to Mitchell, Washington, July 16, 195, Foreign Relations of the United States, 1952-1954, Iran, 1951–1954, Office of the Historian, Department of State, United States of America. https://history.state.gov/historicaldocuments/frus1951-54Iran/d240 also Memorandum of July 22, 1953 https://history.state.gov/historicaldocuments/frus1951-54Iran/d245

27 Telegram From the Station in Iran [text not declassified] August 16, 1958, Foreign Relations of the United States, 1952-1954, Iran, 1951–1954, Office of the Historian, Department of State, United States of America. https://history.state.gov/historicaldocuments/frus1951-54Iran/d269

28 The small groups beginning the protest were known and identified by local Iranians as being under control of the Chaku Keshan leadership,

a criminal faction not known to act without financial incentive. The released documents make it clear that substantial CIA funds had been supplied to Zahedi to buy protests against the Shah. Richard Cottam, *Nationalism in Iran,* 227. also *James A Bill, The Lion and the Eagle; The Tragedy of American-Iranian Relations,* (New Haven and London: Yale University Press, 1988), 90-91.

29   William Shawcross, *The Shah's Last Ride* (Simon and Schuster, 1988), 43-44.

30   Christopher Andrew and Vasili Mitrokhin, *The World Was Going Our Way: The KGB and the Battle for the Third World,* Perseus Books, New York 2005, 171.

31   Christopher Andrew and Vasili Mitrokhin, *The World Was Going Our Way; The KGB and the Battle for the Third World, 171.*

Chapter Five

1   "Report to the President by the President's Committee on International Information Activities," June 30, 1953, Department of State, Office of the Historian. https://history.state.gov/historicaldocuments/frus1952-54v02p2/d370 and https://www.cia.gov/library/readingroom/docs/DOC_0000476939.pdf

2   Alvin Rubinstein, *Moscow's Third World Strategy* (Princeton University Press, 1990), 19-20; 238-39.

3   Dmitri Volkogonov, *The Rise and Fall of the Soviet Empire: Political Leaders from Lenin to Gorbachev* (New York, HarperCollins, 1998), 228.

4   Alvin Rubinstein, *Moscow's Third World Strategy*, 86-87; http://www.un.org/en/decolonization/declaration.shtml

5   Ibid., 245.

6   Kennedy Sought Dialog With Cuba, The National Security Archive, November 24, 2003. http://nsarchive2.gwu.edu//NSAEBB/NSAEBB103/index.htm

7   "Report to the President on the Covert Activities of the Central Intelligence Agency," Reading Room, Central Intelligence Agency. https://www.cia.gov/library/readingroom/docs/DOC_0000476939.pdf

8   John Prados, *Presidents' Secret Wars: CIA and Pentagon Covert Operations from World War II Through the Persian Gulf War* (Chicago: Ivan R. Dee, Inc., 1996), 317. Also Stuart Brewer, *Borders and Bridges: A History of U.S. Latin American Relations,* (Praeger Security International, 2006), 134.

9   Larry Hancock and Stuart Wexler, *Shadow Warfare; The History of America's Undeclared Wars*, (Berkeley: Counterpoint Press, 2015), 386-96.

10   Robert Chesney, "Military-Intelligence Convergence and the Law of the Title 10/50 Debate," *Journal of National Security Law Policy*, Vol. 14. 1-19. http://jnslp.com/wp-content/uploads/2012/01/Military-Intelligence-Convergence-and-the-Law-of-the-Title-10Title-50-Debate.pdf

11   National Security Council Directive on Office of Special Projects 10/2, June 18, 1948, "Emergence of the Intelligence Establishment," Department of State, Office of the Historian. https://history.state.gov/historicaldocuments/frus1945-50Intel/d292

12   Sources include: "Disposal List Home Addresses," copied from an attachment to dispatch, [ ] to [ ] 1 June 1954. Box 145, (S). It contained 15 name, also [ ] routing slip for the attachment, (Dispatch dated 25 May 1954), Box 145 (Secret, Rybat, [ ] draft memo, "Present Status and Possible Future Course of PBSUCCESS," 1 June 1954, Box 145 (S and See "Contact Report," 2 June 1954, Box 146 (Secret, PBSUCCESS, Rybat). See also [ ] memo for the record, "Points Covered in H/W Discussion of June 1 and 2," 3 June 1954 and [ ] note for the file, "Disposal List Prepared by C/EW," 1 June 1954, Box 145 (S).)

Chapter Six

1   *Memorandum of Conversation with Mr. Joe Montgomery and Mr. Thomas Corcoran of T[sic]*, Created July 22, 1954. http://www.faqs.org/cia/docs/106/0000920234/MEMORANDUM-OF-CONVERSATION-WITH-MR.-JOE-MONTGOMERY-AND-MR.-THOMAS-CORCORAN-OF-T.html

2   *CIA Memorandum to Deputy Director of Plans*, July 22, 1954, Foreign Relations of the United States, 1952–1954, Retrospective Volume, Guatemala, Document 279, Meeting between Mr. Joe Montgomery and Mr. Corcoran and Col. J.C. King, Chief CIA Western Hemisphere. http://history.state.gov/historicaldocuments/frus1952-54Guat/d279

3   Louis J. Halle, Memorandum of the Policy Planning Staff to the Director of Staff Planning (Bowie), Washington, May 28, 1954. http://www.princeton.edu/~bsimpson/2010%20Hist%20380/Memorandum%20by%20Louis%20J.%20Halle,%20Jr.%20of%20the%20Policy%20Planning%20Staff,%20Washington,%20May%2028,%201954,%20OUR%20GUATEMALAN%20POLICY

4 William M. LeoGrande, *Our Own Backyard: The United States in Latin America*, 1977-1992 (The University of North Carolina Press, 1998), 11-13.

5 Gerald K. Haines, *CIA and Guatemala Assassination Proposals: 1952-1953*, CIA History Staff Analysis, June 1995. Key sources for the CIA historical study are referenced as noted in the text. http://en.wikisource.org/wiki/CIA_and_Guatemala_Assassination_Proposals:_CIA_History_Staff_Analysis

6 Ibid.

7 "*Guatemalan Communist Personnel to be Disposed of During Military Operations of Calligeris*," (Armas), September 18, 1952, Box 134 (S) Foreign Relations of the United States, State Department History.

8 "Conferences," December 1, 1952, Box 134 (S); "Current Planning of Calligeris Organization," December 12, 1952, Box 134 (S). See also, Acting Chief, [ ] Branch, Western Hemisphere Division for reports that in November 1952 that Armas was studying PW use of liquidation lists. Memorandum for the Record, "PW Conferences," November 5, 1952, Box 151 (S). The case officer also reported that the Árbenz government had targeted Armas for assassination. March 10, 1953, Box 15D (S). Foreign Relations of the United States, State Department History.

9 Report #3 to [ ] "Liaison between Calligeris and General Trujillo of Santo Domingo," September 18, 1952, Box 134 (S). The CIA study noted that "assassination is a nasty but frequent tool of Guatemalan politics. Árbenz himself benefited from the killing of his archrival for the presidency Francisco Arans in 1949." Foreign Relations of the United States, State Department History.

10 Nicholas Cullather, "Operation PBSUCCESS: The United States and Guatemala, 1952–1954," History Staff, Center for the Study of Intelligence, Central Intelligence Agency, 19.

11 *CIA Memorandum for the Record*, Conversation with Mr. Thomas Corcoran, signed by Stuart Hedden, April 16, 1952. http://www.foia.cia.gov/sites/default/files/document_conversions/89801/DOC_0000924155.pdf

12 Interview with E. Howard Hunt, National Security Archives, Cold War Interviews. http://www.gwu.edu/~nsarchiv/coldwar/interviews/episode-18/hunt1.html

13 Richard Immerman, *The CIA in Guatemala: The Foreign Policy of Intervention* (Austin, Texas, University of Texas Press, 1982), 103, 115, 156. Also Smathers, Congressional Record, Senate, 28 May 1954, 7336–8.

14 George Thayer, *The War Business: The International Trade in Armaments* (New York: Simon and Schuster, 1969), 52.

15 Burton Hersh, *The Old Boys: The American Elite and the Origins of the CIA* (Tree Farm Books, 2001), 344–46.

16 David M. Barrett, "Congress, the CIA, and Guatemala, 1954: Sterilizing a 'Red Infection.'"

17 Gerald K. Haines, *CIA and Guatemala Assassination Proposals: 1952-1953*, CIA History Staff Analysis, June 1995.

18 "Log-PBFORTUNE Meetings," with handwritten notation "PBSUCCESS File—6 November, 1953," released in sanitized form 2003, CIA Historical Review Board. The Grace National Bank, a holding of W. R. Grace and Company, focused specifically on business ventures in Latin America, and was extremely profitable in the 1950s. In August 1965 approval was given for it to merge with Marine Midland, and the existing company is known as HSBC Bank USA. Standard Oil was active in Latin America and specifically in Guatemala, and had the ability to put additional financial pressure on the Árbenz government. These corporate briefings were conducted in the Dolly Madison House, later known as the Wilkins Building. The building officially housed the National Advisory Council on Aeronautics but also contained offices of certain CIA technical staff, and was referred to as the "I Building."

19 Log-PBFORTUNE Meetings," with handwritten notation "PBSUCCESS File—6 November, 1953," released in sanitized form 2003, CIA Historical Review Board.

20 Log-PBFORTUNE Meetings," with handwritten notation "PBSUCCESS File—6 November, 1953," released in sanitized form 2003, CIA Historical Review Board.

21 Unnumbered report issued September 1, 1952, titled *Intermediate Report on Military Plans for Guatemala*, 2003 release under CIA Historical Review Program, 5.

22 H. P. Albarelli, Jr., *A Terrible Mistake: The Murder of Frank Olson and the CIA's Secret Cold War Experiments,* Trine Day, 2009, "A Study of Assassinations,"Appendix 2, 720–29.

23 *Foreign Relations of the United States,* "Dispatch to [ ], 'Training,' 6 June 1954, Box 75 (Secret, PBSUCCESS, Rybat) [ ]"; "Memorandum to LINCOLN Station, 16 May 1954, 'Tactical Instructions (part II)' (S)"; and "Specific Instruction: 'Nerve War Against Individuals,'" June 9, 1954, Box 50 (S), Foreign Relations of the United States, State Department History.

24   Rafael Trujillo, the longtime pro-American dictator of the Dominican Republic, frequently proved eager and cooperative in support of covert American actions in the region.

25   John Prados, *Safe for Democracy; The Secret Wars of the CIA,* 119.

26   Ibid., 121.

27   David Phillips, *The Night Watch,* 42–48; Kate Doyle, "Guatemala—1954: Behind the CIA's Coup," Consortiumnews.com, 1997. http://www.con-sortiumnews.com/archive/story38.html

28   Robert J. McMahon and Glen LaFantasie, "Foreign Relations of the United States, 1958-1960: volume XVII. Indonesia," 1994, State Department of the United States. http://digicoll.library.wisc.edu/cgi-bin/FRUS/FRUS-idx?type=div&did=FRUS.FRUS195860v17.i0002&i-size=M

29   Joseph Smith, *Portrait of a Cold Warrior* (Ballantine Books, 1981), 197.

30   "US Policy towards Indonesia," United States Department of State/*Foreign Relations of the United States, 1958-1960. Indonesia,* (1958-1960), 31. http://digicoll.library.wisc.edu/cgi-bin/FRUS/FRUS-idx?type=turn&id=FRUS.FRUS195860v17&entity=FRUS.FRUS195860v17.p0057&q1=september%2023%201957

31   Kenneth Conboy and James Morrison, *Feet to the Fire: CIA Covert Operations in Indonesia—1957/1958* (Annapolis, Maryland: Naval Institute Press, 1999). The full story of the various insurgent colonels, of their island forces, and their combat with the central government across the archipelago is extremely well told in *Feet to the Fire.* Their research provides one of the most detailed studies of joint CIA/military covert action programs currently available. An equally good companion study of CIA covert military operations is found in Conboy and Morrison, *The CIA in Tibet,* also from the Naval Institute Press.

32   Ibid., 31-32; 180. Precise inventory details of the actual military shipment are provided as well as a yearbook showing the sailing route of the classified mission from Subic Bay to Sumatra.

33   Statements by Allen Dulles, February 27, 1958, United States Department of State/*Foreign Relations of the United States, 1958-1960. Indonesia,* (1958-1960), 49. http://digicoll.library.wisc.edu/cgi-bin/FRUS/FRUS-idx?type=turn&id=FRUS.FRUS195860v17&entity=FRUS.FRUS195860v17.p0075&q1=cia

34   Kenneth Conboy and James Morrison, *Feet to the Fire: CIA Covert Operations in Indonesia—1957/1958,* 43-44, 130-31 and 153-54.

35 Allen Dulles and John Foster Dulles, telephone conversation of March 4, 1958, United States Department of State/Foreign Relations of the United States, 1958-1960. Indonesia, (1958-1960), 52. http://digicoll.library.wisc.edu/cgi-bin/FRUS/FRUS-idx?type=turn&entity=FRUS.FRUS195860v17.p0078&id=FRUS.FRUS195860v17&isize=M

36 Lincoln White, Department of State Spokesperson, Press Briefing, Telegram 2499, Central Files, 756D.00/3-758 also United States Department of State/Foreign Relations of the United States, 1958-1960. Indonesia, (1958-1960), 57. http://digicoll.library.wisc.edu/cgi-bin/FRUS/FRUS-idx?type=turn&entity=FRUS.FRUS195860v17.p0083&id=FRUS.FRUS195860v17&isize=M

37 United States Department of State/Foreign Relations of the United States, 1958-1960. Indonesia, (1958-1960), 97, 110-13, also 131. http://digicoll.library.wisc.edu/cgi-bin/FRUS/FRUS-idx?type=turn&entity=FRUS.FRUS195860v17.p0123&id=FRUS.FRUS195860v17&isize=M

38 Kenneth Conboy and James Morrison, *Feet to the Fire: CIA Covert Operations in Indonesia – 1957/1958,* 115-16, 120.

39 "Telegram from the Embassy in Indonesia to the Department of State," May 6, 1958, United States Department of State/Foreign Relations of the United States, 1958-1960. Indonesia, (1958-1960), 139-41. http://digicoll.library.wisc.edu/cgi-bin/FRUS/FRUS-idx?type=turn&entity=FRUS.FRUS195860v17.p0167&id=FRUS.FRUS195860v17&isize=M

40 Telegram from the Embassy in Indonesia to the Department of State," May 6, 1958, United States Department of State/Foreign Relations of the United States, 1958-1960. Indonesia, (1958-1960), May 15, 178-80. http://digicoll.library.wisc.edu/cgi-bin/FRUS/FRUS-idx?type=turn&entity=FRUS.FRUS195860v17.p0204&id=FRUS.FRUS195860v17&isize=M

41 Kenneth Conboy and James Morrison, *Feet to the Fire: CIA Covert Operations in Indonesia – 1957/1958,* 133.

42 Telegram From the Embassy in Indonesia to the Department of State, Djakarta, July 15, 1958. https://history.state.gov/historicaldocuments/frus1958-60v17/d134

43 Kenneth Conboy and James Morrison, *Feet to the Fire: CIA Covert Operations in Indonesia – 1957/1958,* 145.

44 Felix Stump, Telegram from the Commander in Chief Pacific, Honolulu, May 26, 1958. *Foreign Relations of the United States, 1958-1960, Indonesia*, vol. XVII, document 205.

Chapter Seven

1 Duncan Campbell, "Inside Echelon," July 25, 2000. https://www.biblio-tecapleyades.net/ciencia/echelon01.htm

2 "Edward Snowden: Leaks that exposed US spy programme" *BBC News*, January 17, 2014. http://www.bbc.com/news/world-us-can-ada-23123964

3 Pete Earley, *Comrade J: The Untold Story of Russia's Master Spy in America After the End of the Cold War*, (New York: G. P. Putman Sons, 2007), 21-23.

4 Ibid., 17-18.

5 Francis Stonor Saunders, "Stuck on the Flypaper; MI5 and the Hobsbawm File," *London Review of Books*, Vol. 37 No. 7· 9 April 2015, 3-10. https://www.lrb.co.uk/v37/n07/frances-stonorsaunders/stuck-on-the-flypaper

6 HTLINQUAL Soviet mail intercept program, New York; 1952-1953, Central Intelligence Agency. https://www.cia.gov/library/readingroom/document/0001420864

7 Supplementary Detailed Staff Reports of Intelligence Activities and the Rights of Americans, Book III, Final Report of the Select Committee to Study Governmental Operations with respect to Intelligence Activities, United States Senate, April 23, 1976. http://www.randomcollection.info/cointeldocs/churchfinalreportIIIh.htm

8 John Prados and Tom Blanton, "The Family Jewels Then and Now," National Security Archive, October 25, 2013. https://nsarchive.word-press.com/2013/10/25/the-family-jewels-then-and-now/

9 Zimmermann Telegram - Decoded Message Record Group 59: General Records of the Department of State, 1756 - 1979 National Archives and Records Administration National Archives Identifier 302022 https://www.archives.gov/education/lessons/zimmermann

10 Barbara Tuchman, *The Zimmermann Telegram* (New York: Random House, 1985).

11 Ladislav Bittman, *The KGB and Soviet Disinformation: An Insider's View* (Pergamon Press, 1985), 237-38.

12 Thomas Rid, "Disinformation: A Primer in Russian Active Measures and Disinformation Campaigns," Hearings Before the United States Select Committee on Intelligence, United States Senate, March 30,

2017. https://www.intelligence.senate.gov/sites/default/files/documents/os-trid-033017.pdf

13 "Expulsion of Soviet Diplomats from Foreign Countries," 1970-1981, Foreign Affairs Note, United States Department of State, February 1982. http://insidethecoldwar.org/sites/default/files/documents/Report%20on%20the%20Expulsion%20of%20Soviet%20Representatives%20from%20Foreign%20Countries%201970-81%20February%201982.pdf Also Rowland Evans and Robert Novak, "Soviet Backfire in Mexico," *The Washington Post*, 1971. https://www.cia.gov/library/readingroom/docs/CIA-RDP73B00296R000200170086-8.pdf

14 Rob Cameron, "Former Dissident's Database Opens Old Wounds in Czech Republic," *DW*, October 30, 2009. http://www.dw.com/en/former-dissidents-database-opens-old-wounds-in-czech-republic/a-4812564

15 Ladislav Bittman, *The Deception Game* (New York: Ballantine Books, 1981), 23.

16 Ladislav Bittman, *The KGB and Soviet Disinformation: An Insider's View* (1985), 223-24.

17 "Memorandum for President Johnson," CIA Situation Report, October 1, 1965, Foreign Relations of the United States, 1964–1968, Volume XXVI, Indonesia; Malaysia-Singapore; Philippines, Office of the Historian, U.S. State Department. https://history.state.gov/historicaldocuments/frus1964-68v26/d142

18 "Memorandum of Telephone Conversation Between Acting Secretary of State Ball and Secretary of Defense McNamara," October 1, 1965, Foreign Relations of the United States, 1964–1968, Volume XXVI, Indonesia; Malaysia-Singapore; Philippines, Office of the Historian, U.S. State Department. https://history.state.gov/historicaldocuments/frus1964-68v26/d143

19 "Editorial Note," Foreign Relations of the United States, 1964–1968, Volume XXVI, Indonesia; Malaysia-Singapore; Philippines. https://history.state.gov/historicaldocuments/frus1964-68v26/d185

20 John Barron, *KGB; The Secret Work of Soviet Secret Agents*, (New York: Bantam Books, 1974) 237.

21 Jason Grotto, Chris Groskopf, Ryan Mark, Joe Germuska, and Brian Boyer, "U.S. troops, Vietnamese nationals exposed to dangerous chemicals", *Chicago Tribune*, December 4, 2009. http://www.chicagotribune.com/chi-091204-agentorange-map-htmlstory.html

22 John Barron, *KGB Today: The Hidden Hand* (New York: The Berkeley Publishing Group, 1987), 29-30.

23 Emizet Francois Kisangani, Scott F. Bobb, *Historical Dictionary of the Democratic Republic of the Congo*, Historical Dictionaries of Africa, No. 112, (Lantham, Toronto, Plymouth: Scarecrow Press, 2010), 461.

24 John Barron, *KGB: The Secret Work of Soviet Secret Agents,* 312-40.

25 Anne Goodpasture, "Mexico City Station History," Central Intelligence Agency, November 16, 1978. https://maryferrell.org/showDoc.html?docId=146763&search=page_1#relPageId=1&tab=page. Major sources on Winston Scott and the intelligence collection tools and practices of the station include Jefferson Morley's *Our Man in Mexico: Winston Scott and the Hidden History of the CIA* and Chapter Four of Bill Simpich's *State Secret: Wiretapping in Mexico City, Double Agents, and the Framing of Lee Harvey Oswald*, "Mexico City Intrigue: The World of Surveillance."

26 Jefferson Morley, *Our Man in Mexico: Winston Scott and the Hidden History of the CIA* (Lawrence, KS: University Press of Kansas, 2008), 88.

27 John Whitten, "I do not know whether you informed yourself about the magnitude of our political action program at the time—absolutely enormous…", *Lopez Report*, House Select Committee on Assassinations (HSCA), 1978, 178. Also see Anne Goodpasture, *Mexico City Station History*, 521. NARA Record Number: 104-10414-10124.

28 Jefferson Morley, *Our Man in Mexico: Winston Scott and the Hidden History of the CIA,* 90.

29 Ibid, 91.

30 Anne Goodpasture, "Mexico City Station History," 374. NARA Record Number: 104-10414-10124, also "Intelligence to Sources on Oswald's Visit to Mexico City in 1963," 3. HSCA Segregated CIA Collection, Box 36/NARA Record Number: 104-10103-10359.

31 "Debriefing of David M. Wilsted," Russ Holmes Work File/National Archives Records Administration (NARA) Record Number: 104-10413-10053.

32 Bill Simpich, "State Secret," Chapter 4, "Wiretapping in Mexico City," Mary Ferrell Foundation. https://www.maryferrell.org/pages/State_Secret_Chapter4.html

33 "CIA Cryptonyms, LI—Operations, organizations, and individuals related to Mexico City," Mary Ferrell Foundation. https://www.maryferrell.org/php/cryptdb.php

34 Bill Simpich, *State Secret*, Chapter 4, "Wiretapping in Mexico City."

35 HSCA Segregated CIA Collection/HSCA Segregated CIA Collection, Box 47/NARA Record Number: 104-10132-10224.

36 "Request for Renewal of LIENVOY Project," January 1, 1964, HSCA Segregated CIA Collection (microfilm - reel 23: LIENVOY, LIFEAT, LIONION)/NARA Record Number: 104-10188-10049.

37 Bill Simpich, *State Secret*, Chapter 4, "Wiretapping in Mexico City," Mary Ferrell Foundation https://www.maryferrell.org/pages/State_Secret_Chapter4.html

38 Levister memo, 12/30/63, 55. HSCA Segregated CIA Collection, Box 6/ NARA Record Number: 104-10052-10276.

39 Jefferson Morley, *Our Man in Mexico: Winston Scott and the Hidden History of the CIA,* 117.

40 Ibid., 108.

Chapter Eight

1 William M. LeoGrande, *Our Own Backyard: The United States in Central America, 1977–199* (Chapel Hill, North Carolina: The University of North Carolina Press, 2000), 43-45.

2 Ibid., 89.

3 President Ronald Reagan, National Security Decision Directive, NSDD-17, January 4, 1982. https://fas.org/irp/offdocs/nsdd/nsdd-17.pdf

4 Peter Kornbluh, *The Price of Intervention in Nicaragua: Reagan's Wars Against the Sandinistas,* (Washington, DC: Institute for Policy Studies, 1987), 19–20.

5 John Prados, *The Presidents' Secret Wars: CIA and Pentagon Covert Operations Since World War II though Iranscam* (New York: William Morrow and Company, 1988), 386–86.

6 In reality there were three separate Boland amendments offered between 1982 and 1984. Each was aimed at limiting funding to the Contras. The first was attached as a rider to the Defense Appropriations Act of 1983. In December 1983, for the fiscal year 1984, a second Boland amendment limited the amount spent in Nicaragua for military aid. In December 1984, a third Boland amendment prohibited covert assistance for military operations in Nicaragua.

7 Kornbluh, *The Price of Intervention in Nicaragua*, 56.

8 Prados, *The Presidents' Secret Wars*, 389.

9 Ibid., 46.

10 Prados, *The Presidents' Secret Wars*, 390–91.

11 Leslie Cockburn, *Out of Control,* (New York: The Atlantic Monthly Press, 1987), 12.

12 Kornbluh, *The Price of Intervention in Nicaragua*, 47–48.

13 Ibid., 50.

14 Martin Tolchin, "Senate, 84 to 12, Acts To Oppose Mining Nicaraguan Ports; Rebuke to Reagan," *The New York Times*, April 11, 1984. http://www.nytimes.com/1984/04/11/world/senate-84-12-acts-to-oppose-mining-nicaragua-ports-rebuke-to-reagan.html

15 Kornbluh, *The Price of Intervention in Nicaragua*, 61.

16 Larry Hancock with Stuart Wexler, *Shadow Warfare: The History of America's Undeclared Wars*, Chapter 12, "Autonomous and Deniable" (Counterpoint Press), 195-215.

17 Peter Kornbluh, *The Price of Intervention in Nicaragua* (Washington: Institute for Policy Studies, 1987), 198-201.

18 William LeoGrande, *Our Own Backyard: The United States in Latin America, 1977-1992* (The University of North Carolina Press, 1998), 403.

19 Peter Kornbluh, *The Price of Intervention in Nicaragua* (Washington, DC: Institute for Policy Studies, 1987), 71.

20 Scott Anderson and Jon Lee Anderson, *Inside the League*, (New York: Dodd, Mead and Company, 1986), 151-152.

21 Ibid., 260-61.

22 Ibid., 268-69.

23 Oliver L. North with William Novak, *Under Fire; An American Story* (New York, Harper Collins, 1991), 265.

24 Peter Kornbluh, *The Price of Intervention in Nicaragua* (Washington, DC: Institute for Policy Studies, 1987), 81-83.

25 Steve Coll, *Ghost Wars* (New York, Penguin Books, 2004), 55.

26 Ibid., 62.

27 John Prados, *Safe for Democracy*, (Chicago: Ivan R. Dee, 2006), 482.

28 Readers are referred to *Ghost Wars* by Steve Coll for a much broader discussion of the religious elements of the warfare in and around Afghanistan. Coll delves into the personalities and motives of many of the key figures and also explores the belief system that united the fundamentalist Muslims with the intensely religious Director of the CIA during this period, William Casey. Coll's insight into how Casey's personal beliefs reinforced the broader American relationship with the two countries is fascinating. However, the personal relationship also produced a level of reliance on Pakistani and Saudi intelligence structures and operatives which have had a major impact long beyond Casey's tenure.

29 Steve Coll, *The Bin Ladens: An Arabian Family in the American Century* (New York: The Penguin Press, 2008), 250.

30 Ibid., 253–54.

31   The detailed story of the fundamentalist seizure of influence, including an exploration of the personalities that enabled it, is addressed in *Ghost Wars*. It carries through to the ultimate emergence of both the Taliban and the pan-Arabic fundamentalist movement that led to al-Qaeda and 9/11.

32   Ibid., 201.

33   Steve Coll, *Ghost Wars* (New York: Penguin Books, 2004), 127-28.

Chapter Nine

1   John Prados, *Safe for Democracy: The Secret Wars of the CIA* (Chicago: Ivan R. Dee Inc., 2006), 595.

2   Richard Clarke, *Against All Enemies: Inside America's War on Terror* (New York: Free Press), 79.

3   Gary Berntsen and Ralph Pezzullo, *Jawbreaker: The Attack on bin Laden and al-Qaeda: A Personal Account by the CIA's Key Field Commander* (New York: Crown Publishing, 2005), 18, 26. CIA Officer Gary Berntsen writes that bin Laden experts had begun to be well aware of the potential of NGOs such as Al-Haramain as early as the massive terror bombings against multiple American embassies in Africa in 1998. However it was not until 2004 that the U.S. Department of the Treasury officially moved globally against Al-Haramain and certain of its senior figures (including two within its U.S. branch) on the basis of its documented links to bin Laden and al-Qaeda. The United Nations also placed the organization on its list of al-Qaeda and Taliban affiliates. In another terror attack, in Africa, one of the principal figures involved had been operating under the cover of yet another charitable NGO called "Help Africa People."

4   Richard A. Clarke, *Against all Enemies*, Free Press, 2004, 96.

5   Philip Shenon, *The Commission: The Uncensored History of the 9/11 Investigation* (New York: Twelve, 2008), 357.

6   James Risen and David Johnston, "Threats and Responses: Hunt for Al Qaeda; Bush Has Widened Authority of C.I.A. to Kill Terrorists," *The New York Times*, December 15, 2002. http://www.nytimes.com/2002/12/15/world/threats-responses-hunt-for-al-qaeda-bush-has-widened-authority-cia-kill.html

7   Jeremy Scahill, *Dirty Wars: The World Is a Battlefield* (New York: Nation Books, 2013), 114.

8   Nicholas Schmidle, "Getting Bin Laden; What Happened that Night in Abbottabad," *The New Yorker*, August 8, 2011 Issue. https://www.newyorker.com/magazine/2011/08/08/getting-bin-laden

9   "Freedom Agenda," Fact Sheet: President Bush's Freedom Agenda Helped Protect the American People, The White House. https://georgew-bush-whitehouse.archives.gov/infocus/freedomagenda/

10 "President Bush's Freedom Agenda Helped Protect The American People; President Bush Has Advanced Liberty And Democracy As The Great Alternatives To Repression And Radicalism", The Bush Record, The White House, January, 2009. https://georgewbush-whitehouse.archives.gov/infocus/bushrecord/factsheets/freedomagenda.html

11 "First Chechnya War—1994-1996," Global Security. https://www.globalsecurity.org/military/world/war/chechnya1.htm

12 Andrei Soldatov and Irina Borogan, *The New Nobility: The Restoration of Russia's Security State and the Enduring Legacy of the KGB* (New York: Public Affairs A Perseus Books Group, 2010), 20.

13 Ibid., 109.

14 Andrei Soldatov, "The Confession of Disinformation from Lubyanka" *Vesiya*, March 2002.

15 "Attorney General, Manhattan U.S. Attorney, and FBI Announce Charges Against Russian Spy Ring in New York City," U.S. Attorney's Office Southern District of New York, January 26, 2015. https://www.fbi.gov/news/pressrel/press-releases/attorney-general-manhattan-u.s.-attorney-and-fbi-announce-charges-against-russian-spy-ring-in-new-york-city

16 Adam Goldman, "FBI breaks up a Russian spy ring in New York City," *The Washington Post*, January 26, 2015. https://www.washingtonpost.com/world/national-security/fbi-breaks-up-a-russian-spy-ring-in-new-york-city/2015/01/26/d3f8cee8-a595-11e4-a2b2-776095f393b2_story.html?utm_term=.b9e5dda5a682

17 "Smoke Billows from Russian Consulate Chimney in San Francisco," CBS News, San Francisco Area, KPIX 5, September 1, 2017. http://sanfrancisco.cbslocal.com/2017/09/01/smoke-russian-consulate-chimney-san-francisco/

18 Pete Earley, *Comrade J: The Untold Story of Russia's Master Spy in America at the End of the Cold War*, (New York: G. P. Putnam's and Sons, 2007), 161-66.

19 "Foreign Intelligence Service," The Russian Government, Government of the Russian Federation. http://government.ru/en/department/112/

20 John Barron, *KGB: The Secret Work of Soviet Agents*, Chapter VI, "Seduction and Surveillance" (New York: Bantam Books, 1974), 158-192.

21 Pete Earley, *Comrade J: The Untold Story of Russia's Master Spy in America at the End of the Cold War,* 165-66.

22 Donald Trump's security chief testified that during their visit to Moscow for the Miss Universe pageant in 2013, his Russian contacts had offered to send several women to Trump's hotel room. Keith Schiller told Trump about the offer, treating it as a joke. Given the long-term KGB/FSB practices of targeting foreign businessmen for compromise, such an offer might well have been something more serious; certainly international intelligence/security officers would have treated it so during the Cold War. "Manu Raju and Jeremy Herb, Ex-Trump security chief testifies he rejected 2013 Russian offer of women for Trump in Moscow," CNN, November 9, 2017. http://www.cnn.com/2017/11/09/politics/keith-schiller-russian-offer-women-2013-moscow/index.html

23 Mikhail Zygar, *All the Kremlin's Men* (New York: Perseus Books, 2016), 20.

24 "UK Charity teaching Chechens to make bombs, Russians say," *Reuters,* August 10, 2000.

25 Simon Saradzhyan and Kevin O'Flynn, "FSB: Four British Spies Uncovered," *Moscow Times,* January 4, 2006.

26 Andrei Soldatov and Irina Borogan, *The New Nobility: The Restoration of Russia's Security State and the Enduring Legacy of the KGB,* 210-211.

27 Ibid., 212-13.

28 Federal Security Service (FSB), "FSB History," Global Security. https://www.globalsecurity.org/intell/world/russia/fsb.htm

29 Andrei Soldatov and Irina Borogan, *The New Nobility: The Restoration of Russia's Security State and the Enduring Legacy of the KGB,* 32-34.

30 Order of Honor, awarded for "many years of service in the economic sphere," Vladimir Putin, Decree No. 545, April 26, 2007.

31 Andrei Soldatov and Irina Borogan, *The New Nobility; The Restoration of Russia's Security State and the Enduring Legacy of the KGB,* 212-13, 279, endnote 7.

Chapter Ten

1 Andrei Soldatov and Irina Borogan, *The New Nobility; The Restoration of Russia's Security State and the Enduring Legacy of the KGB,* chapter thirteen, "The Beslan Crisis" (New York: Public Affairs, Perseus Books Group, 2010), 155-63.

2 Mikhail Zygar, *All the Kremlin's Men: Inside the Court of Vladimir Putin* (New York: Public Affairs, 2016), 79-80.

3 Arthur Sitov, "X-files, Yuri Roshki, portrait of the political body," *Moldaviski Vedomesti*, April 3, 2009.

4 Orkhan Djemal, "The Choice of Klashnakov," *Novaya Gazeta*, November 4, 2004.

5 Roman Yakovlevsky, "General Uushakov is connected," *Belorusskaya Delovaya Gazeta*, April 2003.

6 "Belarus, NGOs Deny Plot to Overthrow Government," *IPS News*, May 14, 2005. Also Patrushev, "New Color Revolutions are Financed by the West," *RIA Novesti*, May 12, 2005.

7 Andrei Soldatov and Irina Borogan, *The New Nobility: The Restoration of Russia's Security State and the Enduring Legacy of the KGB* (New York: Public Affairs, 2010), 213-14.

8 "Alisher Usmanov handed over from Kazan to Uzbekistan," RIA Novasti, October 24, 2005.

9 Andrei Soldatov and Irina Borogan, *The New Nobility: The Restoration of Russia's Security State and the Enduring Legacy of the KGB* (New York: Public Affairs, 2010). It should be noted that Soldatov's work and his website on Russian intelligence was highly respected, often quoted in print. However, in 2008 his position was terminated with no advance notice and the Russia media outlets which had been carrying his reports disassociated themselves from him. http://www.wow.com/wiki/Agentura. Ru The work of Argentura.Ru continues at: https://www.facebook.com/groups/37241744834/

10 "After the Color Revolutions Political Change and Democracy Promotion in Eurasia," *Policy Perspectives*, The Elliott School of International Affairs, George Washington University, 2010. https://www2.gwu.edu/~ieres-gwu/assets/docs/PONARS_Eurasia_After_the_Color_Revolutions.pdf Readers wishing a comprehensive and scholarly discussion of the full scope of the color revolutions may wish to refer to this project, a series of studies organized and made available on the internet by George Washington University.

11 Robert Perry, "Why Russia Shut Down NED Fronts," *ConsortiumNews*, July 30, 2015. https://consortiumnews.com/2015/07/30/why-russia-shut-down-ned-fronts/

12 David Ignatius, "Innocence Abroad: The New World of Spyless Coups," *The Washington Post*, September 21, 1991. https://www.washingtonpost.com/archive/opinions/1991/09/22/innocence-abroad-the-new-world-of-spyless-coups/92bb989a-de6e-4bb8-99b9-462c76b59a16/?utm_term=.84a0af468579

13 U.S. State Department Dispatch, Vol. 4, No. 4, January 3, 1999, *Dispatch Magazine,* Bureau of Public Affairs. http://dosfan.lib.uic.edu/ERC/brief-ing/dispatch/1993/html/Dispatchv4no04.html

14 Tim Weiner, "The Solo File; Declassified Documents Detail the FBI's Most Valued Secret Agents of the Cold War," National Security Archive Electronic Briefing Book No. 375, *The National Security Archive*, April 10, 2012. http://nsarchive2.gwu.edu/NSAEBB/NSAEBB375/

15 "Memorandum from A. H. Belmont to L. V. Boardman, "Communist Party, USA, International Relations, Internal Security-C," March 5, 1958. https://vault.fbi.gov/solo/solo-part-01-of/view

16 Childs' Account of his April 1958 Trip to Soviet Union and China, SAC, New York, to Director, FBI, July 23, 1958. https://vault.fbi.gov/solo/solo-part-02-of/view

17 John Haynes and Harvey Klehr, *In Denial: Historians, Communism and Espionage* (San Francisco: Encounter Books, 2003), 69.

18 Mikhail Zygar, *All The Kremlin's Men: Inside the Court of Vladimir Putin* (New York: Perseus Books, 2006), 103-04.

19 Ibid., 104.

20 Ronald Grigor, *The Making of the Georgian Nation* (Indiana University Press, 1994), 303-05.

21 Vladimer Papava, "The Political Economy of Georgia's Rose Revolution," *Orbis* 50 (4): 661 https://www.revolvy.com/main/index.php?s=Rose%20Revolution&item_type=topic

22 Cory Welt, "Georgia's Rose Revolution: From Regime Weakness to Regime Collapse," Center for Strategic and International Studies, 2006.

23 Theodor Tudoroiu, "Rose, Orange, and Tulip: The Failed post-Soviet Revolutions," *Communist and Post-Communist Studies*, 2007.

24 The reality of Soros's and his "Open Society" Foundations (a network with activities in over a hundred countries) involvement with and fund-ing for popular and democratic movements is factual and quite public. Those with more populist/freedom of expression-oriented worldviews tend to endorse many of its activities. In contrast those with conservative viewpoints favoring regime stability tend to vilify it, linking Soros to a host of conspiracy theories. In regard to our focus on political warfare there is little doubt that a considerable amount of Soros's funding has gone and continues to go to open election activism, which in itself is certainly a form of political action and regime change. https://www.open-societyfoundations.org/people/george-soros

25 David Anable, "The Role of Georgia's Media and Western Aid in the Rose Revolution," *The Harvard International Journal of Press/Politics*, 2006. http://journals.sagepub.com/doi/abs/10.1177/1081180X06289211

26 Ibid.

27 Angus Rosburgh, *The Strongman: Vladimir Putin and the Struggle for Russia* (London: I. B. Tarus 2012), 108.

28 Ibid., 112.

29 William Liefert, Olga LIefert, Ralph Seeley, and Ed Alle, "Black Sea Grain Exports: Will They Be Moderate or Large?" United States Department of Agriculture, October 2004. http://usda.mannlib.cornell.edu/usda/ers/WRS//2000s/2004/WRS-10-12-2004_Special_Report.pdf

30 H. Von Zon, *The Political Economy of Independent Ukraine: Captured by the Past*, Studies in Economic Transition (UK: Palgrave McMillan, 2000), 141.

31 Alexandra Mclees and Eugene Rumer, "Saving Ukraine's Defense Industry," Carnegie Endowment for International Peace, July 20, 2014. http://carnegieendowment.org/2014/07/30/saving-ukraine-s-defense-in-dustry-pub-56282

32 John Armstrong, "Collaborationism in World War II: The Integral Nationalist Variant in Eastern Europe," The Journal of Modern History, Vol. 40, No. 3, September, 1968, 409.

33 Mikhail Zygar, *All the Kremlin's Men: Inside the Court of Vladimir Putin,* 88.

34 Dr. Andreas Umland, "Understanding the Orange Revolution; Ukraine's Democratization in the Russian Mirror," GEO Politika, September 24, 2009. http://www.academia.edu/204229/Understanding_the_Orange_Revolution_Ukraine_s_Democratization_in_the_Russian_Mirror

35 Mikhail Zygar, *All the Kremlin's Men: Inside the Court of Vladimir Putin*, 89.

36 Katie Sanders, "The United States Spent $5 Billion on Ukraine Anti-Government Riots," PolitiFact, March 19, 2014. http://www.politifact.com/punditfact/statements/2014/mar/19/facebook-posts/united-states-spent-5-billion-ukraine-anti-governm/

37 Taras Kuzio, "Russian Policy Toward the Ukraine During Elections," George Washington University. https://www2.gwu.edu/~ieresgwu/assets/docs/demokratizatsiya%20archive/GWASHU_DEMO_13_4/D761010XT7H55W67/D761010XT7H55W67.pdf

38 The FEP had been involved with the Russian FSB in early internet political warfare—responding to Chechen hackers by hacking into and

manipulating news on the most active Chechen website. Stephen Mulvey, "Russian Internet Politics," BBC News, March 5, 2001. http://news.bbc.co.uk/2/hi/europe/1198603.stm

39   Mikhail Zygar, *All the Kremlin's Men: Inside the Court of Vladimir Putin,* 92-93.

40   Ibid., 103.

41   Erica Marat, "The Tulip Revolution: Kyrgyzstan one year after," The Jamestown Foundation, Washington DC. https://jamestown.org/wp-content/uploads/2016/09/Jamestown-TulipRevolution.pdf

42   Zaal Anjapardze, "Georgian Advisors Stepping Forward in Bishkek," Eurasia Daily Monitor, Volume 2 Issue 59, March 25, 2005. https://jamestown.org/program/georgian-advisors-stepping-forward-in-bishkek/

43   Craig Smith, "U.S. Helped to Prepare the Way for Kyrgyzstan's Uprising," *The New York Times*, March 30, 2005. http://www.nytimes.com/2005/03/30/world/asia/us-helped-to-prepare-the-way-for-kyrgyzstans-uprising.html

44   Op. cit.

45   "A Tulip Revolution," *The Economist*, May 23, 2005. http://www.economist.com/node/3785139

46   Mikhail Zygar, *All the Kremlin's Men: Inside the Court of Vladimir Putin,* 106.

47   "The Second Term," President Bush's Second Inaugural Address, May 20, 2005, National Public Radio. http://www.npr.org/templates/story/story.php?storyId=4460172

48   Mikhail Zygar, *All the Kremlin's Men: Inside the Court of Vladimir Putin,* 112.

49   Ibid., 113.

Chapter Eleven

1   Joseph Stalin, "The Press as Collective Organizer," *Pravda*, May 6, 1923.

2   Andrei Soldatov and Irina Borogan, *The Red Web: The Kremlin's War on the Internet* (New York: Public Affairs, 2015).

3   Thomas Carothers, "U.S. Democracy Promotion Before and After Bush," Carnegie Endowment for International Peace, 2007. http://carnegieendowment.org/files/democracy_promotion_after_bush_final.pdf

4   Eline Gordts and Nataliya Rostova, "Putin's Press; How Russia's President Controls the News," *The World Post/Huff Post*, October 24, 2015. https://www.huffingtonpost.com/entry/vladimir-putin-russia-news-media_us_56215944e4b0bce34700b1df

5   Jill Dougherty, "How the Media Became One of Putin's Most Powerful Weapons," *The Atlantic*, April 21, 2015. https://www.theatlantic.com/international/archive/2015/04/how-the-media-became-putins-most-powerful-weapon/391062/

6   Andrei Soldatov and Irina Borogan, *The Red Web: The Kremlin's War on the Internet*, 102-04.

7   Jonathan Sturn, "The Russian-Ukrainian Gas Crisis of January, 2006," Oxford Institute for Energy Studies, January 16, 2006. https://www.oxfordenergy.org/wpcms/wp-content/uploads/2011/01/Jan2006-RussiaUkraineGasCrisis-JonathanStern.pdf

8   Mikhail Zygar, *All the Kremlin's Men; In the Court of Vladimir Putin* (New York: Public Affairs, 2016), 125.

9   Jonathan Sturn, "The Russian-Ukrainian Gas Crisis of January, 2006," Oxford Institute for Energy Studies.

10 "Putin's Prepared Remarks at 43rd Munich Conference on Security Policy," *Washington Post*, February 12, 2007. http://www.washington-post.com/wp-dyn/content/article/2007/02/12/AR2007021200555.html

11 Robert Perry, "Why Russia Shut Down the NED Fronts," *Consortium News*, July 30, 2015. https://consortiumnews.com/2015/07/30/why-russia-shut-down-ned-fronts/

12 "Foreign Agents Registration Act," The United States Department of Justice. https://www.fara.gov/ The Foreign Agents Registration Act (FARA) was placed into U.S. law in 1938, and requires that all persons "representing the interests of foreign powers…in a political or quasi-political capacity" register themselves and provide information in regard to any activities and finances which might be associated with their foreign connections. The individuals must fully and publicly disclose their relationships as well as provide "periodic" reports on their activities including details of financial receipts and disbursements. Registrations are overseen by the National Security Division of the Department of Justice.

13 "Percentages of Unfavorable Views of the United States," Pew Global Indicators, PEW Research Center, as reported by Theodore P. Gerber and Jane Zavisca, "We Are Losing Hearts and Minds in the Former Soviet Empire," *Newsweek*, August 2, 2015. http://www.newsweek.com/we-are-losing-hearts-and-minds-former-soviet-empire-358989

14 Op. cit.

15 Niccolò Machiavelli, *The Prince* (Simon and Brown, 2011), 13-14.

16 "Accessing Russian Intentions and Activities in Recent US Elections," CIA, FBI, NSA, Office of the Director of National Intelligence, January 16, 2017. www.dni.gov/files/documents/ICA_2017_01.pdf

17   There is an uncomfortable irony in such accusations given that it was the Nazis, and in particular Adolph Hitler, who used the purported plight of native German speakers to argue for the resettlement of Germans living in Estonia and Latvia to areas under German military control. Those Nazi-Soviet population transfers allowed Stalin to establish Russian military bases in Estonia and Latvia in 1939. Lynn H. Nicholas, *Cruel World: The Children of Europe in the Nazi Web* (Vintage Books; A Division of Random House, 2006), 207-09.

18   "Sergei Ivanov Meets with Youth Movements," *Kommersant*, June 7, 2007.

19   Richard Stengel, "Choosing Order Before Freedom," *Time*, December 19, 2007. http://content.time.com/time/specials/2007/personoftheyear/article/0,28804,1690753_1690757,00.html

20   "Relations with Russia," North Atlantic Treaty Organization, June 16, 2017. https://www.nato.int/cps/en/natohq/topics_50090.htm

21   Mikhail Zygar, *All the Kremlin's Men: Inside the Court of Vladimir Putin* (New York: Public Affairs Perseus Books, 2007), 154.

22   Condoleezza Rice, *No Higher Honor* (New York: Crown Books, 2011), 685.

23   Andrew E. Kramer, "Russia Claims Its Sphere of Influence in the World," *The New York Times*, August 31, 2008. http://www.nytimes.com/2008/09/01/world/europe/01russia.html

24   Andrei Soldatov and Irina Borogan, chapter seven, "Internet Rising," *The Red Web: The Kremlin's War on the Internet* (New York: Public Affairs, Perseus Books), 101-07. The emergence of the Russia social media complex, and the efforts of the Russian regimes in power to control them are examined in great detail by Soldatov and Borogan.

25   "FSB Does Not Consider Hackers as Hackers," *Interfax*, Newsru.com, February 2, 2002.

26   Andrei Soldatov and Irina Borogan, *The New Nobility: The Restoration of Russia's Security State and the Enduring Legacy of the KGB* (Public Affairs, Perseus Books), 227-28.

27   Andrei Soldatov, "Cyber Surprise,"*Novaya Gazeta*, May 21, 2007.

28   A Look at Estonia's Cyber Attack in 2007, *NBC News*, July 8, 2009. http://www.nbcnews.com/id/31801246/ns/technology_and_science-security/t/look-estonias-cyber-attack/#.Wf0Zk1H_q1s

29   Andy Greenberg, "When Cyber Terrorism Becomes State Censorship," *Forbes*, May 14, 2008. https://www.forbes.com/2008/05/14/cyberattacks-terrorism-estonia-tech-security08-cx_ag_0514attacks.html

30 Jason Richards, "Denial-of-Service: The Estonian Cyberwar and Its Implications for U.S. National Security," *International Affairs Review*, George Washington University. http://www.iar-gwu.org/node/65

31 Yelena Cernenko and Darya Guseva, "Tensions on the Internet," *Newsweek* Russian edition, August 17, 2009.

32 Julia Ioffe, "Why Does the Kremlin Care So Much About the Magnitsky Act," *The Atlantic*, July 27, 2017. https://www.theatlantic.com/international/archive/2017/07/magnitsky-act-kremlin/535044/

33 Mikhail Zygar, *All the Kremlin's Men: Inside the Court of Vladimir Putin*, 249.

Chapter Twelve

1 Richard Stengel, "Choosing Order Before Freedom," *Time*, December 19, 2007. http://content.time.com/time/specials/2007/personoftheyear/article/0,28804,1690753_1690757,00.html

2 Monroe Doctrine, 1823, Our Documents, National Archives and Records Administration. https://www.ourdocuments.gov/doc.php?-flash=true&doc=23

3 Joshua Partlow, "The Soviet Union Fought the Cold War in Nicaragua; Now Putin Is Back," *The Washington Post*, April 8, 2017. https://www.washingtonpost.com/world/the_americas/the-soviet-union-fought-the-cold-war-in-nicaragua-now-putins-russia-is-back/2017/04/08/b43039b0-0d8b-11e7-aa57-2ca1b05c41b8_story.html?utm_term=.e7a8bd89ca78

4 Drew Sullivan, "Journalism or Propaganda: Let's Help Russian Media the Right Way," *Global Investigative Journalism Network*, August 19, 2015. https://gijn.org/2015/08/19/journalism-or-propaganda-lets-help-russian-media-the-right-way/

5 Mikhail Zygar, *All the Kremlin's Men: Inside the Court of Vladimir Putin*, 258.

6 Ukraine 2014, "Supporting Democracy Around the World," National Endowment for Democracy, 2014 NED Annual Report. https://www.ned.org/region/central-and-eastern-europe/ukraine-2014/

7 "Ukraine Crisis Timeline," BBC News, November 13, 2014. http://www.bbc.com/news/world-middle-east-26248275

8 Sam Frizell, "Ukraine Protesters Seize Kiev as President Flees," *Time*, February 22, 2014. http://world.time.com/2014/02/22/ukraines-president-flees-protestors-capture-kiev/

9 "Putin Acknowledges Russian Military Servicemen Were in Crimea," RT/ Russia Today news, April 17, 2014. https://www.rt.com/news/crimea-defense-russian-soldiers-108/

10 "Crimea's Integration in Russia is Quicker than Expected—Official," TASS, November 19, 2016. https://www.rbth.com/news/2016/11/19/ crimeas-integration-in-russia-is-quicker-than-expected-official_649175

11 Ryan Browne, "US show of force sends Russia a message in Black Sea", February 20, 2018, CNN Politics https://www.cnn.com/2018/02/19/ politics/us-russia-black-sea-show-of-force/index.html

12 Paul Sonne, "'Novorossiya' Falls From Putin's Vocabulary as Ukraine Crisis Drags Revival of Czarist-era term for 'New Russia' fades ahead of European decision on sanctions," *The Wall Street Journal*, May 29, 2015. https://www.wsj.com/articles/novorossiya-falls-from-putins-vocabulary-as-ukraine-crisis-drags-1432936655

13 The Russian idea that Ukraine could be separated by creating a "construct" state was not dissimilar from the American effort to split Vietnam in a purely political North/South construct. No such "state" as South Vietnam existed before the United States literally declared it into being. As with the British and French experience in the Middle East, the creation of construct states via lines drawn on maps has proved to be a very disruptive and inherently unstable practice.

14 Pierre Sautreuil, "Believe It or Not, Russia Dislikes Relying on Military Contractors", War is Boring, March 9, 2018 https://warisboring.com/ believe-it-or-not-russia-dislikes-relying-on-military-contractors/

15 Andrew deGranpre, "Blackwater's founder wants Trump to outsource the Afghanistan war," Why that's so risky, *The Washington Post*, August 23, 2017 https://www.washingtonpost.com/news/checkpoint/ wp/2017/08/10/blackwaters-founder-wants-trump-to-outsource-the-afghanistan-war-why-thats-so-risky/?utm_term=.b5c29710e2a3

16 Eli Watkins, "Key Russian oligarch in touch with Russia, Assad before mercenaries attacked US troops", February 22, 2018 https://www.cnn. com/2018/02/22/politics/russia-syria-us-troops/index.html

17 A. Prokhanov, "Who Are You Shooter?: An interview with the former Minister of Defense of the Donetsk People's Republic," *Zavtra*, November 20, 2014.

18 Mikhail Zygar, *All the Kremlin's Men: Inside the Court of Vladimir Putin,* 287.

19 "Federation Council cancels resolution on using Russian Troops in Ukraine," TASS, June 25, 2014. http://tass.com/russia/737674

20 Shaun Walker, "Putin Admits Russian Military Presence in Ukraine for First Time," *The Guardian*, December 17, 2015. https://www.theguardian.com/world/2015/dec/17/vladimir-putin-admits-russian-military-presence-ukraine

21 Shawn Robert Woodford, "The Russian Army Strike that Spooked the U.S. Army," *Land Warfare*, The DuPuy Institute. http://www.dupuyinstitute.org/blog/2017/03/29/the-russian-artillery-strike-that-spooked-the-u-s-army/

22 Jacek Siminski, "Analysis of Ukrainian Air Force Losses in Eastern Ukraine Clashes," *The Aviationist*, December 2, 2014. https://theaviationist.com/2014/12/02/analysis-of-ukrainian-air-force-losses-in-eastern-ukraine-clashes/

23 "MH17 Ukraine Disaster; Dutch Safety Board blames missile," BBC News, October 13, 2015. http://www.bbc.com/news/world-europe-34511973

24 Ibid., 289.

25 A. Prokhanov, "Who Are You Shooter?: An interview with the former Minister of Defense of the Donetsk People's Republic."

26 Karoun Demirjian, "Putin Denies Russian Troops are in Ukraine; Declares Certain Deaths Secret," *The Washington Post*, May 28, 2015. https://www.washingtonpost.com/world/putin-denies-russian-troops-are-in-ukraine-decrees-certain-deaths-secret/2015/05/28/9bb15092-0543-11e5-93f4-f24d4af7f97d_story.html?utm_term=.c88c22223610

27 Maria Tsvetkova and Aleksandar Vasovic, "Charred Tanks point to Russian Involvement," *Reuters World News*, October 23, 2014. https://www.reuters.com/article/us-ukraine-crisis-tanks-exclusive/exclusive-charred-tanks-in-ukraine-point-to-russian-involvement-idUSKCN0IC1GE20141023

28 Lucian Kim, "The Battle of Ilovaisk: Details of a Massacre Inside Rebel-Held Eastern Ukraine," *Newsweek*, November 14, 2014. http://www.newsweek.com/2014/11/14/battle-ilovaisk-details-massacre-inside-rebel-held-eastern-ukraine-282003.html

29 Amos C. Fox, "The Russian-Ukrainian War: Understanding the Dust Clouds on the Battlefield," Modern War Institute, West Point Military Academy, January 17, 2017. https://mwi.usma.edu/russian-ukrainian-war-understanding-dust-clouds-battlefield/

30   Adrian Bonenberger, "The War No One Notices in Ukraine," *The New York Times*, June 20, 2017. https://www.nytimes.com/2017/06/20/opinion/ukraine-russia.html

31   "EU-Ukraine Association Agreement officially enters into force," *Euromaidan Press*, September 1, 2017. http://euromaidanpress.com/2017/09/01/eu-ukraine-association-agreement-officially-enters-into-force/#arvlbdata

32   UK-EU Relations, *Global Security*, September 1, 2017. https://www.globalsecurity.org/military/world/ukraine/forrel-eu.htm

33   United States Army Europe, Rapid Trident Exercise http://www.eur.army.mil/RapidTrident/

34   "Ukraine's association deal bittersweet with no real hope for EU integration," *RT/Russia Today*, September 1, 2017. https://www.rt.com/business/401736-ukraine-eu-association-agreement/

35   Steven Pifer, "Will Ukraine join NATO? A course for disappointment," Order from Chaos. https://www.brookings.edu/blog/order-from-chaos/2017/07/25/will-ukraine-join-nato-a-course-for-disappointment/

36   "Moscow Threat as Moldova Expels Five Russian Diplomats," *BBC News*, May 30, 2017. http://www.bbc.com/news/world-europe-40091061

37   Luke Coffey, "Where will Putin strike next?," *Newsweek*, October 7, 2016. http://www.newsweek.com/where-will-putin-strike-next-506381

Chapter Thirteen

1   Mikhail Zygar, "The Russian Reset that Never Was," *Foreign Policy*, December 9, 2016. http://foreignpolicy.com/2016/12/09/the-russian-reset-that-never-was-putin-obama-medvedev-libya-mikhail-zygar-all-the-kremlin-men/

2   Mikhail Zygar, *All the Kremlin's Men: Inside the Court of Vladimir Putin*, 249.

3   "Kennedy Sought Dialog with Cuba," Initiative with Castro Aborted by Assassination Declassified Documents SHOW, November 24, 2003, The National Security Archive. https://nsarchive2.gwu.edu/NSAEBB/NSAEBB103/index.htm

4   Sarah N. Lynch, "Flynn pleads guilty to lying on Russia, cooperates with U.S. probe," Reuters, December 1, 2017. https://www.reuters.com/article/us-usa-trump-russia/flynn-pleads-guilty-to-lying-on-russia-cooperates-with-u-s-probe-idUSKBN1DV50N

5   "The Logan Act," *West's Encyclopedia of American Law*, Edition Two. Copyright 2008, The Gale Group. https://legal-dictionary.thefreedictionary.com/Logan+Act

6   Daniel Hemel and Eric Posner, "Why the Trump Team Should Fear the Logan Act," *The New York Times,* December 4, 2017. https://www.nytimes.com/2017/12/04/opinion/trump-team-flynn-logan-act.html

7   Evan Perez and Maegan Vazquez, "Kushner's attorney accuses Senate panel of 'gotcha game' over documents request," *CNN Politics*, November 19, 2017. http://www.cnn.com/2017/11/19/politics/abbe-lowell-kushner-gotcha-games/index.html

8   Natasha Bertrand, "Senate Judiciary Committee; Kushner forwarded emails about Russian backdoor overture and dinner invite," *Business Insider*, November 16, 2017. http://www.businessinsider.com/jared-kushner-emails-russia-backdoor-feinstein-grassley-2017-11

9   Tom Hamburger, Carol D. Leonnig, and Rosalind S. Helderman, "Trump campaign emails show aide's repeated efforts to set up Russia meetings," *The Washington Post*, August 14, 2017. https://www.washingtonpost.com/politics/trump-campaign-emails-show-aides-repeated-efforts-to-set-up-russia-meetings/2017/08/14/54d08da6-7dc2-11e7-83c7-5bd5460f0d7e_story.html?utm_term=.87588284428b

10 Jeremy Herb, Evan Perez, Marshall Cohen, Pamela Brown, and Shimon Prokupecz, CNN, "Ex-Trump campaign adviser pleads guilty to making false statement," CNN, October 30, 2017. http://www.cnn.com/2017/10/30/politics/paul-manafort-russia-investigation-surrender/index.html

11 Tom Winter, Tracy Connor, and Ken Dilanian, "Ex-Trump Adviser George Papadopoulos Pleads Guilty in Mueller's Russia Probe," NBC News, October 20, 2017. https://www.nbcnews.com/news/us-news/trump-campaign-adviser-george-papadopoulos-pleads-guilty-lying-n815596

12 Jeremy Herb, Evan Perez, Marshall Cohen, Pamela Brown, and Shimon Prokupecz, "Ex-Trump campaign adviser pleads guilty to making false statement," CNN, October 30, 2017. http://www.cnn.com/2017/10/30/politics/paul-manafort-russia-investigation-surrender/index.html

13 Jo Becker, Adam Goldman and Matt Apuzzo, "Russian Dirt on Clinton? 'I Love It,' Donald Trump Jr. Said," *The New York Times*, July 27, 2017. https://www.nytimes.com/2017/07/11/us/politics/trump-russia-email-clinton.html

14 Op. cit.

15 Darren Samuelsohn, "Donald Trump Jr. in legal danger for Russia meeting about Clinton dirt," *Politico*, September 10, 2017. https://www.politico.com/story/2017/07/10/donald-trump-jr-russia-meeting-legal-danger-240370

16 Pete Earley, *Comrade J: The Untold Story of Russia's Master Spy in America at the End of the Cold War* (New York: G.P. Putnam's Sons, 2007), 161-66.

17 That advance was enabled by a massive installation of long-distance fiber-optic transmission lines and the implementation of digital switching systems throughout Russia. Those projects had been a priority during the early 1990s and by 1995 were largely in place within four years. Over 70 percent of all Russian intercity switching equipment had been replaced by digital equipment, made in the West. The FSB combined their extensive surveillance capability, which included sophisticated keyword computerized monitoring, with the ability to target communications not just by a location but by the content of the actual communications.

18 "Ukraine Not Investigating Bugging of U.S. Diplomats Phone Talk," Reuters World News, February, 18, 2014. http://www.reuters.com/article/us-ukraine-call/ukraine-says-not-investigating-bugging-of-u-s-diplomats-phone-talk-idUSBREA170G020140208

19 Deripaska was known to be an early supporter and key figure within Putin's inner circle, but he fell out of favor by 2009 due to bad national publicity over labor issues in one of his large refineries. Andrew Roth, "Manafort's Russia Connection: What You Need to Know About Oleg Deripaska" *The Washington Post*, September 24, 2017. https://www.washingtonpost.com/news/worldviews/wp/2017/09/24/manaforts-russia-connection-what-you-need-to-know-about-oleg-deripaska/?utm_term=.5acf1e47c5ca

20 Arthur Phillips, "Paul Manafort's Complicated Ties to the Ukraine Explained," *The Washington Post*, August 19, 2016. https://www.washingtonpost.com/news/the-fix/wp/2016/08/19/paul-manaforts-complicated-ties-to-ukraine-explained/?utm_term=.f2fb85ef9c4a

21 Megan R. Wilson, "Manafort Registers as Foreign Agent for Ukraine Work," *The Hill*, June 6, 2017. http://thehill.com/homenews/administration/339756-manafort-registers-as-foreign-agent-for-ukraine

22 Evan Perez and Jeremy Herb, "Manafort and Gates Charged with Conspiracy against U.S.," CNN, October 30, 2017. http://www.cnn.com/2017/10/30/politics/paul-manafort-russia-investigation-surrender/index.html

23 Even Perez, Jeremy Herb, Marshall Cohen, Pamela Brown, "Manafort, Gates, Charged with Conspiracy Against U.S.," CNN, October 30, 2017. http://www.cnn.com/2017/10/30/politics/paul-manafort-russia-investigation-surrender/index.html

24 Stephen Collinson, "Dread Hangs Over Washington as Manafort and Gates Turn Themselves In," CNN, October 30, 2017 http://www.cnn.com/2017/10/29/politics/indictments-mueller-trump/index.html

Chapter Fourteen

1   "Putin Question and Answer, full transcript," Person of the Year Special Issue, *Time,* December 19, 2007.

2   Percentages of Unfavorable Views of the United States, Pew Research Center's Global Indicators Database, Pew Research. http://www.newsweek.com/we-are-losing-hearts-and-minds-former-soviet-empire-358989

3   Sam Green and Graeme Robertson, "Examining Putin's Popularity; Rallying Round the Russian Flag," *The Washington Post*, September 9, 2014. https://www.washingtonpost.com/news/monkey-cage/wp/2014/09/09/explaining-putins-popularity-rallying-round-the-russian-flag/?utm_term=.8f6cfe9a56c6

4   Address by the President of the Russian Federation, President of Russia, The Kremlin, Moscow, March 18, 2014. http://en.kremlin.ru/events/president/news/20603

5   Mikhail Zygar, *All the Kremlin's Men: Inside the Court of Vladimir Putin* (New York: Public Affairs Press, 2016), 304.

6   Mathew Bodner, "Russia proves nuclear muscle with ballistic missile launch," *The Moscow Times*, September 10, 2014. https://themoscowtimes.com/articles/russia-proves-nuclear-muscle-with-ballistic-missile-launch-39254

7   Dr. Mark Schneider, "Implications for U.S. Nuclear Deterrence and Missile Defense," Russian Nuclear Weapons Policy, RealClear Defense, April 28, 2017. https://www.realcleardefense.com/articles/2017/04/28/russian_nuclear_weapons_policy_111261.html

8   Tylor Rogoway, "Russia fires off multiple cruise missiles and ICBM's during massive nuclear drill," *The War Zone*, October 26, 2017. http://www.thedrive.com/the-war-zone/15507/russia-fires-off-multiple-icbms-and-cruise-missiles-during-massive-nuclear-drill

9   Laurel Wamsley, "Putin says Russia has new Nuclear Weapons that can't be Intercepted," NPR International, March 1, 2018. https://www.npr.

org/sections/thetwo-way/2018/03/01/589830396/putin-says-russia-has-nuclear-powered-missiles-that-cant-be-intercepted

10 Joseph Trevithick, "NATO members train to nuke a fictional enemy after major Russian drills," *The War Zone*, October 26, 2017. http://www.thedrive.com/the-war-zone/15211/nato-members-train-to-nuke-a-fictional-enemy-after-major-russian-drills?iid=sr-link4

11 Chuck Hagel, Secretary of Defense, keynote speech, Reagan National Defense Forum, November 15, 2014, United States Department of Defense. https://www.defense.gov/News/Speeches/Speech-View/Article/606635/

12 Ralph Vartabedian, W. J. Hennigan, and Samantha Masunaga, "A Top Secret desert assembly plant starts ramping up to build Northrups B-21 bomber," *Los Angeles Times*, November 10, 2017. http://www.latimes.com/local/california/la-fi-northrop-bomber-20171110-htmlstory.html

13 Vladimir Putin, "Interview to Channel One, Rossiya-1, NTV, and RBC TV Channels," February 25, 2014.

14 Jill Dougherty, "How the Media Became One of Putin's Most Powerful Weapons," *The Atlantic*, April 21, 2015. https://www.theatlantic.com/international/archive/2015/04/how-the-media-became-putins-most-powerful-weapon/391062/

15 "A Look at Estonia's Cyber Attack in 2007," NBC News, July 8, 2009. http://www.nbcnews.com/id/31801246/ns/technology_and_science-security/t/look-estonias-cyber-attack/#.Wf0Zk1H_q1s

16 Alec Luhn, "Five fibs from Vladimir: How Putin distorted the facts about Ukraine," *The Guardian*, March 4, 2014. https://www.theguardian.com/world/2014/mar/04/vladimir-putin-interview-five-untruths

17 Andrei Soldatov and Irina Borogan, *The Red Web* (New York: Public Affairs, Hachette Book Group, 2015), 281-82. Also Chris Elliott, "The Readers Editor on Pro Russian Trolling," *The Guardian*, May 4, 2014. https://www.theguardian.com/commentisfree/2014/may/04/pro-russia-trolls-ukraine-guardian-online

18 The internet has proved to be a double-edged sword for Russian political action, to a large extent because it still provides the opportunity for independent journalists to continue publishing their work. Much of what we know about the actual practices of the new Russian political warfare comes from the work of certain persistent, astoundingly brave native Russian reporters. Every effort has been made to cite and acknowledge them in this work.

19 Larry Hancock, *NEXUS: The CIA and Political Assassination* (JFK Lancer Productions and Publications, 2011), 34-35.

20 Ronald Reagan, "Address to the Nation on the Iran Arms and Contra Aid Controversy and Administration Goals," August 12, 1986, The American Presidency Project. http://www.presidency.ucsb.edu/ws/index.php?pid=34693

21 Mikhail Zygar, *All the Kremlin's Men: Inside the Court of Vladimir Putin,* 251.

22 Matt Apuzzo and Sharon LaFraniere, "13 Russians Indicted as Mueller Reveals Effort to Aid Trump Campaign," *The New York Times.* 16, 2018 https://www.nytimes.com/2018/02/16/us/politics/russians-indicted-mueller-election-interference.html

23 Mikhail Zygar, *All the Kremlin's Men: Inside the Court of Vladimir Putin,* 283.

24 Devlin Barrett, Sari Horwitz and Rosalind S. Helderman, "Russian troll farm, 13 suspects indicted in 2016 election interference", *The Washinton Post,* https://www.washingtonpost.com/world/national-security/russian-troll-farm-13-suspects-indicted-for-interference-in-us-election/2018/02/16/2504de5e-1342-11e8-9570-29c9830535e5_story.html?utm_term=.7130e30be7c3

25 Mikhail Zygar, *All the Kremlin's Men: Inside the Court of Vladimir Putin,* 283-84.

26 "CyberBerkut broke into the correspondence of Euromaidan activists with American sponsors," NTV, March 25, 2014. Also Vitaly Shevchenko, "Ukraine Conflict, hackers take sides in virtual war," BBC News, December 20, 2014. http://www.bbc.com/news/world-europe-30453069

27 Gordon Corera, "How France's TV 5 was almost destroyed by Russian hackers," BBC News, October 10, 2016. http://www.bbc.com/news/technology-37590375

28 Evan Osnos, David Remnick, and Joshua Yaffa, "Trump, Putin and the New Cold War," Annals of Diplomacy, *The New Yorker*, March 6, 2017. https://www.newyorker.com/magazine/2017/03/06/trump-putin-and-the-new-cold-war

29 Seth Fiegerman, "Russian Meddling on Facebook; what we learned this week," CNN Tech, November 2, 2017. http://money.cnn.com/2017/11/02/technology/business/facebook-russia-meddling/index.html

30 Counter-messaging is one of the oldest of dirty tricks in politics, dating back to ward politics where candidates hired bums to go house to house

and aggressively promote their opponent. Mike Isaac and Scott Shane, "Facebook's Russia-Linked Ads came in many disguises," *The New York Times*, October 2, 2017. https://www.nytimes.com/2017/10/02/technology/facebook-russia-ads-.html

31 Op. cit.

32 Alexa Lardieri, "Putin's Chef suspected of funding fake news operation," *US News and World Report*, October 18, 2017. https://www.usnews.com/news/world/articles/2017-10-18/putins-chef-suspected-of-funding-fake-news-operation

33 Dylan Byers, "Russian Ads Reached 10 Million People," *CNN Money*, October 3, 2017. http://money.cnn.com/2017/10/02/media/facebook-russian-ads-10-million/index.html

34 Seth Fiegerman and Dylan Byers, "Facebook, Twitter and Google defend their role in the election," CNN, November 1, 2017. http://money.cnn.com/2017/10/31/media/facebook-twitter-google-congress/index.html

35 Dylan Byers, Manu Raju and Jeremy Herb, "Twitter tells Congress it took action on 200 Russian accounts," CNN, September 28, 2017. http://money.cnn.com/2017/09/28/media/twitter-russia-capitol-hill/index.html

36 Mike Isaac and Daisuke Wakabayashi, "Russian Influence Reached 126 Million through Facebook alone," The New York Times, October 3, 2017. https://www.nytimes.com/2017/10/30/technology/facebook-google-russia.html

37 Elizabeth Dwoskin, Adam Entous, and Craig Timberg, "Google uncovers Russian bought ads on YouTube, GMail and other platforms," *The Washington Post*, October 9, 2017. https://www.washingtonpost.com/news/the-switch/wp/2017/10/09/google-uncovers-russian-bought-ads-on-youtube-gmail-and-other-platforms/?utm_term=.40a87bff8066

38 "Choose Your Audience," Facebook Business, Facebook.com. https://www.facebook.com/business/products/ads/ad-targeting

39 Curt Devine, "Kill them all; Russian linked Facebook accounts call for violence," CNN Media, October 21, 2017. http://money.cnn.com/2017/10/31/media/russia-facebook-violence/index.html

40 Mike Isaac and Scott Shane, "Facebook's Russia: Linked ads came in many disguises," *The New York Times*, October 2, 2017. https://www.nytimes.com/2017/10/02/technology/facebook-russia-ads-.html

41 Ward Churchill and Jim Vander Wall, *The COINTELPRO Papers: Documents from the FBI's Secret Wars Against Dissent in the United.* (Boston: South End Press, 1990).

42   Dylan Byers, "Russian Bought Black Lives Matter ad targeted Baltimore and Ferguson," CNN, September 28, 2017. http://money.cnn.com/2017/09/27/media/facebook-black-lives-matter-targeting/index.html

43   Megan Trimble, "Russia used Pokémon Go to exploit racial tensions and sow discord in America," *US News and World Report*, October 13, 2017. https://www.usnews.com/news/national-news/articles/2017-10-13/russians-used-pokemon-go-to-heighten-us-tensions

44   Tim Lister and Clare Sebastian, "Stoking Islamophobia and Succession in Texas—from and office in Russia" CNN Politics, October 6, 2017. http://www.cnn.com/2017/10/05/politics/heart-of-texas-russia-event/index.html

45   Casey Michel, "How Russia Created the most popular Texas Succession page on Facebook," Extra Newsfeed, September 7, 2017. https://extranewsfeed.com/how-russia-created-the-most-popular-texas-secession-page-on-facebook-fd4dfd05ee5c

46   Drew Griffin and Donie O'Sullivan, "The fake Tea Party account linked to Russia and followed by Sebastian Gorka" CNN Politics, September 22, 2017. http://www.cnn.com/2017/09/21/politics/tpartynews-twitter-russia-link/index.html

47   Dylan Byers, "Senate Intel Chair: Point of Russian Ads seems to have been to create chaos" CNN Money, October 4, 2017. http://money.cnn.com/2017/10/04/media/facebook-burr-warner-briefing/index.html

48   Priyanka Boghani, "How Russia Looks to gain through political interference," *Frontline*, National Public Radio, December 23, 2016. http://www.pbs.org/wgbh/frontline/article/how-russia-looks-to-gain-through-political-interference/

49   Matt Burgess, "Here's the first evidence Russia used Twitter to influence Brexit," *WIRED*, November 10, 2017. http://www.wired.co.uk/article/brexit-russia-influence-twitter-bots-internet-research-agency

50   "Theresa May accuses Vladimir Putin of election meddling," BBC News, November 14, 2017. http://www.bbc.com/news/uk-politics-41973043

51   Robin Emmott, "Spain sees Russian interference in Catalonia separatist vote," Reuters, November 13, 2017. https://www.reuters.com/article/us-spain-politics-catalonia-russia/spain-sees-russian-interference-in-catalonia-separatist-vote-idUSKBN1DD20Y

52   Andrew Higgins, "It's France's turn to worry about election meddling by Russia," *The New York Times*, April 17, 2017. https://www.nytimes.com/2017/04/17/world/europe/french-election-russia.html

53 Ibid.
54 Donie O'Sullivan, "A notorious Twitter troll came back for a week and Twitter did nothing," CNN Media, November 19, 2017. http://money.cnn.com/2017/11/17/media/new-jenna-abrams-account-twitter-russia/index.html

Chapter Fifteen

1 David Isenberg, "The Pitfalls of U.S. Covert Operations," CATO Policy Analysis #18, The CATO Institute, April 7, 1989 https://object.cato.org/pubs/pas/PA118.HTM
2 Larry Hancock and Stuart Wexler, *Shadow Warfare; The History of America's Undeclared Wars*, "(Berkeley, California: Counterpoint Press, 2014), chapter seventeen "Targeted Infrastructure Warfare in the Southern Cone", 284-325
3 Nicole Machiavelli, *The Prince* (Simon and Brown, 2011), 21-22.
4 "Data-Driven Campaigns," Cambridge Analytica. https://ca-political.com/?__hstc=163013475.14844fa4c9011ffe86e1a7d-de655fda0.1511365275038.1511365275038.1511365275038.1&__hssc=163013475.1.1511365275038&__hsfp=3868151071
5 Issie Lapowsky, "What did Cambridge Analytica really do for Trump's campaign," *WIRED,* October 26, 1917. https://www.wired.com/story/what-did-cambridge-analytica-really-do-for-trumps-campaign/
6 McKenzie Funk, "The Secret Agenda of a Facebook Quiz," *The New York Times*, November 19, 2016. https://mobile.nytimes.com/2016/11/20/opinion/the-secret-agenda-of-a-facebook-quiz.html?_r=0&referer=https%3A%2F%2Fwww.google.com%2F
7 Sydney Schaedel, "Websites that Post Fake and Satirical Stories," FactCheck.org, October 27, 2017. http://www.factcheck.org/2017/07/websites-post-fake-satirical-stories/
8 Chris Cillizza, "Donald Trump just claimed he invented fake news," *CNN Politics*, October 26, 2017. http://www.cnn.com/2017/10/08/politics/trump-huckabee-fake/index.html
9 Christopher Mele, "How Conspiracy Theorists Call Shut Down Part of a Port," *The New York Times,* June 15, 2017. https://www.nytimes.com/2017/06/15/us/port-dirty-bomb-south-carolina.html
10 Oliver Darcey, "Facebook and Google helped spread bad information after Las Vegas attack," *CNN Money*, October 23, 2017. http://money.cnn.com/2017/10/02/media/facebook-google-misinformation-las-vegas/index.html

11   Celeb Ecarma, "Congressman falls for alt-right meme; falsely reports Texas shooter was named Sam Hyde," MEDIAite, November 5, 2017. https://www.mediaite.com/online/congressman-falls-for-alt-right-meme-falsely-reports-texas-shooter-was-named-sam-hyde/

12   Russian bots promote pro-gun messages after Florida school shooting", *CNN US*, February 16, 2018. https://www.cnn.com/2018/02/16/us/russian-bots-florida-shooting-intl/index.html

Index

INDEX

INDEX